JEAN GIRAUDOUX
PLAYS

JEAN GIRAUDOUX

PLAYS

AMPHITRYON · INTERMEZZO
ONDINE

TRANSLATED BY

ROGER GELLERT

NEW YORK

OXFORD UNIVERSITY PRESS

1967

Contents

Amphitryon

AMPHITRYON was first performed at the Comédie des Champs-Elysées on 8 November 1929 and was produced by Louis Jouvet. It was originally entitled AMPHITRYON 38, a private joke of Giraudoux, who claimed that there had been thirty-seven previous versions of the Amphitryon story.

ALCMENA, *wife to Amphitryon*
AMPHITRYON, *Prince of Thebes*
JUPITER
MERCURY
SOSIOS, *a slave*
THE TRUMPETER
THE WARRIOR
ECCLISSA, *Alcmena's nurse*
LEDA, *Queen of Sparta*

ECHO, HEAVENLY VOICES, ETCETERA

SCENE: Amphitryon's palace at Thebes

ACT ONE

A terrace in front of a palace.
Jupiter addresses Mercury.

JUPITER: Mercury! My dear friend, she's there!

MERCURY: Where, Jupiter?

JUPITER: You see that window with the light in it, and the curtain moving in the breeze: that's Alcmena's! Stay quite still, and in a few minutes, with luck, you may see her shadow pass over it.

MERCURY: The shadow will be plenty for me. I must say, though, Jupiter, I take off my hat to you. When you fall for a mortal woman, you put aside all your divine privileges; you waste the whole night squatting in the cactus and brambles just to get a glimpse of Alcmena's shadow, when your ordinary eyes could comfortably pierce through her bedroom walls, to say nothing of her nightdress.

JUPITER: Yes, and touch her body with hands she can't see, and hold her in an embrace she can't feel!

MERCURY: That's how the wind makes love, but it doesn't stop it, or you, being a prime source of fertilization.

JUPITER: You know nothing of earthly love, Mercury.

MERCURY: On the contrary, you order me into human shape so often that I know it only too well. It sometimes happens, waiting on you in this capacity, that I'm attracted by a woman. But in order to get to grips with her I have to make myself agreeable to her, then undress her, then dress her again, then finally make myself disagreeable so that she'll let me go. It's a full-time occupation!

JUPITER: I'm afraid you don't quite grasp the ritual of human love. Only the strictest observation of it leads to pleasure.

MERCURY: I know the ritual all right.

JUPITER: First you must follow her, your mortal woman, with muffled steps exactly matching hers, so that your legs move precisely the same distance apart, setting up an identical rhythmic signal at the base of the spine. Do you do this?

MERCURY: Of course, it's the first rule.

JUPITER: Then you leap forward. With your left hand you squeeze her breast, where virtue and surrender reign side by side, while with your right you cover her eyes, so that her eyelids, being the most sensitive spot of the whole female skin, can read, in the warmth and the lines of your palm, first your desire, then your destiny, the tragic death that awaits you – because a little pity works wonders in seducing women.

MERCURY: Rule two, yes, thank you, I know it by heart.

JUPITER: Then lastly, having broken her resistance, you undo her girdle and you lay her down, with or without a cushion under her head, according to the violence of her circulation?

MERCURY: I have no choice; that is the third and final rule.

JUPITER: And what do you do after that? What do you feel?

MERCURY: What do I feel? Well, nothing out of the ordinary – the same as with Venus!

JUPITER: Then why bother to come to earth?

MERCURY: Oh, you know me – I'm almost human, I like things easy. With this dense atmosphere and green turf, it's much the nicest planet to drop into for a visit, though I must say its metals and oils and inhabitants do have an awfully strong smell – in fact it's the only planet which smells like a wild beast.

JUPITER: Look, the curtain! Look, Mercury, quick!

MERCURY: I know. It's her shadow.

JUPITER: No; not yet. It's only the most unreal, intangible echo of her that the material can hold. It's the shadow of her shadow!

MERCURY: Look, the silhouette's come apart! It was two people embracing! So the shadow wasn't swelling with Jupiter's child, but only with her husband – because that's him – at least I hope it is for your sake – that giant who's closing in and kissing her again!

JUPITER: Yes, that's Amphitryon, her only love.

MERCURY: I begin to see why you do without your divine

vision, Jupiter. It's obviously a good deal less painful to watch the husband's shadow hugging the shadow of his wife than to see the whole performance in flesh-and-blood detail!

JUPITER: Yet there she is, Mercury, playful and loving.

MERCURY: And submissive, apparently.

JUPITER: And so passionate.

MERCURY: And satisfied, I bet.

JUPITER: And faithful!

MERCURY: Yes, but to her husband or herself, that is the question.

JUPITER: The shadow's disappeared. Now Alcmena will be lying down in her languor, abandoning herself to the song of those all-too-happy nightingales!

MERCURY: Don't waste your jealousy on those birds, Jupiter. You know quite well that their contribution to female love is absolutely disinterested. You may sometimes have disguised yourself as a bull to make love to women, but never as a nightingale. Oh no, the one abiding threat is the husband of that gorgeous blonde!

JUPITER: How do you know she's blonde?

MERCURY: Blonde and pink, with the sun shining sweetly in her face, the softness of dawn at her breast, and the depths of night in all the appropriate places.

JUPITER: Are you making this up, or have you really seen her?

MERCURY: While she was having her bath a little while ago, I reverted to my divine vision just for a minute . . . All right, relax. I'm as short-sighted as you are now.

JUPITER: You're not! I can tell by your face – you can see her! Even on a god's face there's a certain glow that's only caused by the reflection of a woman's phosphorescence. Mercury, for pity's sake – what is she doing?

MERCURY: Well, to be absolutely frank, I *can* see her.

JUPITER: Is she alone?

MERCURY: No, Amphitryon's lying there, and she's bending over him. She's lifting his head in her hands, and laughing. Now she kisses it. Now she lets it fall back, her kiss has made

7

it heavier . . . Ah, now I've got a frontal view. I say, I was wrong. She's blonde *all* over.

JUPITER: What about him?

MERCURY: Bronze, all bronze except for two spots of apricot on the nipples.

JUPITER: I meant what is he *doing*?

MERCURY: Patting her, as one pats a young horse. He is, of course, a well-known rider.

JUPITER: And Alcmena?

MERCURY: She's run away. Now she's picked up a gold vase, and – oh, I see, she's sneaking back and she's going to tip the water over his head . . . You could make it freezing if you wanted.

JUPITER: And get him excited, certainly not!

MERCURY: Or boiling.

JUPITER: I should feel I was scalding Alcmena. When a woman loves a man he becomes a part of her.

MERCURY: Yes, but what are you planning to do with the part of Alcmena that *isn't* Amphitryon?

JUPITER: Embrace it and make it fertile!

MERCURY: I know, but how? The main difficulty with respectable women isn't seducing them, it's getting them to yourself in a private place. Their whole virtue depends on half-open doors.

JUPITER: What's your plan, then?

MERCURY: As a human being or a god?

JUPITER: What would be the difference?

MERCURY: Oh well, as a god one would raise her to our height, lay her on clouds, and then a few seconds later let her regain her gravity, heavier by the weight of an embryonic hero.

JUPITER: But I should be missing the most splendid moment of a woman's love.

MERCURY: Is there more than one? Which do you mean?

JUPITER: When she says yes.

MERCURY: Take the human way, then; in at the door, once through the bed, and out at the window.

JUPITER: But she only loves her husband.

MERCURY: So take his shape.

8

JUPITER: Yes, but he's always there. He never leaves the palace. No animal, except possibly the tiger, is so home-loving as the warrior at rest.

MERCURY: Then get him away. There's a formula for conjuring warriors out of their homes.

JUPITER: War?

MERCURY: Have someone declare war on Thebes.

JUPITER: Thebes is at peace with all her enemies.

MERCURY: Then have a friendly nation do it. Neighbours have to do these favours for one another . . . You must face facts, Jupiter. We are gods. Human adventure cuts whatever stylized capers we require. Fate demands far more of us on earth than it does of men. We have to pile up wonders and miracles by the million to get one moment from Alcmena which the clumsiest human being could get by just winking . . . Right, then. Make a man-at-arms appear and proclaim the state of war. Send Amphitryon out at the head of his armies, then assume his shape, and as soon as he's clear let *me* take on the appearance of the slave Sosios, so that I can discreetly inform Alcmena that Amphitryon's only pretending to go away, but he'll be back to spend the night at the palace . . . There, you see: someone's coming already, we'd better hide . . . No, Jupiter, please, *not* a private cloud! You forget that down here we have something that makes us invisible to our creditors, to jealous husbands, even to our worries: that great and perhaps *only* successful democratic institution called Night.

Enter Sosios and the Trumpeter.

SOSIOS: Are you the dawn trumpeter?

TRUMPETER: If you've no objection – yes. And who are you, then? You look like someone I know.

SOSIOS: That would be rather surprising. As it happens, I am Sosios . . . Well, what are you waiting for? Blow!

TRUMPETER: What's your proclamation about?

SOSIOS: You're going to hear, aren't you?

TRUMPETER: Something about lost property?

SOSIOS: Not lost, found. Now kindly blow!

TRUMPETER: You don't seriously imagine I'm going to blow without having a clue what it's about!

SOSIOS: You've no choice. Your trumpet only has one note.

TRUMPETER: It may only have one note, yes, but I happen to be a hymn-writer.

SOSIOS: One-note hymns? Oh, do get on. Orion's coming up.

TRUMPETER: Orion may be coming up, yes, but if there's one thing I'm noted for among one-note trumpeters, it is my habit of pausing before blowing, with my trumpet to my lips, imagining, silently, an entire unheard musical progression of which my note is the triumphant conclusion. This gives it a surprising power.

SOSIOS: Oh, for heaven's sake, hurry, the town will be fast asleep.

TRUMPETER: The town may be fast asleep, yes, but my colleagues, let me tell you, are sick with envy of my technique. I hear that the entire future effort of our schools of trumpeting is to be directed towards improving the quality of their silence. So just tell me what the lost property is, and I will compose a suitable silent hymn.

SOSIOS: The subject is peace.

TRUMPETER: What peace?

SOSIOS: The state known as peace, the interval between two wars! Amphitryon has commanded that I shall read a proclamation every evening to the people of Thebes. It's a hangover from his campaigning days, really, only he's replaced the order of the day by the order of the night. Useful tips on how to guard against insects, or storms, or hiccups. Problems of town planning or religion. All sorts of emergency meetings. And tonight's subject is peace.

TRUMPETER: I see. Something moving, do you think, something sublime?

SOSIOS: Preferably something discreet.

The Trumpeter lifts the trumpet to his lips, beats a few bars with his free hand, and finally blows his note.

My turn now.

TRUMPETER: One normally turns to face one's audience when reciting a speech, not one's author.

SOSIOS: Statesmen think otherwise. Besides, they're all asleep down there, there's not a light showing. Your note can't have carried very well.

TRUMPETER: As long as they heard my silent hymn, that's all I care about.

SOSIOS (*declaiming*): People of Thebes! Here is the one and only proclamation that you can listen to in bed, without even requiring to wake up! My master, General Amphitryon, wishes to speak to you tonight about Peace. Now, what is finer than Peace? What is finer than a general speaking to you about Peace? What could be finer than a general speaking to you about peace of arms in the peace of night?

TRUMPETER: Finer than a general?

SOSIOS: Shut up.

TRUMPETER: Two generals.

Now, behind the very back of Sosios, climbing step by step up the stairway leading to the terrace, the figure of a giant armed Warrior begins looming up.

SOSIOS: Sleep, Thebans! For it is good to sleep on the bosom of a land not ripped by the trenches of war, on unchallenged laws, among birds, dogs, cats and rats who have not known the taste of human flesh. It is good to wear a national face, not as a mask to frighten those who have a different kind of skin or hair, but as the perfect oval for displays of smiles and laughter. It is good, instead of leaping up scaling-ladders, to climb towards sleep up a gentle stairway of lunches, dinners and suppers, to be free to wage in one's own heart, without qualms, the tender civil war of resentments, affections and dreams! Sleep on! What finer panoply than your unarmed naked bodies, flat on their backs, their arms outflung, bearing nothing weightier than a navel. Never was night more clear, more fragrant, more secure. Sleep on.

TRUMPETER: Oh, yes, let's.

The Warrior climbs the last steps and moves towards them.

SOSIOS (*producing a scroll and reading*): We have captured, between the river Ilissus and its tributary, a Thracian roebuck. Between the mounts Olympus and Taygetus, by skilful manoeuvres, we have caused a carpet of green shoots to spring from the furrows, which will grow in due course to be wheat, and we have also launched two waves of bees on the syringas. On the shores of the Aegean, the sight of waves and stars no longer chills our hearts with foreboding, while in the Archipelago we have intercepted many hundreds of signals made from temples to planets, trees to houses, and animals to men, which will take our astrologers centuries to decipher. We are threatened only with centuries of Peace! Accursed be the name of War!

The Warrior is now standing right behind Sosios.

WARRIOR: What's that again?

SOSIOS: I said, as I was commanded to say: Accursed be the name of War!

WARRIOR: I suppose you know who you're talking to?

SOSIOS: No.

WARRIOR: A warrior!

SOSIOS: Ah well – there are many different kinds of war . . .

WARRIOR: Yes, but not warriors . . . Where's your master?

SOSIOS: Up in his room there, the one with the light in it.

WARRIOR: Good old general! Working on his plans of attack, is he?

SOSIOS: Oh, undoubtedly. Smoothing them, stroking them.

WARRIOR: What an artist . . .

SOSIOS: Laying them down and crushing his lips on them.

WARRIOR: It'll be some new theory . . . Well, carry this message to him at once! Tell him to get dressed, and hurry! Is his armour prepared?

SOSIOS: A bit rusty, I should think, but at least it's hung on new hooks.

WARRIOR: Well, what are you waiting for?

SOSIOS: Couldn't it keep till tomorrow? Even his horses are asleep now – laid out on the ground like humans, the peace is so deep. The watch-dogs are snoring in their kennel, while an owl perches on its roof.

WARRIOR: Animals shouldn't trust human peace!

SOSIOS: Listen! Do you hear that faint low murmur from the sea and the countryside? Old men call it the echo of peace.

WARRIOR: These are the very moments when war breaks out.

SOSIOS: War!

WARRIOR: Yes, the Athenians have assembled their forces and crossed the frontier.

SOSIOS: Don't talk such nonsense: they're our allies!

WARRIOR: Have it your own way. So our allies are invading us. They're taking hostages and torturing them. Now wake Amphitryon!

SOSIOS: If it was only sleep I had to wake him from, not happiness as well! And what a time: the very night of the proclamation on peace!

WARRIOR: Oh, nobody heard that stuff. Get on – (*Exit Sosios.*) – and you (*To the Trumpeter*) stay here. Blow your trumpet.

TRUMPETER: What subject, then?

WARRIOR: War!

TRUMPETER: I see. Something moving, do you think, something sublime?

WARRIOR: No. Something youthful.

The trumpet rings out. The Warrior leans over the balustrade and shouts:

Rouse yourselves, Thebans! Here is the one proclamation that can't be heard by sleepers! I want all of you that are fit and able-bodied to stand up, stand apart from the sweating, snoring stew of benighted humanity. Rise up, take up your arms! Add this portion of pure metal which the alloy of human bravery requires! Our theme, people of Thebes, is War!

TRUMPETER: Hark at them shouting!

WARRIOR: Equality, liberty, fraternity – yes, War! All you poor people that fortune has been unkind to, come and revenge yourselves on your enemies! You rich ones, come and taste the supreme joy of staking all your riches, your delights and mistresses, on your country's fate! You gamblers, come and gamble with your lives! You impious sensualists, war gives you carte blanche, you can sharpen your swords on the very statues of the gods, you can take your pick of laws or women! You the lazy ones, be off to the trenches, for war is the triumph of idleness. And you the busy ones, you can be quartermasters. You who love beautiful children, you know that after wars, for some strange reason, more boys are born than girls, except among the Amazons . . . Ah! there it is, down there in that little cottage, the first lamp lighting to the cry of war – and there's the second, the third, all the lamps in the city are coming alive: the first and finest blaze of the whole war, that burns from family to family! . . . Rise up and gather yourselves together. For who would choose, rather than the glory of going and enduring hunger and thirst, of being sucked down in the mud and dying for his country's sake – who, rather than this, would choose the prospect of staying far from the scene of battle, in cowardly peace and comfort . . .

TRUMPETER: I would.

WARRIOR: Besides, there is really nothing to fear. Civilians always exaggerate the risks of war. I am assured that this time at last the soldier's dream will come true, every soldier's certainty as he sets off to war that by some divine conjunction of circumstance not one single man will be killed and any wounds will only be in the left arm, except of course in the case of left-handers . . . Form yourselves into companies! . . . The finest thing nation-hood ever did, when it brought scattered individuals together into one body, was to replace duelling by war. How peace must blush, peace who accepts old, sick, infirm men for death, to realize that war only delivers to death strong men in the prime of human condition! . . . There it is, then. Eat and drink a bit before you go. How sweet it tastes, that last mouthful of rabbit pie washed down with white wine, with your wife in tears and your children getting up from bed one by one, from eldest to youngest, just as they came from nothing! War, we salute you!

TRUMPETER: Here comes Sosios.

Enter Sosios.

WARRIOR: Is your master ready?

SOSIOS: He is. It's my mistress who isn't. The uniform of war is easier put on than the uniform of loneliness.

WARRIOR: Is she the crying type?

SOSIOS: Oh no, she smiles. But her sort of smile heals slower than tears. Here they come now.

WARRIOR: Let's go, then.

Exeunt. Enter Alcmena and Amphitryon.

ALCMENA: I love you, Amphitryon.

AMPHITRYON: I love you, Alcmena.

ALCMENA: That's the whole trouble! If we had just the tiniest bit of hatred for each other, all this wouldn't be so awful.

AMPHITRYON: We may as well face the fact, my darling wife, we don't even begin to hate one another.

ALCMENA: You live with me so absentmindedly, you take it for granted that you have a perfect wife. Are you going to start thinking about me when you're far away? Do you promise?

AMPHITRYON: I'm thinking already, darling.

ALCMENA: Don't stare at the moon like that. You make me jealous. Besides, whatever could you find to think about in that great ball of nothing?

AMPHITRYON: And what can I find in this flaxen head?

ALCMENA: Twin brothers; perfume and memory . . . You've gone and shaved! Does one shave to go to war nowadays? Do you think you look more impressive with a shiny skin?

AMPHITRYON: I shall be wearing my Medusa helmet with its visor down.

ALCMENA: That's the only picture of a woman I'm letting you take . . . Oh, you've cut yourself, you're bleeding! Let me drink the first blood of the war . . . By the way, do you still drink your enemies' blood?

AMPHITRYON: Oh yes, to our mutual health.

ALCMENA: Don't joke about it, darling. Put your visor down, so I can see you like an enemy.

AMPHITRYON: Prepare to tremble!

ALCMENA: There's nothing frightening in that Medusa when

she looks with your eyes . . . Do you think it's attractive, the way she does her hair?

AMPHITRYON: Those are serpents carved in pure gold.

ALCMENA: Real gold?

AMPHITRYON: Unadulterated: and the stones are two emeralds.

ALCMENA: You wicked husband, the way you flirt with war! She gets jewels and nice smooth cheeks; I get bristles and impure gold! How about your greaves – what are they made of?

AMPHITRYON: Silver. Inlaid with platinum.

ALCMENA: Aren't they too tight? Your steel ones are far suppler to run in.

AMPHITRYON: Have you ever seen a general-in-chief running?

ALCMENA: The fact is, you're not carrying one single trace of your wife on you. You might as well be going to a dance, the way you're dressed. I know – you're going to fight the Amazons. And if you die among those mad creatures, they won't find a souvenir of me, not a mark. That would be terrible! I think I'd better bite your arm, before you go . . . Which tunic are you wearing under your cuirass?

AMPHITRYON: The rose-coloured one, with black braid.

ALCMENA: So *that's* what I can see through the joints when you breathe, like glimpses of dawn-tinted flesh . . . Oh, breathe, breathe again, and let me watch that body glimmering through the mournful night . . . You'll stay a bit longer, you do love me, don't you?

AMPHITRYON: Yes, I've got to wait for my horses.

ALCMENA: Lift up Medusa, and try her on the stars . . . Well, look, they shine even brighter. They're lucky; they're getting ready to show you your way.

AMPHITRYON: Generals don't read their way in the stars.

ALCMENA: No, I know, that's admirals . . . Which one will you choose, so that we can both gaze at it this time tomorrow night, and every night. I love you to look at me, even through such a distant and commonplace medium.

AMPHITRYON: Let's choose, then. There is our good friend Venus.

ALCMENA: I really don't trust Venus. In matters of love, I'd rather look after my own interests.

AMPHITRYON: Well, there's Jupiter – a fine name for you.

ALCMENA: Aren't there any *without* names?

AMPHITRYON: There is that little one over there, which astronomers call the nameless star.

ALCMENA: But that's really a name too. Which one shone on your victories? Oh, darling, tell me about your victories – how do you win them? Tell me the secret! Do you win them by shouting my name as you charge through the enemy barricade, to find nothing but the houses and children and wives you also left behind?

AMPHITRYON: No, my darling.

ALCMENA: Then tell me what you do!

AMPHITRYON: I win by encircling their left wing with my right wing, then cutting up their entire right wing with three quarters of my left wing, and finally launching the remaining quarter at them, and that clinches the victory.

ALCMENA: But it's a marvellous battle of birds! How many have you won, my beloved eagle?

AMPHITRYON: Exactly one.

ALCMENA: Dear husband, whose one victory outshines whole lives of conquest! By tomorrow there will be two, won't there? Because you're going to come back – you're not going to be killed!

AMPHITRYON: Better ask the Fates.

ALCMENA: But you can't be killed! It would be too unfair. Commanders-in-chief should never be killed!

AMPHITRYON: Why not?

ALCMENA: Why? Because they have the loveliest wives, the finest palaces, they have glory. Darling, you have the biggest collection of gold plate in all Greece: a human life can't fly away carrying a weight like that! Besides, you have Alcmena to think of.

AMPHITRYON: And I shall think of Alcmena to give me strength to kill my enemies.

ALCMENA: How do you kill them?

AMPHITRYON: I wound them with my javelin, I strike them down with my spear, and I kill them with my sword, which I leave in the wound.

ALCMENA: But then every time you kill an enemy you're disarmed, like a bee after stinging! I'll never sleep again, your methods are far too dangerous! Have you killed many?

AMPHITRYON: Exactly one.

ALCMENA: Oh, darling, you are good! Was it a king, or a general?

AMPHITRYON: Neither. A common soldier.

ALCMENA: You see, you're so modest! You're not the sort to judge men by their class even when you're killing them. Did you leave him a few moments between the spear and the sword to recognize who you were and the honour you were doing him?

AMPHITRYON: Yes, he looked at my Medusa, and there was a sort of sad, respectful smile on his blood-stained lips.

ALCMENA: Did he tell you his name before he died?

AMPHITRYON: He was a nameless soldier. Unlike stars, there are quite a lot like that.

ALCMENA: Oh, why didn't he say his name? I'd have put up a monument to him in the palace. His shrine would have been decked every day with flowers and votive offerings. Of all the shades in the underworld, none would have been so spoilt as the one my husband killed . . . Oh, my darling, I'm so glad you've only had one victim and one victory: perhaps it means you'll only need one woman too . . . Here are your horses! Kiss me!

AMPHITRYON: My horses jog along easier than that; but I don't mind kissing you all the same . . . Gently, love, don't squeeze so hard: you'll do yourself an injury! You forget I'm an iron husband.

ALCMENA: Can you feel me through your cuirass?

AMPHITRYON: I feel your living warmth. It strikes at me through all the joints where arrows could strike. What can you feel?

ALCMENA: A body is a kind of armour too. Even when I've

18

been lying in your arms, I've often felt you were colder and further off than you are now.

AMPHITRYON: And I've often felt you sadder and more upset in my arms when I was only going off to hunt, not to war . . . Now you're smiling! Anyone would think this sudden announcement of war had taken some weight off your heart.

ALCMENA: Do you remember that child that was crying under our window the other morning? Couldn't you see that was a dark omen?

AMPHITRYON: Omens begin with a crash of thunder in a cloudless sky, and a triple lightning to follow.

ALCMENA: The sky was cloudless, and that child was crying. To me that's the worst omen of all.

AMPHITRYON: Don't you start being superstitious, Alcmena! Stick to the official auguries. Has your chamber-maid given birth to a pock-marked, web-footed girl?

ALCMENA: No, but my heart was wrung, and when I thought I was laughing there were tears pouring down my face. I was sure some terrible thing was threatening our happiness . . . Well, thank heavens, it was war, and that almost *is* a relief, because at least war is an honest, straightforward danger; I prefer enemies with swords and spears. It was only war!

AMPHITRYON: But what had you to fear *apart* from war? We have the good luck to be young citizens of a comparatively young planet, where the wicked haven't progressed beyond primary wickedness – rape, parricide, incest, and things like that. We are reasonably well liked. Death would find us both united against him. And what is there about us that could be threatened?

ALCMENA: Our love! I was afraid you'd deceive me. I saw you in other women's arms.

AMPHITRYON: All other women?

ALCMENA: One or all, what's the difference? You were lost to Alcmena. The offence was the same.

AMPHITRYON: You are the loveliest woman in Greece.

ALCMENA: Then it wasn't the Greeks I was afraid of. It was goddesses, and foreign women.

AMPHITRYON: It was *what*?

ALCMENA: Goddesses first. I mean, when they just appear from the sky or the water, all pink and pearly without need of rouge or powder, and their tender young breasts and their heavenly looks, and they clasp you with arms and ankles whiter than snow and stronger than crowbars, it must be quite a job to resist them, mustn't it?

AMPHITRYON: For anyone else but me, quite a job!

ALCMENA: But like all gods, they take offence at nothing, and they demand love. You didn't love them.

AMPHITRYON: Or the foreign women.

ALCMENA: They loved you, though! They love all married men, any man who belongs to anyone else, even to knowledge or fame. Once they arrive in our towns, with their superb luggage, the beautiful ones practically naked under their silks or furs, and the ugly ones wearing their ugliness with the arrogance of beauty because it's a foreign ugliness, that's the end of domestic peace for soldiers or artists. Anything foreign attracts a man far more powerfully than his own home. Foreign women are like magnets, tugging to themselves precious stones and rare manuscripts and expensive flowers and the hands of married men. They even find themselves irresistibly foreign . . . That was my fear for you, my darling husband, when all these omens tormented me! I was afraid of the names of seasons, fruits or pleasures spoken with a foreign accent, all the acts of love touched with a strange perfume or an unfamiliar boldness. I was afraid of a foreign woman! And now war comes, almost like a friend. The least I can do is not to cry in front of her.

AMPHITRYON: Alcmena, my darling wife, listen to me: when I'm with you, you're my foreign woman, and later, when I'm in battle, I shall think of you as my wife. So wait for me and don't be afraid. I shall soon be back, back for good. Every war is the war to end war. This one is between neighbours, and it won't take long. We shall live happy in our palace, and when extreme old age comes at last, I shall get some god to perpetuate it by turning us into trees, like Philemon and Baucis.

ALCMENA: Would you enjoy changing your leaves every year?

AMPHITRYON: We'll choose evergreens. Laurels suit me rather well.

ALCMENA: And when we grow old, I suppose they'll chop us down and burn us?

AMPHITRYON: And the ashes of our bark and branches will mingle in the dust!

ALCMENA: The ashes of our flesh and bones would have done just as well.

The sound of horses' hooves is heard outside.

AMPHITRYON: This time it is them. I must go.

ALCMENA: Them – who? Your ambition, your pride as a commander, your lust for blood and adventure?

AMPHITRYON: No, just Elaphocephalus and Hypsipila, my horses.

ALCMENA: Go, then! I'll feel better, seeing you ride off on those jaunty cruppers.

AMPHITRYON: Is that all you've got to say?

ALCMENA: Haven't I said just about everything? What do other wives do?

AMPHITRYON: They try to make a joke of it. Or they hold out your shield and say: Come back on it or under it! Or they shout out: Fear nothing but the sky falling! Has my wife no gift for noble phrases?

ALCMENA: They frighten me. I can't make phrases to suit posterity rather than you. All I can say are words that softly die as they touch you: Amphitryon, I love you, Amphitryon, come back soon! Besides, there isn't much room left in phrases when one's said your name, it's so *long* . . .

AMPHITRYON: Then put it last. Good-bye, Alcmena.

ALCMENA: Amphitryon!

He goes, and she stays for a few moments leaning on the balustrade, as the horses' hooves die away. Then she turns to go back into the palace; but is stopped by Mercury, disguised as Sosios.

MERCURY: Alcmena – madam.

ALCMENA: Yes, Sosios?

MERCURY: I have a message for you, madam, from my master.

ALCMENA: You have *what*? He's not even out of earshot.

MERCURY: Exactly. But no-one must hear . . . My master has charged me to tell you, firstly, that he is only making pretence of going with the army, and secondly, that he'll be back this very night, as soon as he has given them their orders. The headquarters are encamped only a few leagues off, the war seems likely to be a harmless one, and Amphitryon will make this journey home every night, in secret of course . . .

ALCMENA: Sosios, I don't understand what you're saying.

MERCURY: My master, princess, has charged me to tell you that he is only *pretending* to leave with the army . . .

ALCMENA: Oh, Sosios, you're so stupid. You know absolutely nothing about secrets. The whole point is to pretend not to hear or not to know, when one knows very well.

MERCURY: Of course, madam.

ALCMENA: And besides, I haven't understood a single thing you've said.

MERCURY: You must stay up, princess, and wait for my master. He has charged me to tell you . . .

ALCMENA: Oh, Sosios, do please shut up. I'm going to bed.

She goes into the palace. Mercury beckons to Jupiter, who appears disguised as Amphitryon.

MERCURY: Well, Jupiter, did you hear them?

JUPITER: What do you mean: Jupiter? I am Amphitryon!

MERCURY: You can't fool me. Divinity is clearly visible at twenty paces.

JUPITER: These are an exact copy of his clothes.

MERCURY: As if clothes mattered! Besides, you've even got the clothes wrong: look at them. You've just emerged from the brambles, but they're not even scratched. I see no sign of that uncontrollable tendency to wear and loss of shape that the best fabrics show on their very first day of use. Your garments are frankly eternal. I'm quite sure they're water-proof, non-fading, and unstainable even with lamp-oil. To a good housewife like Alcmena, those are real miracles, and you needn't suppose she'll miss them. Now turn round.

JUPITER: Why turn round?

MERCURY: Men, like gods, imagine that women only see them from the front. They put up a great show of moustaches and gold chains, and throw out their chests. What they fail to realize is that women, while pretending to be dazzled by this splendid façade, are really having a crafty look at the gentleman's back. It's their lovers' backs as they get up or go out, bent, drooping, truthful backs, that betray their tiredness or lethargy. Your back, my good sir, is more flattering than any chest could be! It will have to go!

JUPITER: Gods never turn their backs, Mercury. Anyway, it will be dark.

MERCURY: That remains to be seen. It won't be very dark if you keep the lustre of your divinity at its present pitch. Alcmena is hardly going to mistake this human glow-worm for her husband.

JUPITER: All my other mistresses fell for it.

MERCURY: Not one, I assure you. Besides, you may as well admit that you rather enjoyed giving the secret away by some godlike action, or one of those sudden bursts of light that make your body translucent and spare all the bother of oil-lamps in the room.

JUPITER: Even a god may want to be loved for his own sake.

MERCURY: I'm afraid Alcmena won't oblige you there. Stick to her husband's shape.

JUPITER: I will to begin with; after that, we'll see. You wouldn't believe, Mercury, the surprises one gets from faithful women. You know faithful women are the only ones I ever love. I happen to be the god of justice among other things, and I felt they were entitled to some reward; also, I may say, they seemed to expect it. Faithful women are the ones who expect from the spring-time, from books or perfumes or earth tremors, the sort of revelation that others expect from their lovers. In fact, they are unfaithful to their husbands with the entire physical world, apart from men. Alcmena is unlikely to be an exception to the rule. I shall begin by fulfilling Amphitryon's functions as best I can, and then gradually, by cunningly placed questions about flowers, animals, and the elements, I shall get to know what image haunts her imagination. I shall take its shape; and will then be loved for myself. . . . Are my clothes better now?

MERCURY: Your whole body must be exactly right. Come over into the light, and let me adjust your mortal uniform. No, closer, I can't see you properly.

JUPITER: Will my eyes do?

MERCURY: Your eyes – let's see, now . . . Oh, no, much too brilliant. They're all iris, no cornea, and not a trace of tear-gland – you may easily need to cry, you know – and when you look at something, there's no impact on any optic nerve, it comes straight through your brain from the outside source. Don't go to heaven for your human eyes, whatever you do. Earthly light corresponds to what we in heaven would call total darkness. Down here even murderers' eyes are no better than night-lights. Didn't you ever use pupils on your previous visits?

JUPITER: Never, I forgot . . . Is this right for pupils?

MERCURY: No, for goodness' sake, no phosphorus! They're like cats' eyes! I can still see the pupils through your eyelids when you blink. Nothing reflects in that sort of eye. You must give them a backing.

JUPITER: Sunstone wouldn't be bad – a nice glint of gold to it.

MERCURY: Now your skin.

JUPITER: What's wrong with my skin?

MERCURY: Far too smooth and soft – like a child's. You need a skin that's had thirty years of weathering, thirty years of bathing in the air and sea – in fact a skin with a flavour, because it's going to be tasted. Didn't your other women say anything when they discovered that Jupiter's skin tasted like a child's?

JUPITER: It didn't make their caresses any more motherly, I assure you.

MERCURY: That skin wouldn't stand a couple of night's wear. And do tighten your human envelope: you're floating!

24

JUPITER: Yes, but I hate it tight . . . There, now I can feel my
heart beating, my arteries swelling, my veins getting heavy:
I'm turning into an awful sort of percolator, an hour-glass
full of blood. And this human hour battering away inside me,
it hurts. I hope all wretched humans don't suffer like this.

MERCURY: Only the day they're born and the day they die.

JUPITER: Well, it's extremely unpleasant to feel yourself being
born and dying simultaneously.

MERCURY: It's no pleasanter taken separately.

JUPITER: Do you feel yet that you're looking at a human being?

MERCURY: Not really, no. The main thing that strikes me about
a man, a living flesh-and-blood man, is that he's continually
changing, he's getting a fraction older every second. I can
even see the light in his eyes ageing.

JUPITER: Right, I'll try. And to accustom myself to the idea,
I'll keep repeating: I am going to die, I am going to die . . .

MERCURY: Hey, steady, now you're overdoing it! I can see your
hair growing, and your nails, and wrinkles burrowing into
your face . . . There, that's the way, control your pulse-rate.
You were living at the speed of a dog or cat.

JUPITER: Is that it?

MERCURY: No, too slow now; a fish-pulse. There! That's just
right – the same gentle jog-trot by which Amphitryon recog-
nizes his horses and Alcmena her husband's heart.

JUPITER: Any last tips?

MERCURY: How about your brain?

JUPITER: My brain?

MERCURY: Your brain. It's advisable to lose no time in replacing
divine notions with human ones. What do you think, now
you're a man? What are your beliefs, what is your view of the
universe?

JUPITER: My view of the universe? I believe that the flat earth
is entirely flat, that water is simply water, nature is nature and
spirit spirit. Anything else?

MERCURY: Do you feel an inclination to part your hair and hold
it in place with hair oil?

JUPITER: As a matter of fact, I do.

MERCURY: Do you feel that you alone exist, I mean that you can only be sure of your own existence?

JUPITER: Yes. It even feels odd to be imprisoned inside oneself.

MERCURY: Do you feel that one day you could die?

JUPITER: Certainly not. My friends will die, oh yes, my poor friends – but not me.

MERCURY: And have you forgotten all the women you loved in the past?

JUPITER: Loved – me? I have never loved anyone – anyone except Alcmena.

MERCURY: Perfect! And what about the sky, then?

JUPITER: I think the sky all belongs to me – much more now I'm mortal than when I was Jupiter! I think the solar system is really quite small, and the earth's huge, and I suddenly feel handsomer than Apollo, braver and sexier than Mars, and for the first time I really believe, and see, and feel that I am master of the gods.

MERCURY: In that case you really are a man . . . Good luck!

Exit Mercury. Alcmena appears on her balcony, very wide awake.

ALCMENA: Who's that knocking? Who rouses me from sleep?

JUPITER: A stranger that you'll be pleased to see.

ALCMENA: I know no strangers.

JUPITER: A general.

ALCMENA: What are generals doing out on the road so late? Are they deserting? Or defeated?

JUPITER: Only defeated by love.

ALCMENA: That's their look-out if they start attacking people who aren't generals. Who are you?

JUPITER: Your lover.

ALCMENA: You are addressing Alcmena, sir, not her chamber-maid. I have no lover . . . What's so funny about that?

JUPITER: Would you deny that you opened your window a short time ago, and stared out into the night with something like desperation?

ALCMENA: Perfectly true, I was observing the night. I'm happy to tell you that it's mild and clear.

JUPITER: Would you deny that you also tipped some icy water out of a gold vase on to a reclining warrior?

ALCMENA: As cold as that, was it? Good . . . It's quite possible.

JUPITER: Did you or did you not stand before the portrait of a man, and murmur "If I could only lose my memory till he comes back"?

ALCMENA: I don't remember. I may have.

JUPITER: And as you stood under those youthful stars, didn't you feel your body blossom and your heart contract, thinking of a man who may in some ways, I admit, be very stupid and very ugly?

ALCMENA: He is very handsome and in some ways rather too clever. And yes, my mouth is full of honey when I speak of him. And I do remember about the gold vase, and it was him I was seeing in the shadows. Is that supposed to prove something?

JUPITER: It proves that you have a lover, and that he is there.

ALCMENA: I have a husband, and he is not here. And nobody but my husband will enter my room. Not even him, if he starts disguising his name.

JUPITER: At this hour the very heavens are masked.

ALCMENA: You can't be very intelligent if you really think that night is day with a mask on, or the moon a counterfeit sun, or that a wife's love could disguise itself as lust.

JUPITER: A wife's love is a kind of duty . . . Duty is constraint, and constraint kills desire.

ALCMENA: I beg your pardon? What was that name you just said?

JUPITER: The name of a demi-god: Desire.

ALCMENA: We only like whole gods here. We leave demi-gods to demi-wives and demi-virgins.

JUPITER: Now you're being blasphemous.

ALCMENA: I'm even worse sometimes, because I'm *glad* that there's no god of married love in Olympus. I'm glad I'm a kind of creature the gods never foresaw. I feel no god hovering over this particular joy, only a clear sky. So if you're a lover, I'm terribly sorry, but go. Not that you don't seem very strong and handsome, and you have a nice gentle voice. I should love that voice, if only it spoke to me of fidelity and not desire! I should love to sink into those arms if they weren't a trap that would close brutally on its prey! And your mouth seems fresh and passionate; but it doesn't convince me. I shall not open my doors to a lover. Who are you?

JUPITER: Why don't you want a lover?

ALCMENA: Because lovers are always concentrating more on love than on the beloved. Because I can't bear a limited joy, a tactful pleasure or a controlled abandon. Because I want neither a slave nor a master. Because it's ill-bred to deceive one's husband, even with himself. Because I like clean sheets and open windows.

JUPITER: I must say, for a woman, you certainly put up some reasons for your tastes. Congratulations; and now let me in!

ALCMENA: Unless you are the one at whose side I wake in the morning and whom I let sleep on for another ten minutes on the fringe of my day, whose face is washed by my watching before sun or water ever touch it; unless you are the one of whom I know, by the length and sound of his steps, whether he is shaving or getting dressed, thoughtful or empty-headed, the one I breakfast, lunch and sup with, whose breath is always, whatever I do, a thousandth of a second ahead of mine; unless you are the one I let fall asleep every night ten minutes before I do, ten minutes stolen from the quick of my life, so that at the very moment he slides into dreams I can feel his body still warm and living: whoever else you may be, I shall not let you in. Who are you?

JUPITER: I see I shall have to tell you the truth. I am your husband.

ALCMENA: What – you, Amphitryon! Don't you realize what a risk you're taking, coming back like this?

JUPITER: No one at the camp suspects it.

ALCMENA: That's not the point! Surely you know what a husband is liable to find if he returns unannounced after making an elaborate departure?

JUPITER: Don't joke about it.

ALCMENA: You must know that this is the moment when faithful wives open their clammy arms to some little friend, panting with pride and trepidation?

JUPITER: Your arms are empty, and fresher than the moon.

ALCMENA: Oh, I've been giving him a chance to get away, gossiping here with you. He'll be on the road to Thebes by now, poor boy, whimpering and cursing, with his tunic tangled up in his bare legs.

JUPITER: Let your husband in.

ALCMENA: Oh, you think you can get in just because you're my husband? Have you brought me presents? Jewels?

JUPITER: Would you sell yourself for jewels?

ALCMENA: To my own husband? With the greatest pleasure! But you haven't brought any!

JUPITER: I'd obviously better go back where I came from.

ALCMENA: No, stay! stay! . . . But on one condition, Amphitryon, one definite condition.

JUPITER: Which is?

ALCMENA: That we speak aloud in the presence of night the vows we've only made before by day. I've waited ages for this chance. I don't want this superb assembly of stars, shadows, moths and breeze to think I'm entertaining a lover tonight. Let us celebrate our nocturnal marriage, at the hour when so many false unions are consummated. You start.

JUPITER: What good are vows without priests or altars, spoken against the void of night?

ALCMENA: Imperishable words are cut in glass. Lift your arm, now.

JUPITER: If you only knew, Alcmena, how pathetic human beings seem to the gods, spouting their eternal oaths and brandishing bolts without thunder!

ALCMENA: All they ask is a few nice lightnings with a bit of warmth in them. Lift your arm, and bend the forefinger.

JUPITER: The forefinger bent! But that's the most terrible oath, the one Jupiter uses to call down plagues upon the earth.

ALCMENA: Either you bend it, or go.

JUPITER: I have no choice, then, have I? (*He raises his arm.*)

29

Stay in your vats, thick blacknesses of heaven! Locusts and scorpions – as you were! This little witch Alcmena has forced the gesture from me.

ALCMENA: I'm waiting.

JUPITER: I, Amphitryon, son and grandson of former generals, sire and grandsire of future ones, indispensible buckle in the glorious belt of war . . .

ALCMENA: I, Alcmena, whose parents are dead and whose children not yet born, poor newly-severed link from the chain of humanity . . .

JUPITER: I swear that through my acts the sweetness of Alcmena's name shall live as long as the thunder of my own!

ALCMENA: I swear that I will be faithful to my husband Amphitryon, or else die!

JUPITER: Or what?

ALCMENA: Or die.

JUPITER: Don't call death in where she's no business! Please, I beg you, don't say that word. There are plenty of synonyms, even quite happy ones. Don't talk about dying!

ALCMENA: Too late, it's done. And now no more words, dear husband. The ceremony is over and you can come up . . . How you will complicate everything! I was waiting for you, and the door was open. All you had to do was push . . . What's the matter, aren't you coming? You want me to call you lover, is that it? Well, I'm not going to!

JUPITER: I really can come in, Alcmena? You really want me to?

ALCMENA: I command you to, my darling!

Curtain

30

ACT TWO

Total darkness. Mercury is reclining in lonely splendour at the front of the stage.

MERCURY: I have been keeping watch outside Alcmena's bed-room, listening to – how shall I say ? – a sweet silence, a sweet resistance, a sweet struggle. And now Alcmena carries within herself the germ of a young demi-god. I can't remember any other of Jupiter's mistresses that he's stayed so long with, though . . . I don't know if you find this darkness as oppressive as I do, but the job of keeping it dark around here is beginning to wear me out, especially when I consider that everywhere else is already bathed in morning sunlight. Here we are at the height of summer, and it's seven in the morning. The great flood of dawn is spreading, millions of fathoms deep even over the sea, and among all the little cubes now bathed in pink, only the palace remains a cone of inky black. It's really time I woke my master up, because he loathes being rushed over his leave-taking, and he's bound to insist on telling Alcmena, as he tells all his girl friends the moment he's out of bed, that he's really Jupiter, so as to have the pleasure of her surprise and pride. I have as a matter of fact put it into Amphitryon's mind to come and pay an impromptu call on his wife, so that he can be the first witness and guarantor of the happy event. One owes him the courtesy, I feel, and it will also avoid any misunderstanding. So at this very moment our general is secretly mounting his horse and galloping off in this direction; he'll be here within the hour. Let's see a few of your rays, then, sun, and I'll choose the right one to burn up these shadows. (*The sun offers its rays for inspection, one by one.*) No, not that one! We don't want anything as sinister as green light for waking lovers; they'll each think they've got a drowned body in their arms. Not that, either! Purple and violet are much too stimulating: keep them for tonight. There, that's the right one, the amber; there's nothing like it for

putting a bit of richness into the insipidity of human skin . . .
Carry on, sun!

*Alcmena's room appears in an instant blaze of sunlight. She is
already up, while Jupiter-Amphitryon is still stretched out asleep
in bed.*

ALCMENA: Get up, darling. The sun is up.

JUPITER: Where am I?

ALCMENA: Where husbands are continually surprised to find
themselves on waking: simply in your own bed, in your house,
beside your own wife.

JUPITER. And what's my wife's name?

ALCMENA: Her name by day is the same as her name by night,
it's still Alcmena.

JUPITER: Alcmena, that nice plump blonde who makes love in
silence?

ALCMENA: Yes, and who starts chattering at sunrise, and who's
about to give you your marching orders, husband or no
husband.

JUPITER: She'd far better shut up and come back into my arms.

ALCMENA: I wouldn't bank on it. Nice plump women are like
dreams, they can only be embraced at night.

JUPITER: Shut your eyes and let us enjoy the darkness.

ALCMENA: No, no, my night is not *the* night. Get up, or I'll call
for help.

*Jupiter sits up and gazes out at the landscape sparkling beyond the
windows.*

JUPITER: What a divine night!

ALCMENA: Oh, darling, you're a bit weak on the adjectives this
morning.

JUPITER: I repeat: divine!

ALCMENA: If you call a meal divine, or a bit of beef divine – all
right, one can't be inventive all the time. But for last night I
do think you might have found something better.

JUPITER: What could be better?

ALCMENA: Almost anything except your dreary word divine: it's so absurdly old-fashioned. You could say perfect, you could say charming – or best of all, delightful, which suggests many things at once: What a delightful night!

JUPITER: Far and away our most delightful night together, wouldn't you say?

ALCMENA: That remains to be seen.

JUPITER: I beg your pardon?

ALCMENA: Don't you remember our wedding night, dear husband, and the frail burden I was in your arms, and how we found our two hearts wrapped together for the first time in darkness? That was our most beautiful night.

JUPITER: All right, our most beautiful. But this was still the most *delightful*.

ALCMENA: Do you think so? Oh, surely that night of the big fire in Thebes, when you came back at dawn with its glow still on you, hot and golden like a new-baked loaf – that was the most delightful, definitely.

JUPITER: Well, the most surprising then, if you like.

ALCMENA: Why surprising? Now, the night before last really *was* surprising, when you'd rescued that child who was being carried out to sea by the current, and you came in all glistening with seaweed and moonlight, salted by the gods, and you spent the whole night life-saving me in your sleep. That was surprising enough!. . . No, darling, if I wanted a word for last night I think I'd choose "conjugal". There was such a cosy sense of security about it to me. I've never felt so sure of finding you still there in the morning, all pink and alive and hungry for breakfast; for once I didn't have that sort of divine misgiving I always have that you'll suddenly die in my arms.

JUPITER: I see women do sometimes use the word "divine" then.

ALCMENA: Oh, with the word "misgiving", certainly.

Pause.

JUPITER: What a delightful room this is!

33

ALCMENA: Yes, you would say that the one morning you're not supposed to be here.

JUPITER: Men are so clever! I mean, to invent this system of windows and transparent stones which allows them to see better in their houses than any other creature in this rather underlit planet.

ALCMENA: Not very modest of you to say so, my darling, as you invented it.

JUPITER: And what a marvellous view!

ALCMENA: Yes, you can praise that, it wasn't your doing.

JUPITER: Whose was it, then?

ALCMENA: The Master of the Gods.

JUPITER: And who might that be?

ALCMENA: Jupiter.

JUPITER: You pronounce the names of gods so beautifully! Who taught you to munch them with your lips like that, as if they were some celestial food? It reminds me of a white ewe who's taken a mouthful of broom and stands with her head high, chewing. But your mouth gives perfume to the broom. Say it again. Sometimes, we're told, gods even answer with their presence if you call on them by name.

ALCMENA: Neptune! Apollo!

JUPITER: No, the first one again!

ALCMENA: But I want to munch my way right round Olympus! Besides, I really prefer saying the names of the gods in pairs: like Mars and Venus, Jupiter and Juno. Then I can see them marching on the cloud-crests in pairs, eternally holding hands – oh, it must be so wonderful!

JUPITER: And so gay . . . You like it then, do you, this work of Jupiter, these cliffs and crags?

ALCMENA: Oh, I love it. But did he do it on purpose?

JUPITER: I beg your pardon!

ALCMENA: I know *you* do everything on purpose, darling, whether it's grafting cherry-trees on to plum-stocks or designing a double-bladed sabre. But do you think Jupiter really knew what he was doing on the day of creation?

JUPITER: So we are told.

ALCMENA: He created the earth. But I mean, the earth's beauty re-creates itself all the time. The most miraculous thing about it is its impermanence – and surely Jupiter is too serious to have created anything that wasn't permanent.

JUPITER: Perhaps you don't have a very clear idea of what creation was like.

ALCMENA: No, any more than I do about the end of the world. I'm as far from one as from the other, and neither memory nor foresight helps me. Why, can you imagine it, darling?

JUPITER: I can see it distinctly. In the beginning, chaos reigned. Jupiter's really inspired idea was to split it up into the four elements.

ALCMENA: Do we only have four?

JUPITER: Yes, four, the first being water – and that wasn't the simplest thing to create, I can tell you! I mean to say, water looks natural enough now, doesn't it – but to have thought of creating water, having the *idea* of water, that's another matter altogether!

ALCMENA: What used goddesses to weep with, then – bronze?

JUPITER: Don't interrupt. I'm trying to show you what Jupiter was like. He might appear to you at any moment. You surely wouldn't like him to explain it himself, in all his grandeur?

ALCMENA: Oh, no, he must have explained it so often. I'm sure you put more imagination into it.

JUPITER: Where was I?

ALCMENA: We'd nearly finished: something about chaos, I think.

JUPITER: Oh, yes. Yes, Jupiter suddenly had this brilliant idea of a sort of elastic, incompressible force which would fill up the gaps and absorb all the shocks of an ill-regulated atmosphere.

ALCMENA: Was foam one of his ideas?

JUPITER: No, but once water existed, he had the idea of edging it with irregular coasts, to break up storms, and he also prevented the gods' eyes being tired with a continually glittering horizon by scattering around rocky or soluble continents. The earth and all its wonders were created . . .

ALCMENA: What about pine-trees?

JUPITER: Pine-trees?

ALCMENA: Umbrella pines, cedars, cypresses, all those clumps of blue and dark green without which no landscape is complete. And how about echo?

JUPITER: Echo?

ALCMENA: Well echoed. And colours, did he create colours?

JUPITER: The seven colours of the rainbow are his.

ALCMENA: Yes, but are my favourite ones: purple and bronze, and lizard green?

JUPITER: He left those to the dyers. But by harnessing the various ethereal vibrations to molecular impacts or reverberations, or to refractions and counter-refractions of light, he did manage to spread hundreds of different networks of sound and colour through the universe, whether human organs can catch them or not – after all, what does it matter to him?

ALCMENA: But that's exactly what I said!

JUPITER: What did you say?

ALCMENA: That he did nothing! Except hurl us into a ghastly sea of illusion and bewilderment which we have to do our best with, my dear husband and I.

JUPITER: Alcmena, this is blasphemy. The gods are listening!

ALCMENA: Oh, but they have different acoustics from ours. As far as the supreme being is concerned, I'm sure the beating of my heart drowns all my silly chatter, because it's a heart that's simple and honest. Anyway, why should they be angry with me? I don't have to feel any special gratitude to Jupiter for giving us four elements instead of the twenty we really needed, because that's always been his business; whereas my heart overflows with gratitude to my dear husband Amphitryon, because he found time between battles to invent a system of pulleys for windows or a new way of grafting fruit trees. You've changed the flavour of a cherry for me, and the breadth of a sunbeam: you are my creator . . . Now why are you looking at me like that? Compliments always seem to annoy you; your whole pride is centred on me. I'm too earthbound for you, is that it?

JUPITER (*rising, with great solemnity*) : Would you like to be less so ?

ALCMENA : No, it would make us less close.

JUPITER : Haven't you ever wanted to be a goddess, or nearly a goddess ?

ALCMENA : Certainly not. Whatever for ?

JUPITER : For everyone to honour and revere you.

ALCMENA : They do that for me even as a simple woman, which is far more praiseworthy.

JUPITFR : Your flesh would be lighter, you could walk on air or water.

ALCMENA : Every wife does that, even carrying the weight of a faithful husband.

JUPITER : You would understand the causes of things, of other worlds too.

ALCMENA : Oh, I've never been interested in the neighbours.

JUPITER : You'd be immortal!

ALCMENA : Immortal ? What for ? What good would that do me ?

JUPITER : What good! You wouldn't die, that's what!

ALCMENA : And what would I do, then, if I didn't die ?

JUPITER : You would live eternally, dear Alcmena, transformed into a star; you would twinkle in the night till the world's end.

ALCMENA : Which will be when ?

JUPITER : Never.

ALCMENA : Quite an evening! And what will you be doing ?

JUPITER : I shall be a voiceless shade, sunk in the mists of hell, happy to think that my lady is shining up there in the clear air.

ALCMENA : You usually like to take a more active part in your pleasures. No, my darling, the gods had better not count on me for the job. Besides, the night air is terrible for my fair complexion. I should be extremely chapped in the halls of eternity!

JUPITER : You'll be extremely cold and empty in the halls of death!

ALCMENA : Death doesn't frighten me; it's the stake one plays life for. As your Jupiter, rightly or wrongly, created death in the world, I'm going along with it. I'm too conscious of a connection between my fibres and those of other men and animals and plants, not to want to share their fate. Until there's such a thing as an immortal vegetable, don't talk to me about not dying. It's a sort of betrayal for a human to become immortal. Besides, when I think of the perfect rest death will give us from all our little tirednesses and third-rate sorrows, I'm grateful to it for its fullness, its bounty even. After sixty years of fussing about badly coloured clothes and badly cooked meals, the relief of finding death, peaceful, restful death, is out of all proportion . . . Why are you suddenly looking at me with such respect?

JUPITER: Because you're the first truly human being I've met.

ALCMENA: Oh, that's my speciality in the world; you don't know how right you are. Of all the people I know, I'm the least disposed to quarrel with my destiny. I gladly accept all the ups and downs of human life, from birth to death, I even accept family meals. My senses are moderate and well-controlled. I'm sure I'm the only woman alive who sees fruits and spiders in their true proportions, and tastes her pleasures for what they are. It's the same with my intelligence, too. It seems to lack that element of sport or delusion which only needs a little wine, or love, or fine scenery, to kindle a desire for eternity.

JUPITER: But wouldn't you like to have a son who was less human than you: immortal, in a word?

ALCMENA: It's only human to want your son to be immortal.

JUPITER: A son who would grow to be the greatest of heroes, and even in his infancy would be capable of fighting with lions and monsters?

ALCMENA: In his infancy! In his infancy he will have a spaniel and a tortoise.

JUPITER: He'd kill huge serpents that had come to strangle him in his cradle.

ALCMENA: He'll never be left alone. That sort of accident only happens to working class babies. No, I want him to be a weak whimperer who is frightened of flies . . . What are you getting so worked up about now?

JUPITER: Alcmena, let's try and talk seriously, shall we. Would you really kill yourself rather than be unfaithful to your husband?

ALCMENA: You're very unkind to doubt it!

JUPITER: But killing yourself is dangerous!

ALCMENA: Not for me; I can assure you, my dearest husband, there'll be nothing tragic about my death. Who knows? It may happen this very night, in this very place, supposing the god of war should strike you down, or for any other reason. But I shall make sure that those who see me will find it a peaceful sight, not a nightmare. There must be a way for corpses to smile or fold their hands that makes everything right.

JUPITER: But what if you carried the germ of a son, conceived the night before, into death with you, half alive?

ALCMENA: It would only be a half-death for him. His future fate would have been worse.

JUPITER: How can you talk about it all so simply and calmly, without even having thought about it?

ALCMENA: Without having thought? Have you never wondered what those nice, plump, gay, laughing young women of yours were thinking about? They're thinking about the best way to die simply, without fuss, if their love is betrayed or trampled on.

JUPITER (*rising majestically*): Now listen, my dear Alcmena. You are a god-fearing woman and I can see you understand the mysteries of this world. It is time for me to speak seriously . . .

ALCMENA: Oh, Amphitryon darling, no! You've suddenly gone all solemn. I know what it's leading up to – it's your way of being tender. It always makes me nervous. Do try next time to find a cosier way of being serious.

JUPITER: Stop joking. I must speak to you about the gods.

ALCMENA: The gods!

JUPITER: It is time I explained to you the nature of their relationship with mankind, and the inalienable rights they have over the citizens of the world and their wives.

ALCMENA: You must be out of your mind! Here you are preparing to hold forth about the gods at the one moment of the day when human beings are simply human – drunk with sunlight, hurrying off to plough or fish. And what's more, the army is waiting for you. You haven't got much time left if you want to kill a few enemies before breakfast. Oh, darling, do *go*, so that you can be back with me sooner. Besides, my household calls; I have my rounds of stewardship to make. If you stay here, my dear sir, I shall have to talk seriously to you, not about the gods, but about my maids. I really think we shall have to give notice to Nenetza. Apart from her insistence on only cleaning the black squares in the mosaics, she has, as you would put it, given way to the gods; she's pregnant.

JUPITER: Alcmena! Dear Alcmena! The gods appear at the very moment when we least expect them.

ALCMENA: Amphitryon, dear husband! Women disappear at the very moment when we think we hold them fast!

JUPITER: Their anger is terrible, Alcmena. They accept neither orders nor mockery!

ALCMENA: But you accept everything, darling, that's why I adore you so. Even a parting kiss blown with the hand! Till tonight, then . . . good-bye!

She goes. Enter Mercury.

MERCURY: Jupiter, what *is* going on? I've been waiting for you to sweep out of the bedroom in all your glory, as from so many others, and now Alcmena comes out perfectly composed and apparently putting you firmly in your place.

JUPITER: I can't contradict you.

MERCURY: What's this vertical fold doing between your eyes? Is it a thunder-scar – or the warning of some vengeance you're storing up for mankind?

JUPITER: This fold? It's a wrinkle.

MERCURY: Jupiter can't have wrinkles; it must be left over from Amphitryon's body.

JUPITER: No, Mercury, this is *my* wrinkle, and I know now

where men get their wrinkles from that used to intrigue us all so much: from innocence and pleasure.

MERCURY: You seem very tired, Jupiter, you're quite drooping.

JUPITER: Wrinkles are heavy things to carry.

MERCURY: Are you at last going to experience the famous collapse which men of passion are prone to?

JUPITER: I believe I am experiencing love.

MERCURY: You are known to do that very frequently.

JUPITER: No, Mercury, for the first time I've held a human creature in my arms without seeing, without even hearing her. And I could understand her.

MERCURY: Why, what did you think?

JUPITER: That I was Amphitryon. Alcmena had completely conquered me. From the moment we went to bed till the moment we got up, I simply found myself unable to be any-one else with her but her husband. Just now I had the opportunity of explaining the creation to her: and all I could manage was a schoolmaster's lecture – whereas with you my divine fluency is quite ready to spring forth. I suppose you wouldn't like me to describe the creation to you?

MERCURY: I don't mind you re-creating it, if you feel you absolutely have to; but that's as far as I'll go.

JUPITER: Mercury, mankind isn't at all what gods imagine it is! We think of men as a parody of our nature. Their conceit is such a rewarding spectacle that we even led them to believe there was a raging conflict between the gods and them. We took immense pains to force the use of fire on them so that they'd believe they'd stolen it from us. We carved intricate convolutions in their thankless cerebral dough, so that they could invent weaving, or the cog-wheel, or olive oil, and fondly imagine they had snatched these hostages from us. Well, my friend, this conflict actually exists, and I stand here today as its victim.

MERCURY: Surely you exaggerate Alcmena's power.

JUPITER: I don't exaggerate in the slightest. Alcmena, gentle Alcmena, has a nature less submissive to our laws than stone. She is the true Prometheus.

MERCURY: She simply lacks imagination. After all, it is imagination which illuminates the human brain for our purposes.

JUPITER: Alcmena doesn't illuminate. She isn't susceptible to brightness or appearances. She has no imagination, and possibly not much intelligence either. But she has in her precisely that limited, unassailable thing we can only call infinite humanity. Her life is a prism which transforms the common heritage of gods and men—like courage, love and passion – into purely human qualities like constancy, gentleness and devotion, which we are powerless against. She is the only woman I could tolerate in clothes, veiled from me; whose absence exactly equals her presence; whose business seems to me as attractive as her pleasure. Just to lunch, or even breakfast opposite her, to hand her the salt, honey or spices which nourish and warm her blood, to touch her hand, even if only with a spoon or plate – that's all I can think about now! The simple fact is, I love her, and I don't mind telling you, Mercury, hers will be my favourite son.

MERCURY: The whole world knows that already.

JUPITER: The whole world! But surely nobody knows anything about this yet?

MERCURY: Every creature with ears knows that Jupiter has honoured Alcmena with today's visitation. Every creature that has a tongue is now busy repeating the news. I made a full announcement at daybreak.

JUPITER: You betrayed me! Poor Alcmena!

MERCURY: I followed exactly the same procedure as with your other mistresses; this would have been the first of your loves to be kept secret. You haven't the right to conceal your amorous bounties.

JUPITER: What have you announced, then? That I took on the shape of Amphitryon last night?

MERCURY: Certainly not. Your somewhat ungodly device might not be well received. No, as your obvious desire to spend a second night in Alcmena's arms was fairly bursting through the palace walls, I announced that she would be receiving Jupiter's visit tonight.

42

JUPITER: And who did you announce this to?

MERCURY: First, as is proper, to the air and water. Listen for yourself: wet or dry, the waves are talking in their own language of nothing else.

JUPITER: Was that all?

MERCURY: Oh, and to an old woman who was shuffling round the corner of the palace.

JUPITER: The deaf lodge-keeper? Then we're sunk.

MERCURY: Why react so humanly, Jupiter? You're talking like a lover. Has Alcmena sworn you to silence till the very moment you ravish her from the earth?

JUPITER: That's the whole trouble: Alcmena doesn't *know*. I tried a hundred times during the night to make her realize who I was. And every time some simple, charming phrase of hers changed divine truth into human truth.

MERCURY: Didn't she suspect anything?

JUPITER: Not once – and I can't bear the thought that she might . . . What's all that noise?

MERCURY: My deaf lady has done her work. That is Thebes preparing to celebrate your union with Alcmena. A procession is forming, and seems to be moving up towards the palace.

JUPITER: They mustn't be allowed to get here! Head them off towards the sea, and let them be swallowed up.

MERCURY: How can I? They're your priests.

JUPITER: They'll never have a better proof of my existence.

MERCURY: You're powerless against the laws you yourself laid down. The whole universe knows that Jupiter is today going to give Alcmena a son. It wouldn't be a bad idea to let her in on the secret.

JUPITER: Alcmena would never stand for it.

MERCURY: Then she must lump it. The end justifies the means!

JUPITER: She won't lump it. I know quite well what she will do – she'll kill herself. And my son Hercules will die with her. And I shall be obliged to go through that awful business again as I did with you, of opening my thigh or calf to cradle a foetus for months on end. No, thank you! . . . Is the procession still climbing?

MERCURY: Slowly but surely.

JUPITER: Mercury, for the first time I have the feeling that an honourable god can be a dishonourable man . . . What is that singing?

MERCURY: Those are the virgins, who are coming, transported by the news, in theory to congratulate Alcmena.

JUPITER: You really think I shouldn't drown the priests and prostrate the virgins with early sunstroke?

MERCURY: Well, what do you *want* from all this?

JUPITER: Everything a man wants, I'm afraid: a thousand contradictory desires. I want Alcmena to stay faithful to her husband, and I want her to abandon herself rapturously to me. I want her to be chaste when I kiss her, and I want nameless desires to flare up in her at the sight of me. I want her to know nothing of all these manoeuvres, and I want her to approve them utterly.

MERCURY: It's beyond me. Anyway, I've done my job. The world now knows, as it had to, that you'll be sharing Alcmena's bed tonight. Is there anything more I can do for you?

JUPITER: Yes! See I really do share it!

MERCURY: Including this famous moment when she says yes, which you were discussing yesterday?

JUPITER: Exactly, Mercury. I'm not concerned with Hercules any more. Happily, the Hercules business is over. I'm concerned about myself now. Mercury, you must see Alcmena, you must prepare her for my visit, make her understand my love . . . Appear to her. Use the power of your secondary godhead to set her body's humanity yearning towards me. You have my permission to approach her and touch her. Stir her nerves up first, then her blood, and finally her pride. I may as well tell you, I'm not leaving this town until she has cheerfully laid herself down in my honour. And another thing: I'm sick of wearing this degrading livery! I shall come as a god.

MERCURY: That's my Jupiter! If you'll give up your incognito, I can promise you that in a very few minutes I shall have persuaded her to be ready for you at sunset . . . Ah, there she is now. Leave me to it.

ALCMENA (*off*): Oh, darling! Oh, my darling!

ECHO: Darling!

JUPITER: Who is she calling?

MERCURY: She's talking to her echo about Amphitryon. And you tell me she's not a flirt! She never stops talking to this echo. She even has a mirror for her words . . . Come on, Jupiter, she's almost here.

JUPITER: All hail, thou dwelling pure and lowly! . . . What are you grinning at? Have you heard that line before?

MERCURY: I seem to know it in advance. I hear it on the lips of centuries to come . . . Here she is, quick!

They withdraw. Alcmena and her nurse Ecclissa come in from opposite sides.

ALCMENA: You look very excited, Ecclissa.

ECCLISSA: I brought some vervain, madam – *his* favourite flower.

ALCMENA: Whose favourite? I prefer roses.

ECCLISSA: Do you mean you'd dare to put roses in the room, today of all days?

ALCMENA: Why ever not?

ECCLISSA: I've always understood that Jupiter simply hates roses. But I don't know, perhaps you're right to treat gods like ordinary men. It's good training for them. Shall I get the big red veil ready?

ALCMENA: The big veil? No, don't be silly. The plain linen one.

ECCLISSA: Oh, madam, you're so clever! You're so right to make the palace nice and intimate instead of all dolled up for a party. I've made the cakes and perfumed the bath with amber.

ALCMENA: That's good. It's Amphitryon's favourite scent.

ECCLISSA: Yes, and he's going to be so proud and happy too, your husband.

ALCMENA: What do you mean, Ecclissa?

ECCLISSA: Oh, madam, dear madam, your name will be famous for all the centuries to come, and mine too, perhaps, having been your nurse. My milk put the colour in your cheeks.

ALCMENA: Has something wonderful happened to Amphitryon?

ECCLISSA: Something's going to, as fine as any prince could dream for his glory and honour.

ALCMENA: Is it victory?

ECCLISSA: Certainly it's a victory! Over the greatest of the gods, too! . . . There, do you hear?

ALCMENA: What's all that music and shouting?

ECCLISSA: But madam, all Thebes knows the news. And everyone's so pleased and thrilled that our town is preferred above the others, all thanks to you.

ALCMENA: Thanks to your master, Ecclissa!

ECCLISSA: Yes, he has his share in the honour too!

ALCMENA: He has all of it!

ECCLISSA: No, madam, *you*. The whole of Greece is ringing with your glory. The priests say the sacred cockerels have been crowing a whole tone higher since this morning. Oh, and madam: Leda, Queen of Sparta, the one Jupiter made love to in the shape of a swan, she was passing through Thebes, and she wants to pay her respects. She might be able to give you some useful tips. Shall I send word to her to come up here?

ALCMENA: Yes, of course . . .

ECCLISSA: Oh, madam, one didn't have to see you every day in your bath, as I did, to feel that the gods might one day claim their due!

ALCMENA: I don't know what you're talking about, nurse. Is Amphitryon a god?

ECCLISSA: No, but his son will be a demi-god. (*Music and cheering is heard.*) That'll be the virgins. They've beaten the priests up the hill, all except that little baggage Alexia, of course – they're hanging on to her. I wouldn't show yourself, madam, it's more dignified. Shall I speak to them? . . . What is it, my dears, you want to know if the princess is here? Oh, yes, she's here all right! (*Alcmena paces up and down in growing exasperation.*) Yes, she's comfortably stretched out on her couch, waiting. She's gazing dreamily at a huge golden sphere which has suddenly appeared and is hanging from the ceiling. She has a bunch of vervain in her right hand which she sniffs at from time to time. With her left hand she is feeding diamonds to an enormous eagle which has just come in at the window.

ALCMENA: All right, Ecclissa, you've had your joke. One can celebrate a victory without being completely idiotic about it.

ECCLISSA: What's that, you want to know what she's wearing? . . . No, dear, she's not naked. She's wearing a tunic of a new fabric called silk, with touches of a new dye called red madder . . . Her girdle? . . . Why shouldn't she be needing a girdle? I don't see what there is to laugh at – yes, Alexia, I'm talking to you! Let me just catch you just once more! Her girdle is of green jet and platinum . . . Is she getting him a meal ready? What scent is she wearing?

ALCMENA: Ecclissa, have you quite finished?

ECCLISSA: They want to know what scent you're wearing. (*Threatening gesture from Alcmena.*) . . . I'm afraid that's a secret, my dears, but all Thebes will be perfumed with it to-night . . . She's not to turn into a star we can only see every six months? No, dear, quite, I'll tell her . . . How will it all happen? Don't worry, girls, I'll tell you everything, you have my solemn word. Good-bye, dearies, good-bye . . . Well, Alcmena, there they go, showing us their lovely backs and turning round to smile! Doesn't a smile make the backs even sweeter! Oh, the pretty darlings!

ALCMENA: You are absolutely out of your mind!

ECCLISSA: Yes, madam, with excitement and fear! What shape will he come in, madam? Will he come from the earth, or sky, or sea? As a god, or animal, or man? I mean, I can't even shoo the birds away any more – he may be one of them. I can't scold the pet roebuck, although he chased me here and butted me. He's still out there, the pretty creature, bellowing and prancing all over the ante-room. Perhaps I should let him in? But on the other hand who knows, he may be the wind rustling the curtains! Oh, dear, I *should* have put the red ones up. It may be him caressing your old nurse's shoulders at this very moment. Oh, good gracious, I'm all shaking, this funny draught – I think I'm in the wash of a higher being! Oh, madam, this is how Jupiter's being so clever today: any one of his movements or creatures could be a god!. . . Oh, look, there he is now, coming in at the window!

ALCMENA: For goodness' sake, it's a bee! Get it out of here!

ECCLISSA: Certainly not! It's him – I mean, he's it! Don't move, madam, I beg you!. . . All hail to you, heavenly bee! We guess who you must be.

ALCMENA: It's coming for me, help!

ECCLISSA: Oh, you do look sweet defending yourself! Jupiter's so right to put you through this dance of fear and pleasure; it's the ideal way to show off your lovely simplicity. – I *know* it's going to sting you.

ALCMENA: But I don't *want* to be stung!

ECCLISSA: The beloved sting! Oh, madam, let yourself be stung! Let it settle on your cheek. . . Oh, it must be him, he's going for your breast! (*Alcmena swats the bee, crushes it with her foot and kicks it aside.*) Merciful heavens, what have you done?. . . What, no thunder and lightning, nothing? Well, the rotten little insect, giving us a fright like that!

ALCMENA: Ecclissa, would you kindly tell me what this is all about?

ECCLISSA: Yes, madam, but are you going to receive the procession that's coming up here to congratulate you?

ALCMENA: Amphitryon will receive them with me tomorrow.

ECCLISSA: Of course, it's more natural that way. . . I won't be a moment, madam. I'm just going to look for Queen Leda.

She goes. Alcmena, looking rather anxious, takes a few steps across the room. She turns round to find herself face to face with Mercury.

MERCURY: Hail, princess.

ALCMENA: You must be a god, to have come here with such audacity – and discretion.

MERCURY: A god of ill repute, but still a god.

ALCMENA: Mercury, to judge from your face?

MERCURY: Thank you. Most humans recognize me by my feet,

my winged heels. You are either cleverer or better at flattery.

ALCMENA: I'm very happy to see a god.

MERCURY: If you want to touch one, I have no objection. I can tell by your hands that you have the right to. (*Alcmena gently strokes Mercury's bare arm, and touches his face.*) I gather you find the gods interesting.

ALCMENA: I spent my whole childhood thinking about them, making signs to them. And now one has come! I have heaven under my hand! I love the gods.

MERCURY: All of them? Am I included in this affection?

ALCMENA: Oh, one loves the earth in detail, but heaven *en bloc*. Besides, you have such a beautiful name – Mercury. They say you're the god of eloquence, too. I could see that straight away, the moment you appeared.

MERCURY: You saw from my silence? Yes, and your face is a beautiful word. Do you have a favourite god?

ALCMENA: Oh, of course, just as I have a favourite man.

MERCURY: Which?

ALCMENA: Should I speak his name?

MERCURY: You might prefer me to run through the official list of gods, and you can stop me when I get to yours.

ALCMENA: I'll stop you now. He's the first one.

MERCURY: Jupiter?

ALCMENA: Jupiter.

MERCURY: You amaze me. Are you really all that impressed by his title of god-of-gods? In fact aren't you rather repelled by that sort of super-idleness, being general foreman of the heavenly yards?

ALCMENA: He's more than a general god. He's *the* god.

MERCURY: He knows absolutely nothing about rhetoric, gold-working, heavenly or chamber music. He's quite without talent.

ALCMENA: He's handsome, and melancholy, and serene. He doesn't twitch like gods who are smiths or poets.

MERCURY: He is very handsome, and very lecherous.

ALCMENA: And you're very disloyal to talk like that about him. Do you think I don't understand the meaning of these sudden

passions which hurl Jupiter into the arms of mortal women?
I know quite a bit about cross-grafting from my husband,
who (as you may know up there) discovered the way to graft
cherries. In school they used to make us recite that the only
way to interbreed with beauty and even purity was by these
visits, to women who would be only too honoured by such a
lofty mission . . . Am I annoying you, talking like this?

MERCURY: Quite the reverse . . . So the fate of Leda, Danaë, all
those whom Jupiter has loved or will love, seems to you a
happy one?

ALCMENA: Oh, infinitely happy.

MERCURY: And enviable?

ALCMENA: Highly enviable.

MERCURY: And in fact you envy them?

ALCMENA: Of course I envy them. But why do you ask?

MERCURY: Can't you guess? Can you really not guess why I'm
here, and what I've come to announce to you, as my master's
herald?

ALCMENA: Tell me.

MERCURY: That he loves you – Jupiter loves you.

ALCMENA: Jupiter knows me? Jupiter deigns to be aware of
my existence? I am the happiest woman on earth.

MERCURY: For countless days now he has gazed on you, he has
watched every movement you've made, you are imprinted on
his shining eye.

ALCMENA: Countless days?

MERCURY: And nights . . . You've gone quite pale!

ALCMENA: I'm sorry, I should have blushed. Do forgive me,
Mercury. But I'm so dreadfully upset to think how unworthy
of his eyes I must sometimes have been! Why didn't you
warn me?

MERCURY: What shall I tell him now?

ALCMENA: Tell him that henceforth I shall be worthy of this
favour. A silver altar to him is already being built in the
palace. When Amphitryon comes back, we shall erect a golden
one.

MERCURY: It is not your altar he is asking for.

ALCMENA : But everything here is his! If he will deign to choose any of my most treasured possessions!

MERCURY : He has chosen, and he'll be here at sunset to ask for it himself.

ALCMENA : What is it?

MERCURY : Your bed. (*Alcmena makes no pretence of extravagant surprise.*) Prepare yourself! I have already given the night her orders. She will need all day to assemble enough sounds and splendours for a heavenly bridal night. Not so much a night for you, as a foretaste of future immortality. I'm happy to be able to slip in this fragment of eternity among your perishable moments. Think of it as my engagement present . . . What are you smiling at?

ALCMENA : It's so funny.

MERCURY : Why funny?

ALCMENA : Well, because there's obviously been a mistake, Mercury. I am Alcmena, and Amphitryon is my husband.

MERCURY : Husbands are quite beside the point in the inexorable laws of this world.

ALCMENA : But I'm the most uneducated woman in Thebes. I was no good at school, and what I did learn I've forgotten since. Everyone says how unintelligent I am.

MERCURY : I wouldn't agree.

ALCMENA : May I point out, Mercury, that we're not discussing you, but Jupiter. I'm simply not worthy to receive Jupiter. He's only seen me in the light of his glory. My own radiance is infinitely weaker.

MERCURY : From the sky one can see the Grecian night made day by your body.

ALCMENA : Ah, well, I have certain ointments, certain powders. I can just about get by, with the aid of files and tweezers. But I can't write and I can't think.

MERCURY : You seem to me to talk more than adequately. Besides, our poets of the future will look after tonight's dialogue.

ALCMENA : They'd better look after the rest as well.

MERCURY : Why use this language that cheapens everything it

touches? Do you think you can elude the gods by disclaiming all your nobler and lovelier parts? Don't you realize the gravity of your role?

ALCMENA: That's exactly what I'm trying to tell you! The role doesn't suit me. I live in an atmosphere which is so completely earthbound no god could bear it for long.

MERCURY: Please don't imagine that this is going to be a prolonged affair. We're talking about a few hours.

ALCMENA: What do you know about it? I wouldn't be at all surprised if Jupiter was honourable. It's just his interest that astounds me.

MERCURY: Why, your figure is incomparable.

ALCMENA: My figure is rather good, yes. But does he know that I get revoltingly sunburnt in summer?

MERCURY: Your hands adorn the flowers in your garden.

ALCMENA: My hands are quite nice. But one only has two. And I have one tooth too many.

MERCURY: Your bearing promises untold delights.

ALCMENA: Oh, that doesn't mean a thing. As a matter of fact, I'm rather backward sexually.

MERCURY: There's no point in lying. Jupiter has been studying you in that role too.

ALCMENA: One pretends as best one can.

MERCURY: Oh, come on, that's enough of playing hard to get . . . Alcmena! What's this – tears? Now, when a shower of joys is about to rain down on humanity in honour of you? Because Jupiter has already made his decision. He knows that you're good and you'd prefer this to a shower of gold. Tonight will be the start of a wonderful year for Thebes – no more epidemics, no more famines, no more war.

ALCMENA: That's all it needed!

MERCURY: Besides which, those children of your town that death would have carried off this week – there are eight of them, if it interests you, four little boys and four little girls, including your little Charissa – all these will be saved by your blessed night.

ALCMENA: Charissa! Mercury, this is blackmail.

MERCURY: Happiness and health are the gods' only blackmail
. . . There, do you hear? Singing, music, cheering, all meant
for you. All Thebes knows you're receiving Jupiter tonight,
and they're dressing up and making merry in your honour.
Especially the poor and sick, and all those who will owe their
lives and happiness to you. Jupiter will heal and enrich them
as he passes by at sunset. So now you know. Farewell,
Alcmena.

ALCMENA: *That* was the victory, then! . . . You're going,
Mercury?

MERCURY: Yes, going to tell Jupiter you're expecting him.

ALCMENA: That would be untrue. I can't.

MERCURY: *What?*

ALCMENA: I can't receive him. Mercury, I beg you, turn
Jupiter's favour away from me.

MERCURY: I don't understand.

ALCMENA: I can't be Jupiter's mistress.

MERCURY: Why?

ALCMENA: He would despise me afterwards.

MERCURY: Oh, don't play the innocent.

ALCMENA: I'm not even pious. I blaspheme when I make love.

MERCURY: Liar. Anything else?

ALCMENA: I'm tired, I think I'm ill.

MERCURY: Nonsense. These are deterrents for men – not gods.

ALCMENA: I love a man.

MERCURY: Which man?

ALCMENA: My husband.

Mercury, who had been leaning towards her, straightens up.

MERCURY: Oh, so you love your husband, do you?

ALCMENA: I do.

MERCURY: Good, that's what we thought. After all, Jupiter, not
being a man, doesn't choose unfaithful wives. Besides, don't
pretend to be more innocent than you are. We know all about
your dreams.

ALCMENA: Oh, indeed!

MERCURY: Well, you know you do dream. All faithful wives

dream now and then – and not that they're in their husbands' arms.

ALCMENA: Not that they're in anyone's arms.

MERCURY: And then these faithful wives start calling their husbands Jupiter. We've heard you.

ALCMENA: My husband may be Jupiter to me. Jupiter can't be my husband.

MERCURY: You really are what they call a stubborn spirit! Don't force me to speak crudely to you and point out what lies behind your supposed frankness. Your way of treating all this seems to me remarkably cynical.

ALCMENA: Look, if someone caught me naked, I should have to fight with my legs and body bare. You don't leave me any choice of words.

MERCURY: Then I won't mince mine. Jupiter is not going to insist on entering your bed as a man . . .

ALCMENA: You should have gathered by now that I'm not the type to receive women there.

MERCURY: Granted. But we have noticed that certain natural objects, certain shapes and perfumes, set up a gentle prickling in your soul and body, and often, even in Amphitryon's arms, you start feeling a strange, wild dread of particular people and things. Now, for instance, you like swimming. Well, Jupiter can make himself the water that presses round you and ravishes you. Or if you feel your infidelity would be less noticeable if you received the favours of the king of gods through some plant or animal, say so, and he will grant your wish. Have you any preferences among the cat family?

ALCMENA: Mercury, do please go.

MERCURY: One more word, and I will. Alcmena, a child is to be born of tonight's encounter.

ALCMENA: No doubt it's even been named?

MERCURY: Yes, its name is Hercules.

ALCMENA: Poor little girl, she'll never be born after all.

MERCURY: It is a boy, and he will be born. Hercules will finally destroy the monsters which are still laying waste the earth, and scatter those fragments of chaos that still clutter the work

of creation. Your union with Jupiter was fashioned from
eternity.

ALCMENA: And what will happen if I refuse?

MERCURY: Hercules will still have to be born.

ALCMENA: And if I kill myself?

MERCURY: Jupiter will restore you to life: this child must be
born.

ALCMENA: Not a child of adultery. Even if he were the son of
heaven, he would die.

MERCURY: Alcmena, there are limits to the patience of gods.
You are abusing their courtesy. Well, never mind. After all,
we don't *have* to have your consent. In fact I may as well tell
you, now, that last night . . .

Ecclissa suddenly enters.

ECCLISSA: Madam . . .

ALCMENA: Yes, what is it?

MERCURY: Amphitryon, no doubt.

ECCLISSA: No, my lord, not him. Queen Leda has arrived at the
palace. Should I send her away?

ALCMENA: Leda? No! Tell her to stay!

MERCURY: Yes, Alcmena, you'd better see her, she may be able
to give you some sound advice. I shall go now and tell Jupiter
about our talk.

ALCMENA: And you'll tell him my answer, won't you?

MERCURY: Do you really want to see your city ravaged by
plague and fire, your husband beaten and discredited? I shall
tell Jupiter you'll be expecting him.

ALCMENA: It will be a lie.

MERCURY: What women call lies in the morning they call truth
in the evening. Till tonight, Alcmena.

He disappears.

ALCMENA: Ecclissa, what's she like?

ECCLISSA: Her dress? Silver, very discreetly trimmed with
swan's-down.

ALCMENA: I mean her face. Is it proud and hard?

ECCLISSA: Oh, no, very noble and serene.

ALCMENA: Then hurry, nurse, quick, bring her in: I've had a marvellous idea! Leda may be the saving of me.

Ecclissa goes. Enter Leda.

LEDA: Was it indiscreet of me to come, Alcmena?

ALCMENA: Oh, no, Leda, I did so hope you would!

LEDA: Is this to be the historic room?

ALCMENA: It is my room.

LEDA: The sea – the mountain – you do things rather well here!

ALCMENA: And of course the sky . . .

LEDA: I doubt if the sky means quite so much to him . . . Is it to be tonight?

ALCMENA: So I am informed.

LEDA: Do tell me how it happened! Were you sending up daily prayers full of your grief and longing?

ALCMENA: Not at all. They were full of my satisfaction and happiness.

LEDA: Yes, of course, that's an even better way of calling for help . . . Have you seen him yet?

ALCMENA: No. Did he send you?

LEDA: I was passing through Thebes and heard the news, so I came up to see you, that's all.

ALCMENA: You weren't hoping to see him again?

LEDA: I never did see him! Don't you know the details of my little adventure?

ALCMENA: Is it true what the legend says, Leda – was it a real swan?

LEDA: Ah, that's what interests you! Well, yes, up to a point it was – a sort of cloud-bird, a swan-shaped gust.

ALCMENA: Real swan's-down?

LEDA: To be perfectly frank, Alcmena, I'd rather he didn't take the same shape with you. I mustn't be jealous, but do leave me my uniqueness. There are plenty of other birds – much rarer ones, even!

ALCMENA: Not many as noble as swans, though, or as marvellously aloof.

LEDA: True enough.

ALCMENA: I don't think they seem any stupider than geese or eagles, either. And at least they sing.

LEDA: Oh, they sing all right.

ALCMENA: No one hears them, but they sing. Did he sing? Or talk?

LEDA: A very clearly articulated sort of hiss, which you couldn't quite get the sense of, but the syntax was so pure that you could guess which were the bird-pronouns and which the bird-verbs.

ALCMENA: Is it true that his wing-joints made a musical creak?

LEDA: Perfectly true – like cicadas, but not so metallic. I stroked them with my fingers: it was like a feathery harp!

ALCMENA: Had you been warned of his choice?

LEDA: Well, you see, it was summer. Ever since June there had been these great swans flying high among the stars. As my husband laughingly said at the time, I was right under the sign of the swan.

ALCMENA: Your husband laughs about it?

LEDA: Oh, he doesn't believe in the gods. He sees the whole thing as a fairy story, or an opportunity for puns. It's rather a help, really.

ALCMENA: Were you taken by surprise and just . . . bowled over?

LEDA: Well – let's say assaulted, very gently assaulted. Suddenly I was being caressed by something that was neither those captive snakes called fingers nor those mutilated wings called arms; I was caught up in a motion which wasn't the earth's any more, but the stars', a timeless rolling like the most gorgeous sea trip. However, you'll soon know more about it than I do.

ALCMENA: How did he leave you?

LEDA: I was still lying stretched out, when he rose in the air as high as my eyes could follow; then he granted me a few seconds of superhuman longsightedness to see him to the zenith of zeniths; and there I lost him.

ALCMENA: Nothing more from him, since then?

LEDA: Oh, well, you know, certain favours – his priests are very polite. Now and then, in the bath, the shadow of a swan settles on me, and no amount of soap can wash it off; or a pear-tree that witnessed the visitation bows its branches to me as I pass. Besides, I couldn't have borne a prolonged liaison, not even with a god. A second visit, ah, well, perhaps. But he neglected this point of etiquette.

ALCMENA: He might make up for it yet! Anyway, you've been quite happy since then?

LEDA: Happy! Oh, dear, no. But at least beatific. You'll find that the shock of the experience will have a wonderfully relaxing effect on the rest of your physical life.

ALCMENA: My life isn't all that tense; and besides, I'm not going to see him.

LEDA: No, but you'll feel him. And you'll feel your love-making with your husband saved from that agonizing perfunctoriness, which inevitably sooner or later robs it of the charm of a family game.

ALCMENA: Leda, you know Jupiter – do you think he is open to entreaty?

LEDA: I don't know him: I've only met him as a bird.

ALCMENA: But judging from his bird-behaviour, what would you say is his character as a god?

LEDA: Great coherence in his ideas, not much understanding of women; but he does respond to the slightest hint, and he's grateful for any help you can give him . . . Why did you want to know?

ALCMENA: I've decided to refuse Jupiter's favours. And I'm begging you – please – to rescue me.

LEDA: From what – from glory?

ALCMENA: No. To begin with, I'm unworthy of this glory. Whereas you weren't just the most beautiful of queens, but the most intelligent as well. Who but you could have grasped the syntax of birdsong? And didn't you invent handwriting?

LEDA: It's rather wasted on the gods, they'll never invent reading.

ALCMENA: And then you know about astronomy. You know

your zenith from your nadir. I always get them mixed up.
You already have a fixed place in the stellar system. Knowledge gives the female body a sort of leavening, a gravity
which drives men and gods out of their minds. One only has
to see you to realize that you're not so much a woman, you're
one of those living statues whose marble progeny will one day
grace all the beautiful corners of the world.

LEDA: And you're just as they say you are, youth and beauty
incarnate. But what exactly are you driving at, my dear?

ALCMENA: I shall kill myself rather than submit to Jupiter! I
love my husband.

LEDA: Yes, and of course you'd never be able to love anyone
else once you'd come from Jupiter's bed. No other man or
god would dare to touch you!

ALCMENA: I should feel condemned to love my husband. My
love for him would no longer be the fruit of my free choice.
He'd never forgive me!

LEDA: You may start later on anyway, so why not start with a god.

ALCMENA: Oh, Leda, save me! Save me and get your revenge
on Jupiter for only making love to you once and then thinking
he could fob you off with a lot of bowing pear-trees.

LEDA: How does one revenge oneself on a poor white swan?

ALCMENA: With a black one. Now listen to me: you take my
place!

LEDA: Take your place!

ALCMENA: Look: this door leads to a darkened room where
everything is ready for tonight. Put on my veils, spray my
perfume around. It'll fool Jupiter, and much to his advantage.
One does these good turns for one's friends, doesn't one?

LEDA: Oh, yes, often, without telling them . . . You sweet
woman!

ALCMENA: What are you smiling at?

LEDA: Well, Alcmena, perhaps after all I ought to listen to you.
Because the more I see and hear of you, the more it seems to
me that with so many human charms, a brush with destiny
might be fatal, and the more dubious I am about dragging
you into that company which holds reunions every solstice on

that great promontory down there – the company of Jupiter's former loves.

ALCMENA: That famous company which gives itself up to divine orgies?

LEDA: Oh, come now, my dear, hardly orgies. Orgies of philosophical concepts, at most. We're absolutely *entre nous* down there.

ALCMENA: But what do you *do*, then? Can't I know?

LEDA: Well, dear, you may find it a bit obscure if I tell you. Luckily for you, abstractions don't seem to be your strong suit. Do you understand archetypal words, the word Power-concept, the word Umbilicus?

ALCMENA: I know umbilicus. That means navel, doesn't it?

LEDA: You might understand better if I explained that we spread ourselves out on the rock or the thin grass with its sprinkling of narcissi, and there we lie all day in a glittering shower of primal concepts, like some celestial display of super-beauties; and this time, instead of conceiving, we can feel we're shaping the impulses of the universe and being a mould for all the world's potentialities. Do you follow me?

ALCMENA: I realize it must be an extremely serious-minded gathering.

LEDA: Almost unique, I should say! Most of your charms would be quite wasted on it, Alcmena dear. You're so lively and playful, you're actually glad not to be immortal – and I think you're right. You weren't born to be a basic concept of humanity, only its most enchanting daughter.

ALCMENA: Oh, Leda, thank you! You *will* save me, then! It's always a pleasure to rescue something mortal!

LEDA: I want to save you, my dear, of course I do. But I'd still like to know what it would cost.

ALCMENA: How do you mean, cost?

LEDA: Well, what form is Jupiter coming in? At least it would have to be something I'd fancy.

ALCMENA: But I simply don't know.

LEDA: You should do. He'll take whatever shape haunts your dreams and desires.

ALCMENA: If only there was one.

LEDA: I hope you don't like snakes. Oh, I loathe them. If he's coming as a snake, dear, you can count me right out . . . Well, I might consider a really gorgeous-looking snake, covered in rings.

ALCMENA: I don't seem to be haunted by anything, animal or vegetable.

LEDA: I couldn't be doing with a mineral. Come on, dear, you must have a hidden weakness somewhere.

ALCMENA: No, I haven't. I just love my husband.

LEDA: There's your weakness, then! We needn't look any further. That's how you'll be overcome. You never loved anyone else but your husband?

ALCMENA: I'm afraid that's the way I am.

LEDA: Why didn't we think of it before? Jupiter's trick will be the simplest one of all. Now I've met you I realize that what he loves about you is your humanity; and the most interesting thing with you is to know you as a human woman, in your ordinary, everyday habits and pleasures. Well, there's only one way to manage that: he'll take on your husband's shape. Don't you worry, dear, your swan will be an Amphitryon! The very next time your husband is away for the night Jupiter will get into your palace and deceive you.

ALCMENA: Now you're frightening me! You see, Amphitryon *is* away!

LEDA: Away from Thebes?

ALCMENA: He went off last night to the war.

LEDA: When will he be back? I suppose one can't decently fight a war in less than two days?

ALCMENA: I'm afraid not.

LEDA: Between now and tonight, then, Alcmena, Jupiter will burst through those doors in your husband's shape and you will give yourself to him in perfect trust.

ALCMENA: I shall recognize him.

LEDA: You won't, you know. This man, for once, will be a divine creation.

ALCMENA: Exactly. He'll be a much more perfect, intelligent, noble Amphitryon. I shall loathe him the moment I set eyes on him.

LEDA: He was the most enormous swan, but I couldn't even tell him from the little swan in our river . . .

Enter Ecclissa.

ECCLISSA: News, madam – very surprising news!

LEDA: Amphitryon's back.

ECCLISSA: How did you know ? . . . Yes, madam, the prince will be at the palace any moment now. I saw him from the ramparts, galloping his horse straight at the moat.

ALCMENA: But no one's ever done that!

ECCLISSA: He took it in one leap.

LEDA: Is he by himself?

ECCLISSA: Yes, but you can feel a sort of invisible squadron surrounding him. He glows. He doesn't look a bit tired as he usually does when he gets back from war. Really, the sun's quite pale in comparison. He's like a block of light with a man's shadow. What had I better do, madam? Jupiter is all around us now, and the master's exposing himself to the wrath of the gods. I did think I heard a crash of thunder just when he reached the perimeter road . . .

ALCMENA: All right, Ecclissa, you can go.

Ecclissa goes.

LEDA: Well, does that convince you? Jupiter's here all right – the false Amphitryon!

ALCMENA: In that case he's going to find a false Alcmena . . . Oh, dear Leda, with your help, let's turn this impending divine tragedy into a bit of fun for the girls! Let's get our own back!

LEDA: I say, what's he like, your husband? Have you got a picture ?

ALCMENA (*showing her*): Here he is.

LEDA: Oh, yes . . . not bad at all. He's got those nice eyes I like, with hardly any pupil – you know, like statues. In fact I'd

love statues if they could only talk and feel. Is he dark? Oh, I
do hope he doesn't curl his hair.

ALCMENA: No, Leda, it's as smooth and black as a raven's wing.

LEDA: Military bearing? Nasty rough skin?

ALCMENA: Certainly not! He's got plenty of muscle, but it's
nice and supple.

LEDA: You're sure you won't hate me for holding the image of
the body you love?

ALCMENA: I swear I won't!

LEDA: And you won't mind my depriving you of a god you
don't love?

ALCMENA: He's coming. Save me, please.

LEDA: Is that the room, there?

ALCMENA: That's it.

LEDA: There aren't any steps to go down in the dark, are there?
I'm terrified of tripping.

ALCMENA: No, a smooth level floor.

LEDA: The wall by the couch isn't covered with marble, I trust?

ALCMENA: A rather nice long-piled carpet . . . You're *not* getting cold feet at the last moment?

LEDA: I've given my word, dear, and I'm a conscientious friend
. . . Look out, here he is. Have a bit of fun with him before
you send him in to me. Take it out on the false Amphitryon
for the unhappiness the real one may cause you one day.

Leda slips out, as Amphitryon approaches.

A SLAVE (*calling, off stage*): What about your horses, sir? They're
worn out.

AMPHITRYON: Oh, damn my horses. I'll be off again in a
moment.

ALCMENA: Damn his horses? That's not Amphitryon . . .

Amphitryon comes towards her.

AMPHITRYON: It's me!

ALCMENA: And no-one else; surprise, surprise.

AMPHITRYON: Well, darling, aren't you going to kiss me?

ALCMENA: Not this second, if you don't mind; it's so glaring in here. In a minute, in there.

AMPHITRYON: Now! The mere thought of this has shot me to you like an arrow.

ALCMENA: And made you climb crags, and leap rivers, and stride across the sky. No, come over to the light and let me look at you! Surely you're not ashamed to show your face to your wife? You know she knows all its tiniest beauties and imperfections.

AMPHITRYON: All right, darling, here it is, or a pretty good imitation.

ALCMENA: A very good imitation indeed; good enough to fool any ordinary wife. It's all there. Those two sad furrows that serve for a smile, that funny hollow that holds your tears, and the little mark of age near the temples, some bird's footprint – Jupiter's eagle, no doubt?

AMPHITRYON: A crow, darling – that's my crow's foot. You like to kiss it, as a rule.

ALCMENA: Yes, that's my husband all right! But I don't see that scratch he got yesterday. Curious husband, to come back from the war minus a gash.

AMPHITRYON: The air is a marvellous healer of wounds.

ALCMENA: Oh, the air of battle, yes, of course! Let's see your eyes. Hey, what's this, now? Amphitryon dear, when you went away you had two big, truthful, laughing eyes. How do you account for this strange solemn look that's got into the right one, and this rather suspect glitter in the left?

AMPHITRYON: Married people shouldn't examine each other too closely if they're afraid of surprises . . . Come with me.

ALCMENA: No, just a moment. There are certain clouds hovering behind your eyes, which I never saw there before. I don't know what's the matter with you tonight, my dear, but when I look at you I feel a sort of dizziness, a sort of knowledge of what's past and foreknowledge of what's to come. I seem to sense distant worlds and hidden sciences . . .

AMPHITRYON: You always feel like that before making love. So do I. It'll pass.

ALCMENA: What's it thinking about, this great, unnaturally great brow?

AMPHITRYON: About the beautiful Alcmena, who's such an unchanging miracle.

ALCMENA: And what's this face thinking about, which is growing larger even as I look at it?

AMPHITRYON: About kissing your lips.

ALCMENA: Why my lips? You never used to mention my lips!

AMPHITRYON: And biting your neck.

ALCMENA: Are you out of your mind? You've never had the cheek before to call my features by name!

AMPHITRYON: That's exactly what I've been blaming myself for, so I'm going to call them all. I suddenly had the idea when I was calling the roll of my army, and now they're all going to answer when I say their names: eyelids, throat, neck and teeth. And lips!

ALCMENA: Here is my hand to be going on with.

AMPHITRYON: What's the matter? Are you angry? Was I being offensive?

ALCMENA: Where exactly did you spend last night?

AMPHITRYON: In the brambles, with a bunch of dry shoots for a pillow, which I burnt when I woke up. Darling, I'll have to go in less than an hour: we're joining battle in the morning. Do come on! . . . *Now* what are you up to?

ALCMENA: I'm allowed to stroke your hair, aren't I? I've never known it so dry and shining!

AMPHITRYON: The wind, I suppose.

ALCMENA: Your servant the wind. And what a skull you're getting suddenly! I've never known it so impressive.

AMPHITRYON: Brains, Alcmena, intellect . . .

ALCMENA: Ah, your daughter, intellect.

AMPHITRYON: And these are my eyebrows, if it interests you, and here's my occiput, and this is my jugular vein . . . Dear Alcmena, why do you tremble so when you touch me? You're more like a fiancée than a wife. What can have caused this peculiar new modesty towards your husband? And I must

say you're beginning to strike *me* as quite a stranger. Whatever I discover now is going to be a new experience for me . . .

ALCMENA: I'm sure it is.

AMPHITRYON: Isn't there some present you want, or some wish
you have to make?

ALCMENA: Well, before we go in there, I would like you just to
touch my hair very lightly with your lips.

AMPHITRYON (*taking her in his arms and fiercely kissing her neck*):
There you are!

ALCMENA: What *are* you doing? I said very lightly, on the hair!

AMPHITRYON (*kissing her on the cheek*): There!

ALCMENA: You're breaking your word – or am I quite bald to
you?

AMPHITRYON (*kissing her lips*): All right, there! And now you're
coming with me . . .

ALCMENA: No, not for a minute! Come in in a minute – when
I call you – my lover!

She goes into the bedroom, leaving Amphitryon alone.

AMPHITRYON: What an adorable wife! And what a charming
life this is, flowing along without upsets or jealousies, sweet
ordinary happiness untouched by lust or scheming. Whenever
I come home to the palace, at dawn or dusk, all I find is what
I've hidden there, all that awaits me is peace . . . Alcmena,
can I come in now? . . . No answer. I know her, that means
she's ready. Such delicacy! She summons me with silence –
and what a silence! How it resounds! How it calls out to me!
. . . Yes, my love, my darling, here I am . . .

*He goes into the bedroom. Stealthily, Alcmena reappears, looks
after him with a smile, then draws back the curtains and advances
to the centre of the stage.*

ALCMENA: There we are, then! It's worked, and he's in her
arms. Don't talk to me any more about this being a wicked
world. The simplest schoolgirl trick is enough to outwit it.
And don't talk about fate, either, it's no more than a product
of human feebleness. Neither the wiles of men nor the desires

of gods are a match for the will and love of a faithful wife . . .
Echo, you've always given me the best advice: don't you
agree with me? Would you honestly say I had anything to
fear from gods or men, a true and faithful wife like me? Well,
have I, have I?

ECHO: Yes! Yes!

ALCMENA: *What* did you say?

ECHO: No! No!

Curtain

ACT THREE

The terrace in front of the palace. Sosios is waiting, with the Trumpeter and Ecclissa.

TRUMPETER: What's your proclamation about tonight, then?

SOSIOS: Women.

TRUMPETER: Oh, lovely! The danger of women?

SOSIOS: The state of fidelity natural to married women in time of war. This time, amazingly enough, the proclamation may even ring true, as our war has only lasted one day.

TRUMPETER: Then read it, quick.

He blows his summons.

SOSIOS: The bans! The war, among its many other beneficial effects . . .

ECCLISSA: Sssh!

SOSIOS: How do you mean, sssh? The war is over, Ecclissa. You see before you two of the victors. We've arrived just a quarter of an hour ahead of the army.

ECCLISSA: Be quiet, I tell you, and listen!

SOSIOS: Listen to you keeping quiet, that's a change.

ECCLISSA: It's not me speaking today, it's heaven. A voice from heaven is telling the Thebans all about the exploits of an unknown hero.

SOSIOS: Unknown? Are you referring to little Hercules, that Jupiter's begetting on the lady Alcmena this very night?

ECCLISSA: You know about it!

SOSIOS: The whole army knows – ask the trumpeter.

TRUMPETER: And let me assure you that everyone's thrilled to bits about it. Officers and other ranks realize that our lightning victory can only be due to this happy event. Not one man killed, miss, and even the horses have got left-leg wounds. Amphitryon was the only one who hadn't heard about it, but thanks to these voices from heaven he must be getting the message by now.

ECCLISSA: Don't tell me Amphitryon could hear the voices right out there on the plain!

TRUMPETER: Oh, you can hear every word. The crowd's gathered at the foot of the palace hill, and we heard it with them. Very impressive it was. Specially that bit about the fight between your future young squire and a bull-headed monster – oh, that really had us sweating. Hercules came out on top, but it was a tight squeeze . . . Look out, here's another bit coming up!

VOICE FROM HEAVEN: Hear ye, Thebans! No sooner has the Minotaur been slain, than a dragon appears at your city gates, a dragon with thirty heads all hungry for human flesh – *your* flesh – except for one head which eats grass.

THE CROWD: Ooh! Ah! Oh!

THE VOICE: But Hercules, the child that your Alcmena will this night conceive to Jupiter, takes up a thirty-stringed bow, and shoots all thirty heads.

THE CROWD: Hoo! Haa!

TRUMPETER: I don't see why he had to kill the one that ate grass.

SOSIOS: Look at Alcmena on the balcony – she's not missing a word. Jupiter's so clever! He knows how much our queen wants children, and he's giving her all this about Hercules so that she'll start loving him and let herself be persuaded.

ECCLISSA: Poor madam! You can see what a strain she's going through. He's all round her, this great huge son – he's carrying her as if *she* was the baby!

TRUMPETER: I'd let Hercules speak himself, instead of Jupiter. Alcmena would be twice as moved.

SOSIOS: Hush! It's coming again!

CHILD'S VOICE FROM HEAVEN: I shall have the curly hair and smooth stomach of my father Jupiter.

THE CROWD: Oh! Ah! Ooh!

ECCLISSA: The gods have had the same idea as you, trumpeter.

TRUMPETER: Yes – a bit later.

THE VOICE: I shall have the tender, faithful look of my mother Alcmena.

ECCLISSA: There's your mummy, little Hercules – can you see her?

THE VOICE: I see and admire her.

THE CROWD: Aaah!

SOSIOS: Why ever has your mistress slammed her window like that? That's going a bit far, you know, walking out on a voice from heaven! And anyway, Ecclissa, why is she behaving as if she was at a funeral? And why is there this miserable atmosphere around the palace, when there should be flags and bunting fluttering in the wind? There's been a rumour circulating among the troops, that your mistress invited Leda over to give her some last-minute tips, and that they've spent the day laughing and playing games. Wasn't that true?

ECCLISSA: Oh, perfectly true. But Leda left about an hour ago. It was just after she'd gone that the voices announced that Jupiter would be arriving at sunset.

SOSIOS: And the priests confirmed the news?

ECCLISSA: They're leaving now.

SOSIOS: Alcmena's getting ready, then?

ECCLISSA: I'm really not quite sure.

TRUMPETER: I think you should know, miss, that there's some rather ugly rumours going around Thebes about you and your mistress. It's being said that either from childishness or coquetry, Alcmena is pretending not to appreciate the favour Jupiter's doing her, and that she is even thinking of ways to prevent the liberator from coming to the earth.

SOSIOS: Yes, and that you're abetting her in this child-murder!

ECCLISSA: How dare anyone accuse me of such a thing! I'm simply dying for this child to come! I mean, I shall be the practice-ground for all the duels that will later save the world; I shall spend the first ten years of his life being his Hydra and his Minotaur! I wonder what noises the beastly things make, so that I can get him used to them?

SOSIOS: Calm down, nurse. Tell us about Alcmena. It really wouldn't be decent for Thebes to give the gods a sour, bad-tempered mistress. Is it true that she's trying to find some way to deflect Jupiter from his purpose?

ECCLISSA: I'm afraid she may be.

SOSIOS: I suppose it hasn't occurred to her that if she succeeds, Thebes will be doomed, riot and pestilence will stalk among us, and Amphitryon will be stoned to death by the mob. They're all the same, these faithful wives: they think so much about being faithful, they forget about their husbands.

TRUMPETER: Don't worry, Sosios, how *can* she succeed? Nobody's going to stop Jupiter getting his way, because if there's one thing about gods, they're as stubborn as mules. If men could push their stubbornness to its limit they'd be gods too. Look at our old scholars, plucking divine secrets from air or metal, simply by being pig-headed. Well, Jupiter's pig-headed too. He's going to have Alcmena's secret. Besides, everything's set for his coming. It's as certain as an eclipse. All the little Thebans are busy burning their fingers making smoked-glass splinters, so that they can watch his meteor without hurting their eyes.

SOSIOS: Have you tipped off the musicians and cooks?

ECCLISSA: I'm all ready with cakes and Samian wine.

SOSIOS: Nurses have a splendid feeling for adultery and absolutely none for marriage! You don't seem to realize, this isn't a secret rendezvous – these are nuptials, real solemn nuptials! And what about the crowd, too? Jupiter insists on having a crowd for each of his amorous performances. Who do you think you'll whip up at this hour of night?

ECCLISSA: I was about to set off for the town to collect all the poor, sick, infirm or ill-favoured. My mistress wants them to gather along Jupiter's path to touch him and melt his heart.

TRUMPETER: Greet Jupiter with a lot of hunchbacks and cripples! Show him all the world's imperfections that he doesn't know about – you'll infuriate him! You can't do that!

ECCLISSA: But I've got to. My mistress said I must.

SOSIOS: Then she's wrong, and the Trumpeter's right.

TRUMPETER: Don't you see, miss, it's sacrilege to prove to our Creator that he's made a hash of the world. The only reason he's well disposed towards it is because he thinks it's perfect. I mean, if he sees us all one-armed or bandy-legged, all

71

suffering from jaundice or gravel, he'll be furious with us. Especially as he claims to have made us in his own image; no-one likes unflattering mirrors.

ECCLISSA: But he said himself, through that Voice, he was calling on all the poor down-trodden people in Thebes.

TRUMPETER: Don't worry, he'll get them. I heard what the Voice said, and I gave the matter my personal attention. All that's needed is for these unhappy people to give him a sublime idea of human unhappiness. Don't you fret, Sosios, it'll all be on cue. What I've in fact done is brought along a special troupe of paralytics.

ECCLISSA: You're not telling me paralytics got up to the palace!

TRUMPETER: They got up very nicely, thank you, so I may as well let you see them. Come in then, my darlings, come on in! Come and show your poor sick limbs to the master of heaven.

Enter a troupe of dancing-girls.

ECCLISSA: But these are dancing-girls!

TRUMPETER: Excuse me, they are paralytics. Anyway, that's how they'll be presented to Jupiter. They're to represent the last stage of what he imagines to be human paralysis. And I also have waiting, over there behind the shrubbery, a dozen sopranos who'll yell canticles to represent the dumb. And what with a few giants thrown in as dwarfs, we'll have such a superb collection of cripples that Jupiter will feel downright proud of having created the world, and he'll grant the slightest wish of your mistress and the Thebans. Which way will he be coming from?

ECCLISSA: The priests said he'd have his back to the sun. There'll be two thicknesses of fire when it sets today.

TRUMPETER: Yes, well, I want him to see my bakers' wives with a good strong light on their faces. Put them over there, that's it. They're my lepers.

A DANCING-GIRL: What about us, mister philosopher? What do we have to do?

SOSIOS: Dance, of course. I trust you have no other accomplishments?

A DANCING-GIRL: What dance, though? That symbolic one
with the *grandes jetées*?

SOSIOS: Don't overdo things. Remember that as far as Jupiter's
concerned you're limping.

ANOTHER DANCING-GIRL: Oh, it's for Jupiter! Oh, well, then,
how about the trout-dance, with the wriggles imitating
thunder – that would flatter him.

TRUMPETER: Don't fool yourselves, my dears. Gods see
dancing-girls from above, not below, which accounts for them
being less susceptible to dancing than men are. Jupiter
actually prefers bathing-girls.

ANOTHER DANCING-GIRL: We do have that one called the
wave-dance, executed on one's back, with super-scissor-work
by the thighs.

TRUMPETER: Hey, Sosios, who's that soldier coming up the hill
there? Isn't it Amphitryon?

ECCLISSA: It certainly is Amphitryon. Oh, heavens, I'm shaking.

SOSIOS: Personally, I'm not sorry to see him. He's a sensible
god-fearing man. He'll help his wife to decide.

A DANCING-GIRL: Look at him running!

TRUMPETER: I can understand his hurry. A lot of husbands like
to exhaust their wives so much beforehand that they're
nothing in the god's arms but a body without spirit . . . On
you go, then, girls. We'll follow you and get the music ready.
At last, thanks to the pair of us, this ceremony is going to be
worthy of its guest. We came just in time . . . Now, Sosios,
you can do your proclamation.

He sounds his trumpet.

SOSIOS: Thebans! The war, among its many other beneficial
effects, covers women's bodies with an armour of unjointed
steel through which neither desire nor the human hand can
slip . . .

*Amphitryon appears, dismissing Sosios and the Trumpeter with a
wave of the hand.*

AMPHITRYON: Is your mistress at home, Ecclissa?

ECCLISSA: Yes, my lord.
AMPHITRYON: Up there, in her room?
ECCLISSA: Yes, my lord.
AMPHITRYON: I'll wait for her here, then.

Ecclissa goes, and as Amphitryon waits, the Voice from Heaven rings out again.

THE VOICE: Women. The son that Alcmena is to conceive this night of Jupiter knows them all to be faithless, easily tempted by honours and tickled by glory.
THE CROWD: Ah! Ah! Ah!
THE VOICE: He shall seduce them, suck them dry, discard them, jeer at their outraged husbands, and die at last at women's hands.
THE CROWD: Oh! Oh! Oh!

Enter Alcmena.

ALCMENA: What are we going to do, Amphitryon?
AMPHITRYON: What are we going to do, Alcmena?
ALCMENA: There must be some hope still, if he's let you get here before him!
AMPHITRYON: When is he expected?
ALCMENA: In a few minutes, when the sun goes down. I'm afraid to look at the sky! You can see eagles before they see you – can *you* see anything yet?
AMPHITRYON: One badly hung star, wobbling a bit.
ALCMENA: That'll be him passing . . . Have you any sort of plan?
AMPHITRYON: I've got my voice, Alcmena, I've got words! I shall convince Jupiter! I shall win him over!
ALCMENA: My poor darling, you've never convinced anyone in the world except me, and that wasn't by talking. An argument between you and Jupiter is just what I'm most afraid of. You'd come out of it utterly demoralized, and probably end up giving me to Mercury as well.
AMPHITRYON: But in that case, Alcmena, we're lost!
ALCMENA: We must put our trust in his goodness. Let's wait

for him here, in the place where we receive distinguished guests. I really think he doesn't know about our love. I want him to see us from the heights of his Olympus, just as we are now, side by side on the threshold of our home, and I want the vision of this couple to start destroying in him the image of the woman alone. Take me in your arms and hug me! Kiss me in what remains of the daylight, to show him that unique creature: the married couple . . . Nothing in the sky yet?

AMPHITRYON: The zodiac's shaking: he must have hit the edge. Will you take my arm?

ALCMENA: No, our bond mustn't be as ordinary and artificial as that. Let's leave just a nice friendly gap between us, the gate of human fondness which children and cats and birds like to find between true couples.

Crowd noises and music are heard.

AMPHITRYON: The priests must have given the signal. He can't be far off. Do we say good-bye when he gets here, Alcmena, or now? We must decide what we're going to do!

VOICE FROM HEAVEN (*announcing*): The Farewells of Alcmena and Amphitryon!

AMPHITRYON: Did you hear that?

ALCMENA: I did.

VOICE (*repeating the announcement*): The Farewells of Alcmena and Amphitryon!

AMPHITRYON: Aren't you afraid?

ALCMENA: Oh, darling, haven't you ever heard a strange voice inside you at moments like this, when life seems to expand, giving the moment a sort of title? The day of our first meeting, our first bathe together in the sea, didn't you hear it calling inside you: The Betrothal of Amphitryon! Alcmena's First Bathe! I suppose the nearness of the gods today has made the atmosphere so resonant that you can actually hear the titles without them being spoken. Let's say good-bye, then.

AMPHITRYON: The funny thing is, Alcmena, I feel this is almost as it should be. From the very first moment I knew you I've been carrying this farewell in my heart – not as a last cry of despair, but almost as if it was the declaration of some special tenderness, a new confession of love. As it happens, I'm obliged to say it today, at what may actually be the end of our lives, and so theoretically the most suitable place to say it. But it was nearly always in the middle of our greatest joys, when nothing threatened our unity, that I felt this strange need to say good-bye to you swelling in my heart with the pressure of a thousand unknown caresses.

ALCMENA: A thousand unknown caresses? Tell me more!

AMPHITRYON: I felt that I had some new secret to tell this face I'd never seen a wrinkle on, these eyes where I'd never seen a tear, these lashes not one of which had fallen, even for me to make a wish on it! It was good-bye.

ALCMENA: Don't go into details, darling. All the parts of my body you don't mention will feel they're going to their death unsung.

AMPHITRYON: You really think death is awaiting us?

ALCMENA: No! Jupiter's not going to kill us. He'll more likely revenge himself for our refusal by changing our species; he'll take away all our pleasure and happiness in each other by turning us into quite different creatures. We'll be one of those couples famous for their love, but more divided by nature than they could ever have been by hatred: a nightingale and a toad, a fish and a willow-tree . . . I must stop, or I'll be giving him ideas . . . Good heavens, I even lose my appetite a bit if I see you eating with a spoon while I'm using a fork: so when you're breathing through gills and me through leaves, when you're croaking and I'm warbling, oh, my darling! where will my joy in life be then?

AMPHITRYON: But I shall come to you, and stay with you always. Being together is all that counts for lovers.

ALCMENA: Being together! Being with me will soon be your cruellest torment. When dawn breaks tomorrow we may find ourselves all too wretchedly together, in our same bodies; yours will be intact, but mine will have lost the virginity-to-god that a woman should preserve however often she makes love with her husband. Can you honestly imagine going on

living with a wife who no longer respects herself, dishonoured
by too much honour, and withered by immortality? Can you
imagine there always being a third name on our lips, a name
that can't be spoken, adding a taste of gall to our meals and
kisses? Well, I know I couldn't face it. What sort of a look
would you give me every time you heard thunder, and the
world was filled with cruel, flashing reminders of my defiler?
Even the beauties of creation, the beauties *he* created, will
only remind us of shame. Oh, it would be *far* better to be
changed into primary beings – at least they're clean. You play
your part as a man so faithfully, with so much good will, that
I'm sure I'd recognize you among any number of fishes or
trees, just by the conscientious way you breathe in air, or eat
your prey, or swim.

AMPHITRYON: There's the Capricorn rearing up now. He's
getting near.

ALCMENA: Good-bye, Amphitryon. I would have liked to
stay with you, though, and see old age coming on, see your
back beginning to stoop, see if it's really true that old couples
end up looking the same. I'd have liked us to share the
pleasures of sitting by the fire and remembering, and looking
almost like twins by the time we die. Amphitryon, darling,
why don't we sample one minute of this old age together
we're going to miss? Imagine that we haven't just got twelve
months of marriage behind us, but years and years and years
. . . Did you love me, my old man?

AMPHITRYON: All my life!

ALCMENA: You're quite sure that somewhere around our silver
anniversary you didn't find a sixteen-year-old virgin who was
shy and at the same time bold, who couldn't sleep for thinking
of the way you look and the splendid things you do, an enchanting little flirt, in fact a monster – you're sure she didn't
seem younger than me?

AMPHITRYON: You've always been younger than youth.

ALCMENA: Then when we were in our fifties and I was suddenly
on edge, laughing and crying for no reason at all, and I started
(heaven knows why) urging you to visit certain bad women,

on the pretext that it would liven up our love, you didn't say or do anything, you didn't take me at my word, did you?

AMPHITRYON: No. I wanted you to be proud of us both when we were old.

ALCMENA: And how marvellous old age was, after all! Death can come when it likes!

AMPHITRYON: How clearly we remember those far-off times! Do you remember, Alcmena, the morning I came back from the war to embrace you in the shadows of dawn?

ALCMENA: Dawn? Don't you mean dusk?

AMPHITRYON: Dawn or dusk, what does it matter now! Perhaps it was midday. All I remember is that that day my horses leapt over the widest chasms, and then during the morning I won the victory . . . What's wrong, darling? You're quite pale.

ALCMENA: Please, Amphitryon, I beg you, tell me if you came at dusk or at dawn!

AMPHITRYON: Darling, I'll tell you anything you like. I don't want you to be upset.

ALCMENA: It was night, wasn't it?

AMPHITRYON: Oh, in our room, utter night . . . You're right, my darling: death can come.

VOICE FROM HEAVEN: Death can come.

There is a crash of thunder and Jupiter appears, escorted by Mercury.

JUPITER: Death can come, you say? It's only Jupiter.

MERCURY: May I present to you, sire, Alcmena – the reluctant Alcmena.

JUPITER: What is this man doing with her?

MERCURY: That's her husband, Amphitryon.

JUPITER: The Amphitryon that won the battle of Corinth?

MERCURY: Not yet, he won't capture Corinth for another five years. But that's the one.

JUPITER: Who asked him here, though? What's he up to?

AMPHITRYON (*approaching Jupiter*): Sire!

MERCURY: He's coming to offer you his wife, of course. Didn't

78

you see him, from up there, getting her ready for you – turning her towards you while he kissed her and gradually brought her to the right pitch of excitement and anticipation to make tonight the triumph it should be?

AMPHITRYON: Mercury is mistaken, sire.

JUPITER: Mistaken, is he? You don't seem quite convinced of the need for me to lie with your wife tonight, and fulfil your function with her. I, as it happens, am perfectly convinced.

AMPHITRYON: Well, sire, I'm not!

MERCURY: It's too late now for talking, Jupiter, the sun's going down.

JUPITER: That's the sun's business.

MERCURY: If gods start engaging in individual conversations and arguments with humans, it's the beginning of the end.

AMPHITRYON: Sire, I have come here to protect Alcmena from you, or die.

JUPITER: Now listen to me, Amphitryon. We can talk as man to man. You know my power. You surely realize that I can get into your bed invisible, if I want – even if you're already there. I can make a potion merely from the weeds in your park that will make your wife desire me madly and will even make you want me as a successful rival. So you see, there isn't a real conflict here at all, only (alas) a formal conflict, like all those that provoke schisms or new religions. The question is not whether I shall have Alcmena, but how! Are you going to join battle with the gods over a mere formality, over one short night?

AMPHITRYON: I can't hand her over to you. I prefer the other formality – death.

JUPITER: You must realize how considerate I'm being about this! It's not just Alcmena that I love, or I'd have had her without bothering to consult you. I love you as a couple. I love these pairs of great noble bodies that one finds at the beginning of each new age, carved like figureheads at the prow of humanity. I come between you as a friend.

AMPHITRYON: You were there already, and we worshipped you. No, I refuse.

79

JUPITER: That's your bad luck, then . . . All right, Mercury, the ceremony can begin! Assemble the whole town here. And as he leaves us no choice, proclaim the truth – the whole truth – about last night as well as tonight. We have our divine means of convincing this happy couple.

AMPHITRYON: You'll never convince a general with miracles.

JUPITER: Is that your last word? Are you really determined to fight it out with me?

AMPHITRYON: Yes, if I must.

JUPITER: I'd have thought that you were an intelligent enough general not to commit yourself without having weapons equal to mine. That's the simplest ABC of tactics.

AMPHITRYON: But I have the weapons.

JUPITER: Indeed?

AMPHITRYON: I have Alcmena.

JUPITER: In that case, don't let's waste another minute. I await your weapons with god-like resolution. I even beg you to leave me alone with them . . . Come here, Alcmena. And you two, vanish.

Amphitryon and Mercury do so.

ALCMENA: Alone at last!

JUPITER: You don't know how right you are. At last the moment when I shall possess you.

ALCMENA: My last hour of life, then!

JUPITER: Oh, stop this blackmail. It's unworthy of both of us . . . Yes, here we are for the first time face to face with me knowing your virtue and you my desire. Alone at last!

ALCMENA: You're quite often alone like this, if we're to believe your legend.

JUPITER: But not often in love like this, Alcmena, and never as weak as I feel now. I would never have endured such contempt from any other woman.

ALCMENA: Does the word love exist in the language of gods? I thought it was only the world's supreme regulation that drove them at certain epochs to come and nibble at the faces of the better-looking lady mortals?

JUPITER: Regulation is a crude word. Let's call it fate.

ALCMENA: Well, don't you find fate rather depressing with such a hopelessly unfatal woman as Alcmena? All this darkness over a blonde.

JUPITER: No, you give it for the first time an unexpected colour which I find quite delightful. You're like an eel in its hands.

ALCMENA: And a toy in yours . . . Oh, Jupiter, tell me the honest truth: do you really find me attractive?

JUPITER: If the word attractive means more than just physical attraction, if it also suggests a startled doe or a flowering almond – yes, Alcmena, I do.

ALCMENA: That's my only hope, then. Because if you found me the slightest bit unattractive, you wouldn't hesitate to take your revenge by forcing your love on me.

JUPITER: Do I attract you?

ALCMENA: Can you seriously doubt it? Would I have such a painful sensation of deceiving my husband with a god who repelled me? It might be a disaster for my body, but I should feel my honour untouched.

JUPITER: You mean you renounce me because you love me? You resist me because you're mine?

ALCMENA: That's love, isn't it.

JUPITER: You're certainly driving the gods into metaphysics tonight.

ALCMENA: That won't do them any harm. It seems that the simplest word in your language, one single word, is so cruel it could destroy the world.

JUPITER: I promise you Thebes is in no danger now.

ALCMENA: Then why is Alcmena? Why are you so determined to torture me, break up a perfect couple, take this fleeting pleasure and leave ruins behind you?

JUPITER: That's love, isn't it . . .

ALCMENA: And suppose I offered you something better than love? You can taste love with any of the others. But I'd like to forge a stronger and sweeter bond between us: I'm the one woman in the world who can offer it to you. And I offer it now.

JUPITER: What is it, then?

ALCMENA: Friendship!

JUPITER: Friendship? What is this word? Explain yourself, please. It's the first time I've heard it.

ALCMENA: Really? Oh, then I'm so happy: I won't hesitate any longer! I offer you my friendship – my virgin friendship.

JUPITER: What do you mean by that, though? Is it a common word on earth?

ALCMENA: The *word* is common, yes.

JUPITER: Friendship . . . well, it's true we're so far away up there, certain human practices are still unknown to us. Tell me about it . . . When people hide themselves away from sight, as we're doing, but then take out pieces of gold from under their rags, and count them over and fondle them – is that friendship?

ALCMENA: No, that's avarice.

JUPITER: Then how about the ones who strip naked when there's a full moon, and keep staring at it, running their hands over their bodies and washing themselves in its light – are they friends?

ALCMENA: No, lunatics.

JUPITER: Do speak more plainly! – Well, the ones who don't really love a woman for herself, but concentrate madly on one of her gloves or shoes, and steal it, and wear out the kid or calfskin with their kisses – are they friends?

ALCMENA: Those are fetishists!

JUPITER: Alcmena, tell me what it *means*, this friendship of yours. Is it a passion?

ALCMENA: Oh, a mad one.

JUPITER: But what's the sense of it?

ALCMENA: The sense? All the senses, except sensuality!

JUPITER: We must have that restored to it by a miracle. What does it *do*, though?

ALCMENA: It brings together the most unlikely people and makes them equals.

JUPITER: Ah, now I think I understand! Sometimes, from our observatory, we've seen human beings walking apart in groups of two which seem quite bizarre to us, because they appear to have nothing in common: like a minister who calls every day on a gardener, a lion in a cage who insists on playing with a poodle, a sailor and a professor, a wild boar and an ocelot. And they really do seem absolute equals, and they march on side by side in the face of everyday worries, in the face of death itself. We were beginning to think these people must be joined by some mysterious physical secretion.

ALCMENA: It's quite possible. Anyway, that's friendship.

JUPITER: I can just see that ocelot. He used to leap and prance round that beloved boar of his – and then he'd hide in an olive-tree, and when the boar came grunting past, he'd drop down like velvet on its bristly back.

ALCMENA: Yes, ocelots make admirable friends.

JUPITER: The minister, though, he used to walk up and down one particular path with the gardener. He talked about slugs and grafts, while the gardener talked about taxation and parliamentary procedure. And then, when they'd both said their piece, they used to stop at the end of the path – having presumably ploughed one more furrow in the field of friendship – and they'd look into each other's faces for a moment, stroking their beards and exchanging a friendly wink.

ALCMENA: Friends always do that.

JUPITER: And what shall we do, if I become your friend?

ALCMENA: Well, to begin with, I shall think of you instead of just believing in you. And the thought will be a free thing I owe my heart, instead of a habit I owed my ancestors. My prayers won't be prayers any more, they'll be real words, and my ritual gestures will be signs to you.

JUPITER: You're sure it won't be too much bother?

ALCMENA: Oh, goodness, no! Being friends with the god of gods, being comradely to one who can do or create or destroy anything, those are a woman's minimum requirements in friendship. So naturally we can't get friendship from men.

JUPITER: And what about me, what shall I do?

ALCMENA: Well . . . on days when I'm worn out with human society, I shall see you appear, silently. You'll sit down very calmly at the foot of my divan, and you won't start nervously stroking the paws or tail of my leopard-skin, because if you did, that would be love . . . and then suddenly you'll be gone again. But you'll have been there! – Do you understand what I mean?

JUPITER: I think I do. Ask me some questions. Tell me the sort of occasions when you'll call on me for help, and I'll try and tell you what a good friend should do.

ALCMENA: That's a splendid idea! Are you ready?

JUPITER: Ready!

ALCMENA: When my husband's away?

JUPITER: I detail a comet to guide him. I give you second sight so that you can watch him at a distance, and a secret language so that you can speak to him.

ALCMENA: Is that all?

JUPITER: Oh, no, of course! I bring him back.

ALCMENA: Right . . . Now: when I'm pestered with dreary girl-friends or relatives?

JUPITER: I unleash a plague on the visitors which makes their eyeballs start from their sockets. I send a disease to chew up their livers and also a kind of cerebral colic. Then the ceiling collapses on their heads and the floor caves in under their feet . . . No, that's wrong, isn't it?

ALCMENA: It's either too much or not enough!

JUPITER: Oh, of course, sorry – I take them away.

ALCMENA: A sick child?

JUPITER: Nothing but sadness in the universe. Flowers lose their scent. Animals walk with heads bowed.

ALCMENA: Aren't you going to cure him, then?

JUPITER: Oh – yes! yes! What a fool I am.

ALCMENA: Gods always forget the obvious things, you see. They pity the sick and hate the wicked – it never occurs to them to heal or punish. Still, on the whole you've understood; you've passed your test quite creditably.

JUPITER: Dear Alcmena.

ALCMENA: Don't smile like that, Jupiter, don't be cruel! Haven't you ever yielded to one of your creatures before?

JUPITER: The occasion never arose.

ALCMENA: Well, it has now. Are you going to let it slip?

JUPITER: Stand up, Alcmena. It's time you had your reward. Ever since this morning I've admired your courage and stubbornness, the way you weave good faith into your cunning and sincerity into your lies. You've won me over, Alcmena, and if you can think of some way to explain your refusal to the people of Thebes, I won't impose my presence on you tonight.

ALCMENA: But why mention it to the Thebans at all? Let the whole world think I'm your mistress – don't worry, I shan't mind, and nor will Amphitryon! It will make people jealous of us, but we'll be happy to suffer that for your sake.

JUPITER: Come into my arms, Alcmena, and say good-bye to me.

ALCMENA: Into a friend's arms – oh, Jupiter, I run!

VOICE FROM HEAVEN: The Farewells of Alcmena and her Lover Jupiter.

ALCMENA: Did you hear that?

JUPITER: I did indeed.

ALCMENA: My *lover* Jupiter?

JUPITER: Lover really means friend. Voices from heaven are prone to this rather literary style.

ALCMENA: Jupiter, I'm frightened. That one word has thoroughly upset me!

JUPITER: There's nothing to fear.

VOICE FROM HEAVEN: The Farewells of Jupiter and Alcmena his Mistress.

JUPITER: This is some nonsense of Mercury's. I'll soon put a stop to it . . . But Alcmena, what's the matter? Why are you so pale? Do you want me to tell you again: I accept friendship.

ALCMENA: Without reservations?

JUPITER: Without any reservations.

ALCMENA: You've accepted it very easily! And you seem remarkably satisfied about it!

JUPITER: Oh, I *am* satisfied.

ALCMENA: Satisfied not to have been my lover?

JUPITER: That's *not* what I meant.

ALCMENA: Nor what I think! Jupiter, you're my friend now, be frank with me. Are you absolutely positive you've never been my lover?

JUPITER: Why ask me that?

ALCMENA: You were only playing with Amphitryon just now, weren't you? There was no real struggle between his love and your desire; it was only a game on your side. You'd renounced me before it started. From what I know of men, I'm almost inclined to suspect that was because you'd already had what you came for.

JUPITER: Already? How do you mean, already?

ALCMENA: Are you sure you never got into my dreams, and never took on Amphitryon's shape?

JUPITER: I'm positive.

ALCMENA: Perhaps that's something else you've forgotten. Not surprising, really, with all the adventures you get through.

JUPITER: Alcmena!

ALCMENA: So it doesn't show a very great love on your part. Of course, I wouldn't have asked for more, but to have slept just once with Jupiter, that would have been something for a poor silly woman to look back on. Never mind!

JUPITER: Alcmena, my dear, you are trying to trap me.

ALCMENA: Trap you? Are you afraid of being caught, then?

JUPITER: I can read you like a book, Alcmena. I can see your anxiety and your cunning little plans. I saw that you'd have killed yourself if I'd been your lover – so I wasn't.

ALCMENA: Take me in your arms.

JUPITER: Gladly, little Alcmena. Are you happy there?

ALCMENA: Yes.

JUPITER: Yes who?

ALCMENA: Yes, Jupiter darling. – There now, does that seem natural to you, that I should call you Jupiter darling?

JUPITER: You said it so naturally.

ALCMENA: What made me say it, though? That's what intrigues me. And this trust and pleasure my body feels in you, where does that come from? I feel so at ease with you, it's as if it was *your* ease I felt.

JUPITER: That's right. We're very well attuned.

ALCMENA: No, we're not, though. There are plenty of things I disagree violently about: your creation for one thing, and your dress sense for another. But our bodies do agree. Our bodies are drawn to each other like magnets, like gymnasts after exercise. When was *our* exercise, Jupiter? Come on, confess.

JUPITER: I tell you: never.

ALCMENA: Then why am I so upset?

JUPITER: Because in your arms, in spite of myself, I feel a strange desire to take on Amphitryon's shape. Or possibly because you're beginning to love me.

ALCMENA: Oh, no, it's far from a beginning. You're sure it wasn't you who came all burning into my bed after the great fire in Thebes?

JUPITER: No – nor all dripping, the night when your husband fished that child out of the sea.

ALCMENA: There you are, you see – you know!

JUPITER: As I know everything concerning you. No, I'm afraid it really was your husband . . . The softness of your hair!

ALCMENA: I have the feeling that it's not the first time you've fingered that lock of hair, or bent over me as you are now . . . Was it at dawn or dusk you came and took me?

JUPITER: You know very well it was dawn. Do you think I didn't see through that trick with Leda? I took Leda to please you.

ALCMENA: Oh, master of the gods, can you bestow forgetfulness?

JUPITER: I can give forgetfulness like opium, or deafness like valerian. Whole gods in heaven have much the same power as gods dispersed on earth. But what is it you want to forget?

ALCMENA: Today. Yes, I know everything has gone beautifully and everyone has behaved in perfect good faith, but there's still something suspicious about it that I can't get off my mind. I'm the sort of woman who can't bear to have a haunted day in her life, not even one. My whole body welcomes this

87

day when I came to know you, but my soul is troubled by it. Surely that's the opposite of what I ought to feel? Give Amphitryon and me the power to forget this day – everything except your friendship.

JUPITER: You shall have your wish. Come back into my arms, and this time with all the love you can.

ALCMENA: Yes, I will, because I shall forget.

JUPITER: It's important you should, because I can only give forgetfulness with a kiss.

ALCMENA: Are you going to kiss Amphitryon on the lips as well?

JUPITER: Alcmena, as you're going to forget everything, wouldn't you like me to show you your future now?

ALCMENA: The gods preserve me – no!

JUPITER: It's a happy one, I promise.

ALCMENA: I know what happy futures are like. My beloved husband will live: and die. My darling son will be born, live and die. And I shall live and die.

JUPITER: Why won't you be immortal?

ALCMENA: Because immortality is an adventure, and I loathe adventures.

JUPITER: Alcmena, my dear friend, I want you to share in the life of us gods, if only for a second. As you're going to forget everything, wouldn't you like to see and understand in one flash what the world's really like?

ALCMENA: No, Jupiter, I've no curiosity at all.

JUPITER: Don't you want to see infinity, the great void, a succession, an infinity of voids? If you think you'd feel frightened among all those milky limbos, I can make your favourite flower, a rose or a zinnia, appear in the furthest corner of space, so that for an infinitesimal moment infinity can be stamped with your arms.

ALCMENA: No.

JUPITER: You can't just go off today, you and your husband, and leave me with all this surplus divinity on my hands! Would you like to see humanity at work, from its birth to its extinction? Or the eleven Great Ones who'll adorn its history: the fine Jewish face, or the little nose of a girl from Lorraine?

ALCMENA: No.

JUPITER: My dear obstinate woman, I'm asking you for the last time! Don't you want to know, as you're about to forget it all, what semblances your happiness is built on, what illusions sustain your virtue?

ALCMENA: No.

JUPITER. Nor what I really am to you, Alcmena? Nor what's inside this dear, dear belly?

ALCMENA: Oh, hurry!

JUPITER: Forget everything, then – except this kiss.

He kisses her.

ALCMENA (*coming to herself again*): What kiss?

JUPITER: Oh, now, let's have no nonsense about the kiss. I took special care to place it well this side of oblivion.

Enter Mercury.

MERCURY: The whole of Thebes is out there, Jupiter, under the palace walls, waiting for you to appear in Alcmena's arms.

ALCMENA: Come on, Jupiter, let them all see us and then they'll be satisfied.

MERCURY: They want you to say a few words, Jupiter. You can make it as loud as you like: they're all standing sideways on to avoid any damage to their eardrums.

JUPITER (*very loudly*): At last . . . Alcmena, my dear!

ALCMENA (*very softly*): Yes, dear Jupiter, at last we must say good-bye.

JUPITER: So begins our night that shall enrich the world.

ALCMENA: So ends our day that I was just beginning to enjoy.

JUPITER: And now, before these noble, splendid people of Thebes . . .

ALCMENA: These miserable specimens, who cheer my supposed lapse as loudly as they would hiss my virtue . . .

JUPITER: Now, for the first time, I embrace you, to bid you welcome.

ALCMENA: And I for the third time, to bid you farewell for ever.

For a few moments they move side by side along the balustrade. Then Alcmena leads Jupiter aside to the little door.

JUPITER: And now what?

ALCMENA: Now that our legend's in order, as befits the gods, let's get down to putting history straight, as befits men, by the usual compromises. No one can see us now. Let's get away from the laws of fate . . . Amphitryon, are you there?

Amphitryon opens the little door.

AMPHITRYON: Here I am, Alcmena.

ALCMENA: Darling, say thank you to Jupiter. He insists on personally giving me back to you, intact.

AMPHITRYON: Only the gods could show such courtesy.

ALCMENA: He wanted to try us, that's all! The one thing he's definite about is that we must have a son.

AMPHITRYON: We'll have one in nine months, Sire, I swear we will!

ALCMENA: And we promise to call him Hercules, as you're so keen on the name. He'll be a good, gentle little boy.

JUPITER: Yes, I can just see him . . . Good-bye, then, Alcmena. Be happy! And you, Mercury, as master of the revels, I charge you, before we leave these realms, to prove our friendship to them by giving the reward due to all reunited couples.

MERCURY: Reunited couples: no problem there! And to witness their sporting, I summon here the gods, I summon you, Leda (who have yet to learn the truth), I summon all you good people who have played today the lesser ranks of love and war, you, groom, warrior, and trumpeter! Open your eyes, now, wide, and round the bed, to drown their cries, let song and music chime, and thunder roar . . .

All those summoned come crowding on to the stage.

ALCMENA: Oh, Jupiter, be merciful, stop him! For Alcmena's sake!

JUPITER: Alcmena again! As if anything today could be for

anyone's sake *but* Alcmena's! In that case, obviously, Mercury's got it wrong. In that case let it be the most whispered of asides, the stillest of silences! And we must all disappear, gods to our zeniths, extras to your cellars. And you, audience, must file out without a word, with an affectation of total indifference. Now let Alcmena and her husband appear one last time, alone in a circle of light, where my arm will be seen no more save as a pointer in the direction of happiness; and now, on this couple which no adultery has touched nor ever will, which will never know the taste of sinful kisses, now, to enclose this glade of fidelity in a wall of velvet, now, curtains of the night, who for nearly an hour have held back – now fall.

Curtain

Intermezzo

Intermezzo was first performed on 27 February 1933 at the Théâtre Louis Jouvet (now the Comédie des Champs-Elysées) and was produced by Louis Jouvet. The music was by Francis Poulenc.

ISABELLE

THE SUPERINTENDENT

THE GHOST

THE INSPECTOR

THE CHEMIST

THE MAYOR

ARMANDE MANGEBOIS

LÉONIDE MANGEBOIS

LUCE
GISÈLE
DAISY
GILBERTE
IRÈNE } little girls
NICOLE
MARIE-LOUISE
VIOLA

CAMBRONNE
CRAPUCE } executioners

MONSIEUR ADRIEN

FATHER TELLIER

ACT ONE

In the country. A flowery meadow. Thickets. Dusk.

MAYOR (*appearing alone, shouting*): Hoo-ooo! – I must say this is an odd sort of place. Nobody's answering, not even the echo. Hoo-ooo!

CHEMIST (*coming in behind him*): Hoo-ooo!

MAYOR: My dear Chemist, you gave me quite a fright.

CHEMIST: I'm so sorry, Mr. Mayor – did you think it was *him*?

MAYOR: Please don't joke about it. I know he may not exist, I know that those who claim to have met him round here may have been the victims of a hallucination. But you must admit this is a very curious place!

CHEMIST: Why did you choose it for a meeting-place, then?

MAYOR: No doubt for the same reason that makes him choose it: to get away from inquisitive eyes. Doesn't it make you feel a bit uneasy?

CHEMIST: Not in the least. Everything's perfectly green and calm – you'd think you were on a golf course.

MAYOR: Aren't they ever found on golf courses, then?

CHEMIST: They may be eventually, when the comings and goings of men and women golfers have begun to produce this gradual accretion of commonplace words and true confessions, fag-ends and powder puffs, sympathies and rivalries – the whole humus necessary to humanize still primitive earth. But for the moment, certainly, I'd say that these handsome, well-designed, shaped and tended areas are the least likely to have sinister overtones – especially as they are sown with English grass, which is probably the least mysterious species. You never find henbane, centaury or vertadine. Here, I see, you have all these plants – you even have the mandrake.

MAYOR: Any truth in all that stuff about mandrakes?

CHEMIST: You mean for constipation?

MAYOR: No, I mean about them making you immortal – you

97

know, children conceived by a hanged man over a mandrake becoming demoniac and living for ever.

CHEMIST: There's a reason for all symbols; it's up to us to interpret them.

MAYOR: It looks as if we may be dealing with this sort of symbol.

CHEMIST: How does he generally appear – sickly, malformed?

MAYOR: No: tall and handsome.

CHEMIST: I take it there have been hangings round here in the past?

MAYOR: Since I've been Mayor, all we've had have been two suicides: my vine-dresser, who blew himself up with his bird-scaring gun, and the old lady who kept the grocer's shop. She hung herself – by the feet, though.

CHEMIST: It has to be a hanged man, of between twenty and forty . . . You know, I'm beginning to think our gentleman must have got lost. It's well past the agreed meeting-time.

MAYOR: Don't worry. I asked the Superintendent of Weights and Measures to show the Inspector the way. So there'll be four of us to make up the committee of investigation.

CHEMIST: Wouldn't a commission of three have been plenty?

MAYOR: Well, he's an awfully nice chap, the young Superintendent.

CHEMIST: Oh, awfully.

MAYOR: And he has courage, too. At our dinner on Wednesday evening, when the talk frequently bordered on the indecent, he seized every opportunity to defend female virtue. And yesterday, in a mere couple of sentences, he produced a quite unanswerable vindication of Catherine the Second, in the teeth of the Surveyor of Roads, who deployed all the arguments against her.

CHEMIST: No, I meant the Inspector. Why bring him all the way from Limoges? He is said to be extremely brutal in his methods, and ghosts don't respond well to bullies.

MAYOR: He came on his own initiative. Apparently he makes a point of confronting any local manifestation of the mysterious or abnormal. At the first hint of an unexplained phenomenon in the fauna and flora of the region, or even its geography, the Inspector comes on the scene and restores order. Did you hear about his latest exploits?

CHEMIST: At Berry, with the so-called mermaids?

MAYOR: No, right here in Limousin! First at Rochechouart, where he got the military to block up the singing spring. And then at the Pompadour stud-farm, where the stallions had started using their eyes like humans, exchanging side-glances, giving significant looks via the pupils or eyelids – he made them wear blinkers, even in the stables. So you can imagine how attracted he was by the state of our town. I'm only surprised it's taking him so long to get here.

CHEMIST: Let's give him a shout.

MAYOR: No, no! Don't shout, please. Don't you find the acoustics of this field have something awfully disturbing and confused about them?

CHEMIST: The Superintendent has the finest bass voice in the district; we'll hear him a mile off . . . Hoo-ooo!

The cry is echoed by a shrill chorus of little girls' voices, as Isabelle and her pupils come into view.

MAYOR: Ah, Miss Isabelle! Good evening, Miss Isabelle!

ISABELLE: Good evening, Mr Mayor.

CHEMIST: Well, girls, are you collecting plants?

MAYOR: Since our schoolmistress fell ill three months ago, Miss Isabelle has very kindly been deputizing. But she does insist on taking her lessons out of doors in this fine weather.

ISABELLE: As a matter of fact, Mr Chemist, we are collecting plants too. I want my girls to know Nature by all its names and titles. We've already got a whole bag full of curious plants. Please excuse us, but we're still short of the most vital one for our present lesson. I know where to find it . . .

CHEMIST: Which one?

THE LITTLE GIRLS: The mandrake, the mandrake!

They run out with Isabelle.

CHEMIST: What a delightful girl! It's so touching to see innocence walking safe and fearless among the symbols of evil!

MAYOR: I only wish the Mangebois sisters shared your view.

CHEMIST: What have those two hags got to do with Isabelle?

MAYOR: That's what we're about to find out. They've asked to
have an interview with the Inspector, and they hinted strongly
to me that it not only had to do with Isabelle, but with bringing a grave charge.

CHEMIST: What possible charge could they bring? Isabelle is so
frank and open, so different from the other girls! I mean,
you know the others, Mr Mayor. They spend their afternoons
getting lost in the woods with their cousins, bathing with the
Negro servant from the Sub-Prefect's office, sprawling in the
meadows reading the Marquis de Sade – with illustrations!
Young girls, indeed! Whereas Isabelle, on the contrary, is
without any vague yearnings or curiosity about future experience. Look at the openness of that profile! Isn't she the
key to our understanding of every person or thing she meets?
Look at her now, astride that sapling, making that little
donkey dance by waving a thistle at it, with her pupils skip-
ping round them in a ring – you see, the function of donkeys
in this base world suddenly strikes one with blinding clarity.
Of little girls too, I may say. Look at them, Mr Mayor – those
enchanting little faces, those delicious little backs. . . .

MAYOR: Restrain yourself, Mr Chemist.

CHEMIST: Ah, here comes the Inspector.

Enter the Inspector in conversation with the Superintendent.

INSPECTOR: Proof, Superintendent? You want proof that
neither spirits nor the spirit world exist? Would you like me
to give it to you, here and now?

SUPERINTENDENT: Coming from such a high official, I should
of course treasure it.

INSPECTOR: You would agree that if spirits do exist, they presumably can hear me?

SUPERINTENDENT: Apart from deaf spirits, certainly.

INSPECTOR: Let them hear this, then: Spirits, shapes spun of thin air or white of egg (you see, I'm not mincing my words – if they have a scrap of self-respect they'll know what's expected of them) – I challenge you, on humanity's behalf, to appear to us! Considering the quality of the present company, this is an ideal opportunity for you to enhance your reputation in these parts. I'm not asking you to produce a live parrot from my pocket, which I gather is the classic gambit for spirits. I am merely defying you to make a common or garden sparrow fly out of this tree, thicket, or forest when I count three . . . Now, Superintendent, I'm counting: one . . . two . . three. . . You see, it's pathetic. (*His hat flies off.*) Good heavens, what a wind!

CHEMIST: But Inspector, we can't feel a breath of wind.

INSPECTOR: There is quite sufficient. It's really pitiful.

SUPERINTENDENT: Perhaps ghosts don't believe in men.

MAYOR: Or perhaps your invocation was a bit too generalized.

INSPECTOR: Would you prefer me to call on each of them by name? Shall I call on Asphlaroth?

CHEMIST: Asphlaroth, the most cruel and touchy of spirits, who is said to lodge in the human organism and delight in tormenting it? Do be careful, Inspector! You never know what these games may lead to.

INSPECTOR: Listen to me, Asphlaroth. I defy you today with the lowest and most ludicrous parts of my system. Not my lungs or heart, but my gall-bladder, my adam's apple, my sneezing membrane. Strike just one of them with the slightest pain, the minutest contraction, and I will believe in you. Right: one . . . two . . . three. . . . Well, I'm waiting!

He abruptly sits down.

It's terribly slippery here!

MAYOR: It hasn't rained for three weeks.

CHEMIST: Spirits do have a different conception of time from ours. Perhaps Asphlaroth answered your insults some time in advance. Might I ask when you got those scars on your nose?

INSPECTOR: A tile fell on my head when I was only just out of my cradle.

CHEMIST: That explains his silence. He gave you your answer forty years ago.

INSPECTOR: Exactly what I'd have expected from him: (a) he doesn't exist, (b) he's a coward, and (c) he attacks little children. There, gentlemen, is your incontrovertible proof. You must pardon me for smiling when you tell me that your town is haunted.

MAYOR: It *is* haunted, Inspector.

INSPECTOR: I know what haunted towns invariably are. You find kitchen implements clattering about at night in flats where the landlord wants to get rid of the tenant. You find ghosts appearing on joint estates to persuade one of the parties to give up his share. Then the gossips get to work, after which fear and suspicion lead to slander and finally crime. You recently elected a local councillor, didn't you? No doubt there were brawls around the ballot boxes, possibly resulting in bloodshed. Well, there you are, you see: more than one kind of box can summon up a corpse.

MAYOR: Not at all, Inspector; quite the reverse.

INSPECTOR: Do you mean to say you voted without shedding blood? It's hardly democratic, and certainly not demoniac.

MAYOR: But we didn't vote. Nobody voted or even thought of voting. Not that the electors didn't get up at dawn, conscious of their civic duty, and hurry out to read the notices. But the sun was shining, and everybody swore afterwards that they read on the hoardings: "No abstention from the sun". So they went and walked round the town till evening.

INSPECTOR: Obviously bribed by the conservatives.

CHEMIST: By arrangement with the sun.

SUPERINTENDENT: Certainly not. The Mayor is not trying to convince you, Inspector, that the town has given itself over in recent weeks to that sort of curious delusion. No, some unknown and in my opinion rather congenial influence is at work here, gradually undermining all the principles (false ones, by the way) on which civilized society is based.

INSPECTOR: I don't need your personal comments. Just explain what you mean.

SUPERINTENDENT: I will. For instance, children who are beaten by their parents now leave their parents. Dogs who are ill-treated by their masters bite their master's hand. Women with ugly, old, drunken, hairy husbands simply abandon them for young, sober, smooth-faced lovers. Great strapping fellows, when abused by puny little men, no longer hesitate to smash their teeth in. In short, weakness here is no longer a strength, and affection no longer a habit.

INSPECTOR: And you've waited till now to warn me about this state of affairs?

MAYOR: I should add that there have been several remarkable coincidences which have confirmed the intrusion of occult powers into our municipal life. The other Sunday we drew our regular monthly lottery, and the first prize in silver was won by the poorest man in town – not, as it nearly always had been before, by M. Dumas the millionaire, who was well able to survive the disappointment. The motor bike was won by our young local champion and not, as it invariably had been before, by the mother superior of the local convent. This week two people have died: amazingly enough, they were the two oldest inhabitants. Not only that, they were also the most miserly old man and the most cantankerous old woman. So, you see, for the first time, fate is actually on our side, and chance seems to know what it is doing.

INSPECTOR: But this is the negation of human liberty.

CHEMIST: Perhaps, Mr Mayor, you ought to mention the census.

INSPECTOR: What census?

MAYOR: The official five-yearly census. I haven't yet dared to pass the results on to the Prefecture.

INSPECTOR: Did your townsfolk make false declarations?

MAYOR: On the contrary. They all replied with an extravagant, cynical truthfulness that is a positive insult to the administration. Under the heading of family, to give you one example, most of them didn't put down as children their real sons or daughters, in cases where these were ugly or ungrateful, but put instead their dogs, or apprentices, or canaries – in fact, whatever they really loved like their own children.

SUPERINTENDENT: Some of them put down as their wives not their actual wife but the unknown woman of their dreams, the neighbour they're secretly carrying on with, or even the female animal which to them is the perfect companion – a cat or a squirrel.

MAYOR: Under the heading of residence, rich neurotics put down hovels, while contented paupers put down palaces.

INSPECTOR: And how long have these scandals been going on?

MAYOR: Roughly since the first appearance of the ghost.

INSPECTOR: Please don't use that stupid word. There is no ghost.

MAYOR: Phantom, if you prefer it.

INSPECTOR: There's no phantom either!

CHEMIST: That's not what science teaches us. There are phantoms of everything, even of metal or water. There may very well be one of men.

Off-stage, the voices of the two Misses Mangebois are heard. The elder sister is deaf, and has a deaf-aid slung around her neck, through which her younger sister keeps her in touch with the conversation.

ARMANDE MANGEBOIS (*calling out, still offstage*): May we join you, Mr Mayor?

MAYOR: Please do, ladies, please do! Inspector, here are the Misses Mangebois I told you about, who promised us some important evidence.

ARMANDE (*appearing with her sister*): I do hope, Mr Mayor, that we're not going to disappoint you.

MAYOR: The Misses Mangebois are the daughters of our late magistrate – famous, you know, for having cut the membrane of the female siamese twins whose custody was disputed by the two rival showmen from Limoges.

The Misses Mangebois sit down on folding stools, after exchanging greetings with the gentlemen.

INSPECTOR: My congratulations, ladies. A judgment worthy of Solomon. Now please proceed.

ARMANDE: First, Inspector, I do want to ask you to excuse my sister Léonide. She is rather hard of hearing.

LÉONIDE: What did you say?

ARMANDE: I told the Inspector that you were rather hard of hearing.

LÉONIDE: Why tell me? I know.

ARMANDE: Now look here, Léonide, do you or don't you want me to repeat everything to you?

LÉONIDE: Yes, except when you say I'm deaf.

INSPECTOR: Our reasons, ladies, for asking you to come and meet us here, in a place specially chosen for discreetness . . .

LÉONIDE (*to Armande*): You snore. But do I go and tell him?

ARMANDE: I do not snore!

LÉONIDE: Well, if you don't, you must have suddenly stopped the moment I went deaf.

INSPECTOR: Please ask your sister to be quiet, Mademoiselle, or we'll never get anywhere.

ARMANDE: That's rather difficult, Inspector. You see, she's the elder.

LÉONIDE: What are you saying?

ARMANDE: Nothing to do with you.

LÉONIDE: If it's nothing to do with me, I suppose you're busy telling them you're the younger.

ARMANDE: The Inspector has asked me to say that he would like silence.

LÉONIDE: If he knew what silence was, he wouldn't like it at all. I'll be quiet.

INSPECTOR: Ladies, I gather that you are in close touch with everything that is being said and done in the district.

ARMANDE: Well, we are secretaries to the Marriage Guidance Institute.

INSPECTOR: And what are they talking about at the Institute at present?

ARMANDE: What do you think, Inspector? The ghost, of course.

INSPECTOR: Do you believe in this ghost, then? Have you seen it?

ARMANDE: I've seen people who have seen it.

INSPECTOR: Would you call them trustworthy?

ARMANDE: One of them is a Knight Commander of the Grand Dragon of Annam.

INSPECTOR: If he believes in the Grand Dragon of Annam, I'd call that suspect for a start. Kindly name your witnesses.

ARMANDE: Well, there's our milkman, there's the beautiful Fatma – that's what gentlemen call the grocer's wife – and there's Captain Lescalard. He's the one who's the Knight Commander.

INSPECTOR: I think I might have guessed. And how did the ghost appear to them? Wrapped in a shroud, presumably, with a head made from a scooped-out pumpkin pierced with holes and a torch shining inside?

ARMANDE: Not at all, Inspector. All the accounts tally perfectly. It's a tall young man dressed in black. He appears at nightfall, and always at the edge of the pond – over there where you can see the reeds.

INSPECTOR: And how do you explain these visitations? Have there been ghosts in these parts before?

ARMANDE: No, never. Not before the crime, that is.

INSPECTOR: What crime?

SUPERINTENDENT: A magnificent crime, Inspector, I'd almost call it world-shaking. A young foreigner and his wife had rented the Château for Easter. A friend came to stay with them. Next morning they discovered the wife and the friend murdered – savagely, brutally murdered – and lying by the side of the pond was the husband's hat. I call that a salute to death in the grand style. It is generally supposed that he drowned himself.

ARMANDE: We are all agreed at the Institute that this is the drowned man's ghost. Apart from anything else, he is hatless.

INSPECTOR: He could quite well return without being drowned.

The criminal always returns to the scene of his crime, like a boomerang to the feet of its thrower.

LÉONIDE: What is the Inspector saying?

ARMANDE: That the boomerang returns to the feet of its thrower.

LÉONIDE: How very interesting. Perhaps you'll tell me when you get to the gun with the crooked barrel.

INSPECTOR: And you think that the strange events in your town are all connected with this ghost?

ARMANDE: Oh, goodness, no! That's another story altogether. But we do feel that the two stories will very soon link up. It's the danger of this which has decided us to speak.

MAYOR: Try to be a bit more lucid, Miss Mangebois.

ARMANDE: Inspector, I don't know if these gentlemen have described the scandal to you in all its horror.

INSPECTOR: Yes, Miss Mangebois, yes. Do get to the point. I realize that the entire bourgeois morality of your town has been caught with its knickers down.

LÉONIDE: What did the Inspector say?

ARMANDE: Nothing in particular.

LÉONIDE: I insist on your repeating the last word or two, as usual.

ARMANDE: Just as you wish. You really are a bore. Knickers down.

LÉONIDE: Ah, you're talking about Madame Lambert.

ARMANDE: We are *not* talking about Madame Lambert.

LÉONIDE: Well, if it's not Madame Lambert, it must be the tax-collector's wife.

INSPECTOR: Who is this Madame Lambert?

ARMANDE: The wife of the watchmaker – among others . . .

SUPERINTENDENT: I beg your pardon?

ARMANDE: I said among others.

SUPERINTENDENT (*in a sudden passion*): Excuse me! I'm not going to allow any aspersions to be cast on Madame Lambert.

INSPECTOR: Superintendent, our inquiry is quite trying enough as it is. We are not here to discuss Madame Lambert.

SUPERINTENDENT: Well, I'm sorry, but we're going to. It

wouldn't surprise you in Paris, I imagine, on café terraces or in literary salons, to see a poet suddenly rise, for no particular reason, and make a passionate speech in honour of the spring. Well, Madame Lambert is our town's spring.

ARMANDE: This young man is clearly mad.

MAYOR: My dear Superintendent!

SUPERINTENDENT: Whether we brush past Madame Lambert as she stands in the doorway of her shop pretending to find the correct time from a hundred contradictory dials, or whether we see her through the shop window, prettily nibbling the tip of her tongue with the effort of concentration, as she fastens a wristwatch for a young communicant or springs open an officer's watchcase with her rosy finger-nail, we must agree that France's most soul-stirring national treasure is not her cathedrals, or hostelries, but this young woman in every small town whose bust, softly sheathed in satin or organdie, acts like a magnet at different times of the day to the Sub-Prefect, the schoolboys, and the entire garrison!

LÉONIDE: What is the Superintendent saying?

ARMANDE: Absolutely nothing.

SUPERINTENDENT: I mean, in short, this provincial beauty which nothing will stop me worshipping here and now in the person of Madame Lambert, and under all the names and shapes assumed by Madame Lambert in the course of my still comparatively short career – for instance when she was called Madame Merle and kept a bookshop at Rodez, or Madame Lespinard the truss-manufacturer's wife at Moulins, or Madame Tribourty who sold gloves at Castres – these kid gloves were from her, incidentally – not a hole in them still . . . I will be answerable for Madame Lambert.

INSPECTOR: Gentlemen, I suggest we adjourn. We are not going to achieve anything by this sort of shambles. You, Superintendent, deserve a censure.

ARMANDE: How about Miss Isabelle, Superintendent, are you going to answer for her as well?

CHEMIST: You're surely not going to mix up Miss Isabelle in these scandals?

SUPERINTENDENT: She is the soul of purity and honour.

MAYOR: And I'm delighted that I entrusted her with the young girls' class in the regular teacher's absence.

ARMANDE: Men are so blind! Miss Isabelle is in the field over there. You have a niece in her class, Mr Mayor. Call them here for a moment, and you'll soon find out what little Daisy is being taught?

MAYOR: Why, what is she being taught?

ARMANDE: While you have the Inspector here, I suggest you put her through an examination – then you'll see.

INSPECTOR: Yes, but see what?

ARMANDE: We've had our suspicions for some time that Isabelle was involved with the outrages undermining our town. And since this morning we've been quite positive.

SUPERINTENDENT: This is slander!

ARMANDE: Léonide, tell these gentlemen why we are sure that Isabelle is the guilty one.

LÉONIDE: Because her diary tells us so. She has this diary where she writes down an account of every day's happenings.

INSPECTOR: How did it come into your possession?

ARMANDE: How did it come into your possession?

LÉONIDE: I found it on the pavement.

CHEMIST: And you had the cheek to read it?

ARMANDE: You had the cheek to read it?

LÉONIDE: I didn't ask for your opinion, did I? I looked through it to find the owner's name.

SUPERINTENDENT: This notebook is Miss Isabelle's property! You should have given it back to her.

ARMANDE: This notebook is Miss Isabelle's property, you should have given it back to her.

LÉONIDE: Mind your own business! – Here it is, Mr Mayor! Open it anywhere you like, and you'll see your favourite at work: plotting to separate ill-assorted couples, using drugs to make horses lash out at cruel carters – cruel according to her, anyway – writing endless anonymous letters to inform husbands or wives of their partners' virtues. For instance, if you want to know what made you decide to appoint her as your

new teacher, just open it at March 21st! . . . Well? What
are you saying?

ARMANDE: You're the only one that's talking.

INSPECTOR: Well, read it out, Mr Mayor.

MAYOR (*reading*): March 21st . . . Ah, March 21st! "Organ-
ized small spring festival. Took opportunity to address pupils
on beauty of human body. Emphasized the advantages of
being frankly coquettish. For exercise, made them nominate
the handsomest man in town. Sub-Prefect nominated." Well,
that's not bad, so far.

ARMANDE: Of course, the Superintendent hadn't joined us then.

INSPECTOR: But really, this is quite outrageous! It ought to be
dealt with at once. Superintendent, kindly tell this young
lady to come straight here with her pupils. I shall examine
them on the spot. I was pretty sure we should find women
behind all this disgraceful behaviour. If you give a scrap of
freedom to those termites of the social structure, every beam
is chewed to pulp before you can bat an eyelid.

SUPERINTENDENT (*on the point of going out, turns*): Inspector,
if you will excuse me . . .

INSPECTOR: Are you declining to fetch Miss Isabelle?

SUPERINTENDENT: Of course not, Inspector. I merely wanted,
with respect, to challenge the exactitude of your metaphor
and point out that there really is a certain difference between
women and termites.

INSPECTOR: If you can see the slightest difference, you're a
better man than me. Now do please hurry.

SUPERINTENDENT: Mind you, I've got nothing against ants. I
recognize their exceptional qualities. I know they milk fleas
and train soldiers. But to go on to compare them to women,
to all women – no!

ARMANDE: For once, Superintendent, I say bravo.

SUPERINTENDENT: You made your remark on the spur of the
moment, without thinking. What are the physical characteris-
tics of the ant?

INSPECTOR: Superintendent, I gave you an order.

LÉONIDE: What are they saying?

ARMANDE: The Inspector says he can't tell a woman from an ant.

LÉONIDE: Is he married?

INSPECTOR (*exploding with rage*): No, Madame, I see no difference at all. The same useless bustling about, the same tendency to gossip whenever two of them meet. The same viciousness to any outsider who enters their circle. To say nothing of their waistline, and their passion for carrying parcels. Ants, beyond question!

SUPERINTENDENT: If you turn an ant over on its back, Inspector, and touch it with your fingertip . . .

INSPECTOR: For the last time, sir, I am ordering you to go and fetch Miss Isabelle.

The Superintendent bows and goes out.

MAYOR: But you know, Inspector, our purpose in meeting was to discuss the ghost, not Isabelle.

ARMANDE: It's the same thing!

CHEMIST: I suppose you're going to suggest now that Miss Isabelle is a witch?

ARMANDE: Open the diary at June 14th, and read what it says.

INSPECTOR: June 14th – surely that was yesterday? Today is the 15th, isn't it?

ARMANDE: We had been wondering for some time why Miss Isabelle always chose the edge of the pond for her evening walks. The last page of her diary will leave you in no further doubt.

INSPECTOR: Read it, Mr Mayor.

MAYOR (*reading*): June 14th: "I'm sure now that the ghost understands that I believe in him and can help him. How can one *not* believe in ghosts? Obviously he is looking for me, for there are reports of him appearing everywhere I've taken the girls for walks. He will certainly appear to me at dusk, at the edge of some wood, and who knows what instructions he may not give me for completing the reformation of the town? I'm almost certain it will be tomorrow."

INSPECTOR: And tomorrow is today!

LÉONIDE: What's the Inspector saying?

ARMANDE: That tomorrow is today.

LÉONIDE: Well, that's one point of view.

The Superintendent reappears.

SUPERINTENDENT: Miss Isabelle is coming, Inspector.

ARMANDE: We'd better go, Léonide. Isabelle's coming.

INSPECTOR: I'm extremely grateful to you ladies. I hope that thanks to your evidence we may at last be approaching the naked truth.

ARMANDE: We have nothing more to tell you, gentlemen. We have no information about Madame Lambert . . .

INSPECTOR: You certainly boast a Parthian shot, Miss Armande.

LÉONIDE: What?

ARMANDE: The Inspector is talking about Parthian shots.

LÉONIDE: Another string to his bow!

Exeunt the Misses Mangebois. The Superintendent watches Isabelle approaching.

SUPERINTENDENT: Well, Inspector, if ants crawling in the fields look like the Victory of Samothrace plus her head, or the Venus of Milo plus her arms, if their cheeks are dyed with the blood of pomegranates and their smile with that of raspberries – then; and only then, is there the slightest resemblance between Isabelle and an ant. Just look at her!

Isabelle appears, followed by the Little Girls.

ISABELLE: You wanted to see me, Inspector?

INSPECTOR: Miss Isabelle, there are most unfortunate rumours about your methods of teaching. I intend to find out here and now if these rumours are founded, and take action accordingly.

ISABELLE: I don't understand, Inspector.

INSPECTOR: That can't be helped. Let us begin the examination. Tell your pupils to come in. (*The little girls laugh.*) Why are they laughing like that?

ISABELLE: It was you saying come in, Inspector, when there isn't a door.

INSPECTOR: This open-air teaching is quite absurd. One's official vocabulary loses half its force. (*Whispering among the little girls.*) Be quiet over there! The next one to talk will sweep out the classroom – I mean the field, the countryside. (*Laughter.*) Mademoiselle, your pupils are insufferable!

MAYOR: But they're so sweet, Inspector – just look at them.

INSPECTOR: They've no business to be sweet. Behind all that sweetness, there isn't one who hasn't got her particular way of smiling or winking. I expect a class of pupils to show its master as grave and uniform a face as a set of dominoes.

CHEMIST: You'll never manage it, Inspector.

INSPECTOR: And why not?

CHEMIST: Because they're gay.

INSPECTOR: They've no business to be gay . . . You are supposed to be concentrating on your examinations, not shrieking with laughter. The reason they're gay is that their mistress doesn't punish them enough.

ISABELLE: Whatever should I punish them for? In outdoor schools there's hardly any occasion for punishment. Things which are naughty in a classroom become signs of intelligence and initiative in a field. How can you punish a pupil here for staring at the ceiling? Just look at the ceiling!

SUPERINTENDENT: Yes, indeed, look.

INSPECTOR: The whole educational point of a ceiling is to emphasize the difference in stature between an adult and a child. An open-air teacher frankly admits that he is smaller than a tree, weaker than an ox, slower than a bee, and thus sacrifices his most convincing claims to dignity. (*Laughter.*) *Now* what is it?

MAYOR: Only a caterpillar climbing up you, Inspector.

INSPECTOR: A fine moment to choose! It must take what's coming to it.

ISABELLE: Oh, Inspector, don't kill it. That's the *collata azurea*. It's only fulfilling its destiny as a caterpillar.

INSPECTOR: Nonsense. It has never been the *collata azurea*'s mission to climb over inspectors. (*He crushes it: the little girls sob.*) Now what's the matter with them, are they crying?

LUCE: Yes, because you've killed the *collata azurea*!

INSPECTOR: Whereas, of course, if a blackbird had carried off the *collata azurea*, they would all find it quite splendid. They'd be thrilled to bits.

LUCE: Well, caterpillars are blackbirds' food!

SUPERINTENDENT: Quite right. No sympathy can be wasted on caterpillars in their nutritional capacity.

INSPECTOR: So that's the effect your teaching has on your pupils, Miss Isabelle. They want to see an inspector eat the caterpillars he kills! Well, I'm sorry, they're going to be disappointed. I shall continue to kill caterpillars without eating them, and, girls, I had better warn all your regular classmates, whether insects, reptiles or rodents, not to go tickling my neck or crawling into my socks if they don't want to be killed! So you with the brown hair, keep an eye on your moles, because from now on I shall crush moles; and you, little redhead, if one of your squirrels comes within my reach, I shall break his squirrel neck with these bare hands, as sure as I shall be dead when I am dead. . . . (*The little girls burst out laughing.*) I don't see anything funny in that.

ISABELLE: It's just the idea of your being dead when you're dead, Inspector.

MAYOR: Shall we start the examination?

INSPECTOR: Call the first one here. (*Confused movements among the class.*) What are they fidgeting about now?

ISABELLE: The thing is, Inspector, that we don't have a first, or second, or third. You don't think I would be so cruel as to wound their pride like that? We do have the biggest, and the most talkative – but they are all first.

INSPECTOR: Or all last, more likely . . . You over there, you can start! What are you first in?

GILBERTE: In botany, Inspector.

INSPECTOR: Botany, eh? Then tell me the difference between monocotyledons and dicotyledons.

GILBERTE: Inspector, I said botany.

INSPECTOR: Listen to that! Do you suppose she even knows what a tree is?

GILBERTE: That's exactly what she knows best, Inspector.

ISABELLE: If you know it, Gilberte, speak up. The gentlemen are listening.

GILBERTE: The tree is the motionless brother of man. In tree language, murderers are called woodcutters, undertakers' mutes are known as charcoal-burners, and fleas as woodpeckers.

IRÈNE: The seasons send us unmistakable messages through its branches. And through its roots the dead breathe their dreams and longings up to its topmost point.

VIOLA: And these are the flowers that cover all plants in spring.

INSPECTOR: Yes, especially spinach. So, my dear, if I understand you aright, the roots are the real leaves, and vice versa.

GILBERTE: Exactly.

INSPECTOR: Nought out of ten! (*She laughs.*) What is there to laugh about, you impertinent little girl?

ISABELLE: Well, in my marking I have adopted nought as the top mark because of its connexions with the infinite.

SUPERINTENDENT: Fascinating idea.

INSPECTOR: Really, Mr Mayor, I can't take much more of this . . . Mademoiselle, will you please take over the examination.

ISABELLE: Daisy, tell us about flowers.

DAISY: The flower is man's noblest conquest.

INSPECTOR: Very good; a promising start.

DAISY: What I particularly look at, in a flower, are the pistil and the stamen. They take in pollen from other flowers through the wind's agency. And that's how plants are born – quite differently from birds.

GILBERTE: Or duck-billed platypuses . . .

VIOLA: Or carnivores, particularly!

INSPECTOR: Mr Mayor, this is scandalous, absolutely scandalous! I have reached my decision about the happenings in your town!

MAYOR: Let's take geography next, Inspector . . . Viola, my dear, who causes volcanoes to erupt?

VIOLA: The All-Rounder, Mr Mayor.

INSPECTOR: Who?

VIOLA: The All-Rounder!

LITTLE GIRLS: The All-Rounder!

INSPECTOR: The All-Rounder? Are they mad?

ISABELLE: You see, Inspector, I'm particularly anxious that these children shouldn't think of Nature as unjust. I explain the major catastrophes to them as regrettable details, certainly, but necessary to achieve a universe satisfying in its all-round effect, so that we've come to know the spirit or power which causes them as the All-Rounder.

SUPERINTENDENT: Quite right! Extremely sensible!

INSPECTOR: So, Mademoiselle, if I understand your method, you must also have thought up a second spirit, to explain all life's little shocks and trials; the cunning invisible one who bangs shutters at night, or induces an old gentleman to sit down in a plum tart accidentally left on a chair?

VIOLA: Oh yes, Inspector! That's Arthur.

INSPECTOR: Is it Arthur or the All-Rounder who makes caterpillars crawl over visiting inspectors?

THE LITTLE GIRLS: Arthur! That's Arthur!

INSPECTOR: And is it Arthur who makes the Inspector kill the caterpillar?

LITTLE GIRLS: No, no, the All-Rounder! The All-Rounder!

EVERYONE ELSE: The All-Rounder!

INSPECTOR: It makes you want to give up, Mr Mayor! I've never seen anything like it.

MAYOR: Perhaps they might be stronger in history . . .

INSPECTOR: History? But don't you see what all this education's aiming at? Nothing less than freeing these young minds from the net of truth that our wonderful nineteenth century spread over our country. History! It would be just the same as their arithmetic or geography. Well, see for yourself . . . You there, what is between France and Germany?

IRÈNE: Eternal friendship and peace.

INSPECTOR: To put it mildly . . . You, what is a right angle?

LUCE: There is no such thing as a right angle. The right angle

doesn't exist in Nature. The only more or less right angle is
the one obtained by extending an imaginary straight line from
the Grecian nose to the Grecian earth.

INSPECTOR: Naturally! . . . You, what do two and two make?

DAISY: Four, Inspector.

INSPECTOR: There, you see, Mr Mayor? . . . Oh, I do beg
your pardon! These little idiots have got me mixed up. Anyway, come to think of it, how is it possible that two and two
should also make four for them? What new aberration, what
refinement of sadism has made this woman dream up a false
multiplication table which tallies exactly with the true one?
I'm sure her four is really not a four at all, but a shameless
incognito five . . . Two and two make five, don't they, my
dear?

DAISY: No Inspector, four.

INSPECTOR: Obstinate, too . . . You there, sing me the
Marseillaise!

MAYOR: Is that really in the syllabus, Inspector?

INSPECTOR: Let her sing the Marseillaise.

ISABELLE: She knows it, Inspector. The little girls' Marseillaise,
of course.

DENISE: I know it, Mr Mayor. I know it! (*She sings.*)
          "The only State that little girls adore
          To dream about is the married state.
          Be his name Paul, Jacques or Dimitri,
          He must love and dress like the great."

ISABELLE: Now the chorus, children!

LITTLE GIRLS: "Marseilles! We love Marseilles!
          It's sunny all the day!
          The only state we think is great
          Is summer in Marseilles!"

INSPECTOR: How disgraceful! And look at their hair, all over
the place! And what are these red pencil marks on their necks
– some sort of vaccination?

LUCE: Oh no, Inspector, that's for ghosts!

INSPECTOR: Now we're coming to it. Those Mangebois sisters
were right . . . Ghosts, did you say?

LUCE: Ghosts, yes, phantoms. This is the mark they recognize their friends by. Mademoiselle puts it on us every morning!

INSPECTOR: Wipe it off this minute!

LITTLE GIRLS: Never! Never!

VIOLA: We'd be frightened.

LITTLE GIRLS: We'd be frightened: the ghost is around here somewhere.

INSPECTOR: Wipe it off, unless you want me to slap you!

LITTLE GIRLS: We're frightened! The ghost's around!

INSPECTOR: Be quiet. Kindly understand, you wretched little girls, that after death there are no ghosts, only carcasses; no returned spirits, only bones and worms. Now, you will all repeat what I have just told you. You there, what is left after death?

CHEMIST: Don't spoil their idea of life, Inspector.

INSPECTOR: Their idea will always be far too favourable, Mr Chemist. I'm going to teach these silly little girls what life is really like. A deplorable adventure which consists, for men, of a miserable starting salary, snail-paced promotion, non-existent retirement and rebellious collar-buttons; and for little ninnies like them, it's wheedling and needling, poultry and adultery . . . There now, they've made me rhyme for the first time in my life. You certainly teach your pupils happiness, Mademoiselle!

ISABELLE: I teach them what God has appointed for them.

INSPECTOR: Nonsense. God never intended his creatures to be happy: all he meant them to have were a few compensations, such as fishing, love, and dotage . . . Mr Mayor, I have come to my decision. As the Superintendent's functions don't seem to absorb all his energies, he will provisionally take over direction of the class . . . Now where are you going, girls? Does the All-Rounder wish you to leave without saying goodbye?

ISABELLE: Do your curtsey, children.

INSPECTOR: Two by two, and keep your mouths shut. Aerophagia is rampant in the district . . . What are you carrying away there?

GILBERTE: The blueboard, Inspector.

INSPECTOR: Leave the blueboard here! Together with the gold chalk, the pink ink, and the goose-shit pencil. From now on you will have a blackboard! And black ink! And black clothes! In our lovely country, black has always been the colour of youth . . . And kindly look at me! That's better, at last they're beginning to look more indistinguishable. A month of discipline and you couldn't tell one of them apart. As for you, Mademoiselle, I shall lose no time in writing to inform your parents that you are a disgrace to your family and to our university.

ISABELLE: I'm an orphan, Inspector.

INSPECTOR: Well, that's lucky for them. At least they can't see what you're up to.

ISABELLE: They can, Inspector, and they thoroughly approve.

INSPECTOR: Bravo. That gives us a splendid impression of the level of primary education in hell.

ISABELLE: Will you kindly go, Inspector!

INSPECTOR: I am going, Mademoiselle. In spite of there being no door, I'm going, but we shall meet again. I shall not go home till I have scotched this scandal. Come along, gentlemen . . . Where is my hat? Who replaced it with this hedgehog?

VIOLA: Arthur, Inspector . . .

LITTLE GIRLS: Arthur, Inspector, Arthur!

All go out, except Isabelle and the Chemist.

ISABELLE: Did you have something to say, Mr Chemist?

CHEMIST: No. Absolutely nothing.

ISABELLE: To do, then?

CHEMIST: Nothing to do either. I'm just staying on for a moment, for the transition.

ISABELLE: I'm sure you're always very welcome.

CHEMIST: That's not quite what I meant. But I feel that my presence serves as a kind of lock-gate between two moments which are on different levels, or a buffer between two incidents which would otherwise clash, between happiness and unhappiness, precision and confusion, or vice-versa. This is well known in town. It's always me who has to carry the news of her lover's fatal car-crash to the woman playing bridge, or tell the man with the weak heart that he's drawn first prize in the lottery. I had to announce the outbreak of war to the Military Mothers' Union. My mere proximity is enough to make the past link hands with the most unexpected of presents.

ISABELLE: And you feel the need for a transition now?

CHEMIST: Absolutely imperative. Here we are, thanks to the Inspector, becalmed in a present which is at once absurd, trivial and cruel, and yet you don't have to be a genius to sense that even now a moment of supreme sweetness and calm is searching through the dusk for somewhere to settle. And then there's another transition to be made between the Isabelle we already know, so alive and earthy, and some new, romantic, other-worldly Isabelle who's still a stranger to us.

ISABELLE: How will you set about it?

CHEMIST: With you, nothing could be simpler. With the bereaved woman playing bridge, I must admit it took me a good quarter of an hour. Well, naturally she redoubled. It was no easy matter to lead her down from her triumph to poor dead Emmanuel. But with you, Isabelle, the lightest touch is enough to add a dimension of mystery to the most trivial moment: a mere gesture, like this – (*Gesture.*) – a mere silence, like this – (*Short silence.*) – there, you see, it's almost done. My transitional colleagues, the bat and the owl, are beginning their gentle roundelay. You have only to give this moment a name, and all will be ready.

ISABELLE: Aloud?

CHEMIST: Yes, we must hear it.

ISABELLE: I seem to remember that its name is twilight.

CHEMIST: You remember correctly. And what sound do you hear at twilight, coming from the little towns?

ISABELLE: The sound of bugle-practice. (*Bugles are heard.*)

CHEMIST: There, you see. There are three sounds that make up the mystic harmony of France: the sound of paths being raked in the drowsiness of dawn, the evening cannon-shot, and bugles at dusk.

ISABELLE: They've stopped now.

CHEMIST: And when the last bugle dies away, who will loom up among the reeds and willows, straighten his inky cloak and move through the yews and cypresses, against the thickening shades of night?

ISABELLE (*smiling*): The ghost! The ghost!

CHEMIST (*disappearing*): There, now I can go.

Isabelle sits down on a hummock. She takes out her mirror and looks at herself, looks at her eyes and hair. Suddenly the Ghost appears behind her. She sees him in the mirror: a handsome young man, in a velvet waistcoat, with a pale clean-cut face. There is a moment of confrontation, like a mute dialogue. Isabelle lowers the little mirror, then raises it again, flashing a reflected beam from the setting sun into the Ghost's face. The Ghost appears discomfited.

ISABELLE: I'm sorry about that bit of sun!

GHOST: It's gone now. The moon's here instead.

ISABELLE: Can you hear what living people say – all living people?

GHOST: I can hear you.

ISABELLE: Good. I've been wanting so much to talk to you.

GHOST: What about?

ISABELLE: About your friends – my friends too, I'm sure – the dead. You must know a lot about the dead.

GHOST: I'm beginning to.

ISABELLE: Will you tell me, then?

GHOST: I will if you'll come here every evening at this time. What's your name?

ISABELLE: My name is really not important. I hope you'll tell me all these things a bit less solemnly. I simply won't believe that they never smile.

GHOST: Who don't?

ISABELLE: I thought we were discussing the dead.

GHOST: What would they have to smile about?

ISABELLE: Well, funny things must sometimes happen in Hell.

GHOST: Funny – in Hell?

ISABELLE: Funny, or touching, or unexpected. I'm sure there

must be clumsy spirits and comic ones and absent-minded ones.

GHOST: I don't know. Would they have anything to drop or slip on?

ISABELLE: Whatever corresponds in Hell to cut-glass or banana-skins. A memory, perhaps . . . or a small piece of oblivion.

GHOST: Oh, no. The dead are extremely adroit. They never bump into the void or get caught on shadows. They never twist their ankles in space. Nothing shines in their face and dazzles them . . .

ISABELLE: What I simply can't understand is why the dead themselves should believe in death. You'd expect that sort of folly from the living, of course. It's natural to imagine there being an end to lies and fatness and stupidity; one could even believe that goodness and beauty must pass away – their fragility is their glory. But I'd have expected something different from the dead! I mean, the dead, who are purified, pure and noble through and through – really, I did expect something better.

GHOST: In fact, they should believe in life?

ISABELLE: The life of the dead – certainly. May I be quite frank with you? I often get the impression that they rather let themselves go to pieces. I don't mean you, of course, because you're here, and I'm grateful to you for being here. But I believe if they only had a little more gaiety and determination they might be able to get across to meet us. Hasn't there been anyone down there who's been able to make them want to?

GHOST: They're waiting for you.

ISABELLE: Oh, I shall come, I shall certainly come in time. But I don't have the feeling that I shall be particularly strong or determined once I've passed over. On the contrary, I know that the very thing I shall like about death is its laziness, its sort of thick, fluid numbness, so that no one's really dead, it's as if they'd been drowned. All I can do for death must be done while I'm alive. Now listen. Ever since I was a child I've dreamed of one great enterprise. It's the only thing that makes me worthy of your visit. What I mean is: has there ever yet been a spirit of genius, a spirit who could inspire the other dead with his power and reality – an emperor, a Messiah of the dead? Don't you think everything might be changed, marvellously changed, for you and for us, if one young spirit could arise, a young dead man or woman – or a couple, that would be beautiful – who could make them love their state and realize that they are immortal?

GHOST: But they aren't.

ISABELLE: Why not?

GHOST: They die too.

ISABELLE: Isn't it extraordinary what a false idea all races have of themselves! Indians think they're red, Negroes think they're white, and the dead think they're mortal.

GHOST: Finally a sort of weariness takes hold of them, a kind of spirit-pestilence breathes over them, a tumour of nothingness eats them away. Their fine shadowy grey turns silvery, then greasy; and after that the end soon comes, the end of everything.

ISABELLE: Oh, come on, you surely don't believe that! There must be an explanation for this decay.

GHOST: It's the end of death.

ISABELLE: It can't be! Don't be so obstinate. Tell me about it, I'm sure I shall be able to explain it all quite satisfactorily.

GHOST: First tell me your name.

ISABELLE: I told you, it's not important. My name's just like everyone else's . . . No, come on, you know you can trust me!

GHOST: After the death of death . . .

ISABELLE: Good. Now this is where it starts getting interesting. What happens after the death of death? I'm waiting . . . Well? (*She glances over her shoulder.*) Nobody can hear you . . . no-one at all . . . (*But while she is turned away the Ghost disappears.*) Where are you? Where are you? (*She looks desperately around, then cries:*) Isabelle! My name's Isabelle!

Curtain

ACT TWO

Different country scene. Beech thickets. Hedgerows. Dusk some way off. Enter the Superintendent, followed by the Little Girls carrying electric torches.

SUPERINTENDENT: Get into your Triangle, children.

The Little Girls form up in a sort of triangle, and sing.

LITTLE GIRLS (*singing*):
>"The biggest thrill for Bougainville,
>While Noumea grew chillier,
>Was gazing at the Triangle
>Through leaves of bougainvillea!"

SUPERINTENDENT: Excellent. Now the Scales!

LITTLE GIRLS (*singing as they form up in Scale formation, with the tallest girl as the beam*):
>"If I could have my childhood's wish
>To weigh the night all starry bright,
>I'd twinkle as the southern Scales,
>My boredom balanced by delight."

SUPERINTENDENT: Now, the Four Wolves!

CHEMIST (*entering*): Good afternoon, children. Are you playing at four corners?

SUPERINTENDENT: The four corners of heaven, yes.

LITTLE GIRLS: Goodnight, Mr Chemist, goodnight.

CHEMIST: Why goodnight? It's still broad daylight. Whatever is that one doing standing with her legs apart, holding a torch?

GILBERTE: I am the Southern Compass, Mr Chemist.

SUPERINTENDENT: You find us in the middle of our astronomy lesson. Now, shine your torch, Gilberte. You are first magnitude, remember?

CHEMIST: Well, you've chosen a fine evening for it. You'll be able to see the stars come out one by one. A perfect night for little girls who want to learn to count up to a milliard. You'll even have Orion.

SUPERINTENDENT: Unfortunately not. The Inspector insists on my pupils going to bed at sundown.

CHEMIST: So you have to talk stars to them under an empty sky? That's a very bad system, and risks breeding covetousness in these young ladies. They'll start lusting after stars like diamonds.

SUPERINTENDENT: I'm taking all precautions. I'm well aware that little girls only believe what they can see. Their eyes won't take them through air to the vault of heaven even in broad daylight, but it's child's play for their imagination to see through the earth to every detail of the other hemisphere. So here we are, deep in the southern night.

CHEMIST: And do they know their way around?

SUPERINTENDENT: Daisy, where are the Flying Scales?

DAISY: Just underneath Mr Chemist.

LUCE: That's why we can see him so well.

SUPERINTENDENT: The great advantage of these southern constellations is that the ancient astronomers never saw them, and they finally got christened by some astronomer who must have been a physicist or a freemason. So it's a completely modern firmament. Instead of mythical heroes, it's full of useful objects: the sun-dial, the triangle, the scales, the compasses. You'd think you were in a workshop – and of course children adore workshops . . . Now, Viola, jump from the Triangle to the Air-pump!

VIOLA: Through the Compass?

SUPERINTENDENT: No dear, through the Southern Fish.

VIOLA: But that's twenty-five thousand million miles.

SUPERINTENDENT: Then do it in two strides, silly. Right you are, then, form up again into the Southern Cross.

The Little Girls form a cross and sing.

LITTLE GIRLS: "As La Pérouse so wisely said,
　　　　　You needn't know the Hebrew laws
　　　　　To sail to the Antipodes;
　　　　　The Southern Cross will guide your course."

SUPERINTENDENT: The bad thing about this system, of course,

is that I end up showing them the sky as if it were a floor and not a ceiling, and the night as if it were something to walk on.

CHEMIST: Don't let that worry you. After one complete heart-beat they will find it back over their heads. They're very logical.

SUPERINTENDENT: They're certainly logical in always giving me the opposite answer to the one I expect. This week, for instance, in order to get into their heads the most useful of human concepts, that of weight and volume, I made them hold fresh iron-castings, and I also broke a thermometer and poured mercury into their thimbles. However, they insisted on picking me up between them to see what a man weighs. The result now is that they're all madly in love with the ghost.

LUCE: Just like Miss Isabelle!

SUPERINTENDENT: Luce, I must punish you for that. Switch off your torch. You will spend ten minutes as a dead star. Will you switch it off?

LUCE: But dead stars go on shining two million years after they're dead.

SUPERINTENDENT: Yes, and humans for two seconds. Put it out. Oh, anyway, it's time for your recreation. Off you go.

The Little Girls disappear.

CHEMIST: Do you take a particular interest in Miss Isabelle?

SUPERINTENDENT: I'm afraid I'm not the only one. I've had the impression since this morning that the Inspector has also entered the field.

CHEMIST: What field?

SUPERINTENDENT: Don't pretend you don't know what I mean. You know perfectly well that the ghost is still appear-ing, and that Isabelle is found rather too often in his vicinity.

CHEMIST: Surely that's her business.

SUPERINTENDENT: No, it is not her business. She belongs to all of us, she is the town's better self – Nature's, even – she has no business at all. I mean, surely, my dear Chemist, you're not going to tell me *you* believe this ghost exists.

CHEMIST: I'm not sure that he's existed up to now. But I think he may very likely exist tonight.

SUPERINTENDENT: I'm not quite with you.

CHEMIST: I have a distinct feeling that tonight we may witness the birth of a ghost.

SUPERINTENDENT: The birth of a ghost! How? Why?

CHEMIST: Don't ask me how. That's a surprise in store for us. As for why: well, I don't imagine all this atmosphere can have gathered over our town for nothing. Each time that Nature had adopted this curious ironic tone towards a human community, this comic but rather disturbing furrowing of the brow, like an elephant which is losing patience with its keeper, the outcome has always been something mysterious – the birth of a prophet, a ritual murder, the discovery of some new species of animal. It was at such a moment, no doubt, that the first horse appeared in the mouth of one of our ancestors' caves. We shall be no exception.

SUPERINTENDENT: I agree with you there. Our town is certainly out of its mind.

CHEMIST: Or rather, in that precise state where dreams come true, and madness becomes reality. With a person, you'd call it a state of inspiration. Our town is in a poetic delirium. Haven't you observed it in yourself?

SUPERINTENDENT: I have indeed! When I got up this morning I found myself thinking, God knows why, of the ape which is called a mandrill, the one with the three-coloured behind. And what did I meet the moment I opened my front door? A mandrill. A tame mandrill, actually, which some gypsies were walking on a leash – but never mind, there was a mandrill on my doorstep.

CHEMIST: Yes, and if you'd have been thinking of armadilloes, you'd have met an armadillo; if you'd thought of a girl from Martinique, there would have been a girl from Martinique – and it would have had the most natural explanation: a circus passing through, or a retired colonial governor moving house. The town is quite simply on a winning streak, like a roulette player who wins at every throw.

SUPERINTENDENT: But surely, in that case, we ought to keep an even closer watch over Miss Isabelle?

CHEMIST: We most certainly should. Nature's pregnancies are never mere wind. Mountains don't give birth to mice, or storms to sparrows: the offspring are lava and thunder. Every element will combine to produce a ghost for us – light and shade, stupidity and imagination, even ghosts themselves, if they exist – not to mention the Inspector.

SUPERINTENDENT: Our winning streak continues. Here he comes . . .

Enter the Inspector and the Mayor.

INSPECTOR: Something rather urgent, gentlemen. I have here a letter from the Government, sent by special messenger . . . Read it out, Mr Mayor, it really concerns you.

MAYOR: Are you sure it does?

INSPECTOR: Quite as much as me – especially the end.

MAYOR: But the end particularly . . .

INSPECTOR: Please read it out, will you?

MAYOR: You seem to be on very intimate terms with the Government.

INSPECTOR: I'm happy to say I am.

MAYOR: According to this, it kisses your gorgeous mouth, asks for a hundred francs and signs itself "Your ever-loving Adèle".

INSPECTOR: Do forgive me! I got them muddled up. Here is the letter I meant. Now please, gentlemen, do be serious. This is a solemn moment.

MAYOR (*reading*): "The Supreme Council has made a close study of the remarkable events which have been troubling your constituency. As a resolutely secular body, it is happy to learn that in France collective hysteria has found another outlet besides miracles. It would have expected no less from the Limousin, a district which has been able, while contributing three popes to the Christian Church, to build an archway of local poetic beliefs joining druidical naturalism to contemporary radicalism, and towering clear above all clerical superstition."

SUPERINTENDENT: How beautifully put! Who is the Supreme Council composed of?

INSPECTOR: Supremely intelligent people, as the title indicates.

MAYOR (*reading out*): "It does not, however, feel that the disturbances provoked by this apparition in the life of your community are of a sufficiently democratic nature to justify an official policy of tacit approval. The council therefore invests you with full powers to ventilate the district once and for all, and places the civil and military authorities at your disposal."

INSPECTOR: So, gentlemen, to work. Our hunt must be brought to a conclusion.

MAYOR: Haven't we come to that already, Inspector? We've spent the last fortnight hunting down every human or animal in the town that could conceivably be suspected of strangeness, and we're running out of quarry.

INSPECTOR: Really? What was yesterday's tally?

MAYOR: Negligible!

INSPECTOR: How many humans?

SUPERINTENDENT: Well, we confiscated the secret ledger of the Registrar of Mortgages, in which he recorded both the moral and demoniac mortgages of our countrymen.

INSPECTOR: And animals?

MAYOR: We lassoed, and unfortunately strangled in the process, a dog which bore the strangest resemblance to one of our foremost publicity agents. I should add, though, that in death it resumed the expression of faithful humanity natural to its kind. It isn't much.

INSPECTOR: It certainly isn't. Tell me, my dear Mayor, what did you dream about last night?

MAYOR: What did I dream? Why?

INSPECTOR: If the town's atmosphere has really been purged, its citizens should be dreaming the most normal dreams in France. Well, can you remember what you dreamed?

MAYOR: I certainly can! I was fighting two gigantic maybugs which finally eluded me by turning into my two feet. It was infuriating. They started cropping the grass, and I can tell you it's no easy matter to walk on grazing feet. They then turned into centipedes, and after that everything went fine, almost too fine.

INSPECTOR: And what about you, Superintendent?

SUPERINTENDENT: I rather hesitate to tell you.

INSPECTOR: It is an official order.

SUPERINTENDENT: I was madly in love with a woman in an overcoat who kept jumping through a hoop with her right breast showing. The woman was you.

INSPECTOR: Well, gentlemen, there you have it – very flattering for me, I admit – but that's what you call a normal French dream! Are you seriously suggesting that this nocturnal residue, multiplied by forty-two million, is worthy of the most judicious and practical race in the world?

SUPERINTENDENT: Compared with the residue of sixty-four million German dreams, I should think it probably is.

CHEMIST: So in fact, Inspector, you are at last taking the super-natural seriously?

INSPECTOR: I was just coming to you, Mr Chemist. We've had about all we can take from you, too. Your perpetual smile of silent detachment has probably been the greatest single reason why our fight against Isabelle's influence has failed to make any progress in the sub-prefecture. I get the impression that you are no stranger to these continual mystifications which might once have seemed rather piquant on some old Thuringian estate, but which turn the stomach of any enlightened citizen today. At midnight, for instance, when the town clock strikes twelve, some facetious hand adds a thirteenth stroke. A senior official has only to sit down on a bench for the bench to become coated in wet paint, or if he sits down at a café table the sugar declines to melt in his coffee, however hot. Only just now I received a violent blow on the chest from a carpet-beater, which had no doubt grown accustomed to sailing through your ghosts. Unfortunately I interposed my human density, but my spare pince-nez are shattered beyond repair. I shudder to think what affronts to normal good sense await us tomorrow when your monthly lottery is drawn! But I had better warn you of one thing. Tonight I intend to put a stop to these humiliating aberrations, by eliminating Miss Isabelle once and for all.

MAYOR: What has Isabelle to do with all this?

INSPECTOR: Mr Mayor, everyone in town except you knows that for the last two weeks Miss Isabelle has been keeping a nightly rendezvous.

SUPERINTENDENT: What nonsense!

MAYOR: You're joking, of course.

INSPECTOR: I'm not joking. Every evening about six o'clock – about now, that is – Isabelle slips out of town, with the would-be casual air of one taking food to an escaped convict. But her face is fresher than ever, her eye at once more alert and more misty, and as she goes empty-handed one can only conclude that the victuals she is taking to her protégé are simply her warm blood, life and tenderness. A meal, in fact, for a ghost – possibly with dessert to follow.

SUPERINTENDENT: Inspector!

MAYOR: Now look here, Inspector. This morning I arranged for you to have lunch with Isabelle, for the very purpose of convincing you how real and alive everything about her is. Have you ever seen, for instance, a more human appetite?

INSPECTOR: Obviously you were fooled by that. I watched her rather more closely. Oh, I agree, she had a second helping of jugged hare, and caused serious casualties among the profiteroles. But I also noticed that besides the real meal of meats and pastries, she was nibbling away – obviously unaware of what she was doing – at tiny crumbs of bread, grains of rice and fragments of hazelnut: in fact she was taking exactly the sort of meal that the ancients used to leave on tombs. Now, who did she have inside her that needed that kind of food? Again, I noticed the way she dressed: besides her frock and necklace there was a second Isabelle, all pale, dressed up and ready for an infernal rendezvous. So she thinks, at least. And at this very moment she'll be stealing deceitfully towards the edge of this wood, where we must lose no time in confronting her.

MAYOR: What do you consider we ought to do, then?

SUPERINTENDENT: Please, Inspector, let us avoid creating any sort of incident or scandal. Miss Isabelle and I often chat quite freely. Let me speak to her and make her see the danger of her conduct? I'm sure I can make her understand.

CHEMIST: And may one ask, Inspector, precisely how you plan to break Isabelle's resistance?

INSPECTOR: Oh, by force. I've had my reasons for delaying any final action till the Government put the local militia at my disposal. This ghost story must be liquidated once and for all. That's the only way I can strike at Isabelle's prestige, and where my opinion differs from yours is that I believe we are not dealing with a ghost at all, but with your country-house murderer. This is the time and place of their meetings, and I've laid an ambush for him. I shall have policemen stationed behind this thicket, and they will seize him when I give the signal.

MAYOR: You'd better not count on the garde champêtre, Inspector. The fishing season opens today, and he'll be on his rounds.

INSPECTOR: Then I shall call on the constabulary.

MAYOR: The gendarmes are at present in quarantine, from good citizens and criminals alike. A case of scarlet fever has been reported at the barracks.

INSPECTOR: Who cares if an inspector gets scarlet fever?

MAYOR: The Public Prosecutor cares, for one, because the captured criminal will then contaminate his entire office, from the Deputy Prosecutor right down to the Concierge. A healthy judiciary demands healthy criminals.

INSPECTOR: You won't stop me now, Mr Mayor. I suspected that nobody here would go out of their way to back me up, so I've taken my own precautions.

MAYOR: What else have you thought of, then?

INSPECTOR: The most obvious thing of all. I've found out that there is a man living in a near-by town who is probably more ready than anyone else in France to come to grips with bandits living or dead.

MAYOR: You mean the old executioner, who is living there in retirement?

132

INSPECTOR: Precisely. I've sent him a message offering five hundred francs if he'll come here. Do you know him?

MAYOR: Nobody does. He keeps very much to himself. But I'm afraid your message is bound to have its effect. Where is he to meet you?

INSPECTOR: Here, any time now. And he's coming armed.

MAYOR: But supposing our suspect puts up a fight?

SUPERINTENDENT: Please, Inspector, I beg you, before it's too late – let me speak to Miss Isabelle.

INSPECTOR: Hush, gentlemen, here she comes now – you see, just as I said she would! Well, Superintendent, I'll give you five minutes to convince her. If you fail, I shall go into action. For the moment, she's yours. The rest of us had better go and find this executioner: he's late already.

CHEMIST: Executioners are only punctual at dawn.

They go out, leaving the Superintendent alone. Enter Isabelle.

SUPERINTENDENT: How lightly you walk, Miss Isabelle! Even on gravel or brushwood, you are practically inaudible. Like burglars who know how to avoid making staircases creak by treading exactly on the heads of nails, you must walk only on the seams of the countryside.

ISABELLE: How beautifully you talk, Superintendent. It's a pleasure to listen to you.

SUPERINTENDENT: Yes, I do talk well when I've got something to say. Not that I ever manage to say precisely what I mean; in spite of myself, I end up saying something different. But yes, I do say it well . . . I don't know if you're following me?

ISABELLE: Well, I realize that when you spoke of the seams of the countryside you were trying to convey some sympathy for me. You're always nice to women. It was very nice, what you said about Madame Lambert.

SUPERINTENDENT: Exactly! And when I spoke of her, I wasn't only thinking of Madame Lambert.

ISABELLE: No, you wanted to take the opposite view to the Inspector, and I'm grateful to you for that. Everything that man does is beastly and incomprehensible to me. Do you know why he's spying on me?

SUPERINTENDENT: Yes, he's just told us. He thinks it abnormal to believe in ghosts.

ISABELLE: And what about you, Superintendent? Don't you ever believe in the abnormal?

SUPERINTENDENT: I'm beginning to get used to it. It's abnormal, for instance, that there should exist such a perfect creature as Isabelle.

ISABELLE: Very well said; but I'm sure it's not what you meant.

SUPERINTENDENT: Oh, Miss Isabelle . . .

ISABELLE (*smiling at him, rather touched*): Abnormal to believe in ghosts! What I call abnormal is the indifference of living people for the dead. Either we're all hypocrites, and those millions of Christians who keep saying that the dead have another life don't mean a word of it, or else they speak of them in a completely selfish, short-sighted way.

SUPERINTENDENT: But you're not short-sighted now, are you, Miss Isabelle? You see them?

ISABELLE: I don't see very clearly yet. I only see one.

SUPERINTENDENT: But a good-looking one, so they say in town.

ISABELLE: Not bad.

SUPERINTENDENT: And young too, perhaps?

ISABELLE: About 30. Surely you can just as well embark on eternity at 30 as you can with a white beard.

SUPERINTENDENT: Does he come up to you? Do you let him touch you?

ISABELLE: He doesn't come very close, and I never move towards him. I know how many things human breath can tarnish.

SUPERINTENDENT: And do you stay looking at each other for long?

ISABELLE: Oh, hours.

SUPERINTENDENT: And does this really seem to you very sensible?

ISABELLE: Dear Mr Superintendent, I spent my whole childhood obeying my teachers by refusing any demands but this world's! All my schoolfellows and I were taught was a self-centred sort of civilization and an ant-like form of courtesy. As little girls, even in our teens, we were supposed to avert our eyes from birds with too brightly-coloured feathers, clouds with too definite shapes, men who were too manly – from everything in Nature which can be construed as a call or sign. All we really had a thorough knowledge of when we finally left the convent was a somewhat narrow corner of the universe: the inner lining of our own eyelids. Of course it's very pretty, with its stars and gold circles and purple or blue diamonds, but it is a bit limited, even if you get your best friend to press her finger on your eyeballs.

SUPERINTENDENT: But you got top marks in the Examination, Miss Isabelle. You must have been taught some human knowledge?

ISABELLE: What they call knowledge is, at best, human religion. And it's so dreadfully self-centred; the whole aim of its teaching is to make it impossible or at least sterile to form relationships with any but human beings, and to make you unlearn all the languages (apart from human ones) that a child already knows. We may have rejected marvellous offers from all the natural orders and stages of life, simply through this false modesty or absurd kowtowing to prejudice. I'm the only one who's dared to give an answer, and my answer to the dead will be the first of many.

SUPERINTENDENT: And do you plan to answer the living one of these days?

ISABELLE: I answer anyone who speaks to me.

SUPERINTENDENT: Suppose a living person asks you to live with him, to marry him, will you answer then?

ISABELLE: I shall answer that I'll only take a husband who will allow me to be in love with life and death at once.

SUPERINTENDENT: Well, life and death, that might just get by; but a living man and a dead man would be going a bit far – because if I understand you aright, you mean to go on seeing this ghost.

ISABELLE: Certainly. As I'm lucky enough to have friends in regions outside the earth, I intend to make the most of it.

SUPERINTENDENT: Aren't you afraid that this may have an embarrassing or belittling effect on your married life?

ISABELLE: In what way? Why ever should a husband feel slighted or humiliated to come home from hunting or fishing to a wife who believes in the afterlife, or close the shutters at night, after attending a political meeting, on a wife who believes in a higher radiance? And why shouldn't that empty hour of the day that other wives devote to receiving more dangerous visitors – memories, hopes, phantoms of their own lives, even their lovers – be an hour of invisible friendship?

SUPERINTENDENT: Because your husband wouldn't want anything to stand between you and him, however invisible and intangible.

ISABELLE: There are so many intangibles already between husband and wife. What's one more or less?

SUPERINTENDENT: Between husband and wife!

ISABELLE: Even their dreams . . . even their shadows . . . Don't you ever amuse yourself by treading on the shadow of people you love – without their knowing – and staying there, caressing it?

SUPERINTENDENT: Your husband's shadow belongs to him. It won't feel a thing.

ISABELLE: His voice, then?

SUPERINTENDENT: His voice!

ISABELLE: There's bound to be some note in my husband's voice that I like but that isn't really him, and I shall love it without telling him. And then there's his eyes. You surely don't think, Mr Superintendent, that I shall always think of my husband when I look at his eyes? I want a husband as I'd want a diamond, for the different gleams of pleasure he'd give me without ever being aware of it. Any number of things in him would keep beckoning disloyally to me. By comparison, the ghost would be infinitely more trustworthy than his own appearance.

SUPERINTENDENT: All we know about ghosts is that they are

appallingly faithful; their lack of employment makes it possible. You'll see his grey shadow appearing at times when he's
nothing but a nuisance. All you'll have got finally by looking
death in the face will be the sort of spots before the eyes you
get by looking straight at the sun.

ISABELLE: But there are two suns. I don't find the dark one any
less warming or vital to me.

SUPERINTENDENT: Take care, Isabelle, take care!

ISABELLE: Of whom? Of what?

SUPERINTENDENT: Beware of the dead, real or pretended, who
prowl round young girls. Their intentions are not pure.

ISABELLE: The *real* dead's are, surely?

SUPERINTENDENT: Their game is well known. It is to separate
a being from the mass of humans. Through pity or curiosity
they lure him away from the herd which takes pleasure in ties
and dresses, bread and wine; and they seem to absorb him.
This is precisely what your ghost is after.

ISABELLE: Don't go on, dear Superintendent. Remember that
out of this immeasurable crowd of spirits my ghost, as you
call him, is the only one who has succeeded in reaching me.
You can be sure that he isn't the only one who's been tempted
to make the journey. In the ocean of shades I often feel that
there are currents forming, surging towards this young woman
who believes in them. And I feel in each of them a desire to
break free of the others and find itself a visible body. I feel
that they understand my position, and that they're pointing
me out to countless thousands of others. They all know by
now that I'm not going to receive them with exorcism and
chattering teeth, but simply and humanely. All spirits want,
when they come here, is to be told: "Take a rest from your
eternal rest! Sit down! I shall carry on just as if you weren't
there." They want to look at a piece of bread, listen to a
canary in a cage, rub shoulders with what must seem to them
a model of furious activity – a retired Civil Servant – to
breathe in the latest perfume worn by a young girl, which
living people have made from flowers and essences. "Let's go
and see Isabelle," those millions of silences down there are

saying. "She's waiting for us. Come along! We may even be lucky enough to see the Inspector of Roads and the Tax Collector." But they simply haven't the strength to make the journey. They hesitate voiceless within earshot of the Tax Office, or blind within sight of the Sub-Prefecture, and a ground-swell scatters them or carries them away. Only my ghost, by some prodigy of strength or will, has managed to swim clear over the abyss. How could I have the heart to reject him now?

SUPERINTENDENT: Isabelle, don't try to probe human life to its limits. Its whole greatness consists in being a brief interlude of fullness between two gaping chasms. Its miracle is to be solid, colourful and healthy in the midst of an infinity of nothingness. If you introduce into it one drop, one single drop of spirit blood, you'll be doing something every bit as momentous as that inevitable future inhabitant of our solar system who will one day upset our laws of gravity by making some unfortunate experiment, by a chance synthesis of some new and heavier metal, or by some hitherto unknown way of laughing or sneezing. The slightest deviation is enough to throw human reason out of true. Human beings should be no more than watchmen at its gates. You may be betraying all humanity by opening the gates, and yielding to the push of the first ghost who arrives.

ISABELLE: Only one has got through. Millions were pushing.

SUPERINTENDENT: Exactly, and now millions may follow.

ISABELLE: Well, what would be the harm? Please, dear Superintendent, don't say any more. You asked me what I felt about the man who would one day want to take me in his arms. Well, I told you. If he tries to keep me from everything that calls out to me, if he uses his mouth to stop my words and his eyes to stop me seeing, if he wants us to join in the miserable human blockade, with all those other couples who present united backs to the world, I'd rather he kept away. So if he happens to be a friend of yours, perhaps you'd warn him. I shall continue to see my ghost – so it's up to him to choose. Goodbye! The ghost will be waiting for me.

SUPERINTENDENT: Waiting? Miss Isabelle, I beg you – not today, at least not today.

ISABELLE: I must go.

SUPERINTENDENT: Please, for heaven's sake! For *his* sake, don't go. The Inspector has set a trap for both of you! You mustn't see him again!

ISABELLE: I shall see him again, this very day and this very hour. In fact I'd be grateful, Superintendent, if you'd leave me alone now, because the hour is nearly come.

SUPERINTENDENT: In that case I shall stay. I shall see him too.

ISABELLE: I very much doubt it. I should be most surprised if he were visible to anyone but me.

SUPERINTENDENT: I shall see him and touch him. I shall prove to you that he's an impostor.

ISABELLE: You'll never see him.

SUPERINTENDENT: Why?

ISABELLE: Why? Because he's there already.

SUPERINTENDENT: Where?

ISABELLE: There, quite near. He's looking at us and smiling.

SUPERINTENDENT: This is no time for jokes! The Inspector is busy posting armed men to take him dead or alive.

ISABELLE: A ghost, dead or alive: that really is a joke . . . Oh, here's the moon! The real moon, Superintendent! Look at the pock-marks!

She disappears. Enter Inspector, Mayor and Chemist.

INSPECTOR: Well, Superintendent? I gather from your expression that you haven't had much success.

SUPERINTENDENT: I shall have better luck tomorrow.

INSPECTOR: Tomorrow, quite so! Today, however, perhaps you would oblige me by collecting your pupils, who are roaming round the forest and will certainly get lost when night falls.

The Superintendent goes out. The Inspector motions to two Executioners who are still off-stage.

You can join us now, my merry men. (*Enter Executioners.*) – You, I gather, claim to be the former executioner?

FIRST EXECUTIONER: I am!

CHEMIST: What's he, then?

SECOND EXECUTIONER: Me? *I'm* the former executioner!

INSPECTOR: One of you is lying. One of you, I'm afraid, is an impostor with an eye on the five hundred francs reward. (*Both Executioners protest.*) Your papers, please . . . Ah, here we have it. Your papers have given you away, my good fellow. You were the first bassoonist at the Enghien Casino!

FIRST EXECUTIONER: You don't seriously imagine that the Department puts our real status on the documents? They make our lives easier by inventing harmless professions for us, generally in music.

SECOND EXECUTIONER: That's right. I'm down as a piccolo.

INSPECTOR: Will you please turn out your pockets? . . . Now, Mr Mayor, let's see if these clues will tell us which is the real executioner.

MAYOR: Well, this one has a free-gift corkscrew, an old scallop-shell and two tooth-picks.

INSPECTOR: Perfectly normal!

CHEMIST: This one has a little piece of dark blue pencil, two sugared almonds and a woman's comb.

INSPECTOR: More or less what you find on anyone who's suddenly asked to empty his pockets.

MAYOR: Really, I'd have thought it would be child's play to tell an executioner from an ordinary law-abiding citizen.

INSPECTOR: You try, then!

CHEMIST: I believe that a dog's hackles rise when it meets an executioner. Let's get hold of a sheepdog!

MAYOR: We haven't got time! Inspector, ask them a few questions about their trade. Examining is up your street.

INSPECTOR: Right, then: an executioner's exam. Preferable to little girls, anyway . . . You, what wood is the guillotine made of?

FIRST EXECUTIONER: The same as the Christian cross, the oak – except for the actual blade-casing . . .

SECOND EXECUTIONER: Which is made of teak, like the Hindu cross.

INSPECTOR: You, what did Madame Dubarry say as she

140

climbed the scaffold?

FIRST EXECUTIONER: "A moment's grace, Mr Executioner, a moment's grace . . ."

INSPECTOR: Your turn now. Who said: "Mind my beard, executioner. I don't want it damaged. My beard has not offended the King."

SECOND EXECUTIONER: Thomas More, or Morus, in the year 1535.

INSPECTOR: I'm not going to catch them out . . . You, what was the statute of January 1847?

FIRST EXECUTIONER: The statute of Dunoyer de Segonzac, reminding those sentenced to death that executions are serious matters.

SECOND EXECUTIONER: And forbidding them to laugh or joke on the scaffold, or in any way occasion merriment among the onlookers.

INSPECTOR: You, what is the executioner's song?

FIRST EXECUTIONER: Which one, the song of the dandy executioner?

SECOND EXECUTIONER: Or the song of the female executioner?

INSPECTOR: The dandy executioner. Do you know it?

SECOND EXECUTIONER: It's the only one we do know!

FIRST EXECUTIONER (*singing*):

> At daybreak in the market square
> I'm busy at my guillotine,
> And rosy dawn anoints my hair
> With rosy-fingered brilliantine.

SECOND EXECUTIONER:

> No toilet water or Cologne
> Over my cheeks is shed.
> Some wretch might die complaining I
> Was going to his head!

FIRST EXECUTIONER: But neither Mary Queen of Scots

SECOND EXECUTIONER: Nor Ravachol, I think,

FIRST EXECUTIONER: Objected to the rosy dawn

SECOND EXECUTIONER: Dying my fingers pink.

INSPECTOR: Oh, to hell with the examination. As you insist on being a double act, you'd better divide the fee. Will that be agreeable? (*The Executioners beam.*) You have your arms with you? (*They nod.*) Pistols? Admirable! Get them loaded and hide in this coppice.

FIRST EXECUTIONER: We shan't have to wait too long, shall we? If I stay awake after midnight, I'm always sick.

INSPECTOR: It'll all be over in a quarter of an hour. A young girl will come along this path . . .

SECOND EXECUTIONER: Ah, love, the only true executioner!

INSPECTOR: And then a young man will appear by that thicket . . .

FIRST EXECUTIONER: Ah, the lover, the only true condemned man!

INSPECTOR: You will let them talk together for five minutes, then, on an agreed cue, you will shoot him down. He is a dangerous murderer, and we have official authorization.

SECOND EXECUTIONER: Could we shoot, for instance, the moment he says "Obelisk and Pyramids"?

INSPECTOR: What a curious choice!

SECOND EXECUTIONER: Well, they go nicely together. My assistant and I always swore by them.

INSPECTOR: But it might be several years before he had occasion to say Obelisk and Pyramids! However, there is one particular word dear to this class of person, which often crops up in the conversation.

MAYOR: What word?

INSPECTOR: The word "alive".

FIRST EXECUTIONER: Right then, the moment he says "alive".

SECOND EXECUTIONER: "Alive!"

CHEMIST: You'd better caution them, Inspector.

INSPECTOR: I must caution you, yes. One last question, then, my friends: Who was Axel Petersen?

FIRST EXECUTIONER: The butcher-executioner of Göteborg.

SECOND EXECUTIONER: Who well and truly guillotined a ghost.

INSPECTOR: There, you've had your warning. Don't let's waste any more time. We'd better start looking out for Isabelle. She's sure to lead us to him.

The Chemist bursts out laughing.

Yes, Chemist, you'd better get to work too!

CHEMIST: What can I do for you?

INSPECTOR: I gather that your speciality in this base world is to produce the right phrase or gesture to modify the atmospheric pitch and make the most surprising occurrences seem natural. If so, get to work! Give us a suitable flat or sharp – I leave it to you!

CHEMIST: You can count on me.

The Inspector goes out with the Executioners.

MAYOR: Why do you smile at a moment like this, Mr Chemist?

CHEMIST: You see, Mr Mayor, they were lost and I've found them again!

MAYOR: Found what?

CHEMIST: My tuners!

MAYOR: Is this really a moment for tuners? You must have heard, surely, that we're dealing with a murder.

CHEMIST: Look at them. I still prefer this kind you blow – no, not yet, my friend – which looks like the original Pan-pipe, the one with a single note. This metal one looks more like a lyre or a magnet . . . No, Mr Mayor, not that way, you're holding it like a curling tong.

MAYOR: How odd. I've never held a curling tong. A man's life is at stake, Mr Chemist, and you still refuse to be serious!

CHEMIST: I thought they were lost, and I had them on me all the time. If a couple of sous had got lost in the lining of my pocket, I'd have been tinkling like a cow-bell – yet here I had all the music in the world hiding on me in perfect silence. So, thank heaven, we're saved!

MAYOR: You really think your tuners can protect Isabelle?

CHEMIST: My dear Mayor, do you really think Isabelle *needs* protecting? Doesn't the Inspector's fury over her remind you of anything?

MAYOR: Yes. It's like insects of prey, in captivity, trying to get at each other through the glass partitions.

CHEMIST: Precisely. They're on such totally different levels of reality that they can't possibly harm one another. They're separated by more than glass. They move in diametrically opposite worlds: what one sees as ghost the other sees as flesh and blood, and vice-versa. The only danger is that the Inspector, with his irrational excitement and his jarring voice, may have left behind enough dissonances to upset Isabelle's atmosphere when she arrives. It would be appalling if the whole of Nature, which normally yields her up its inmost truths, were suddenly to ring false under her touch. But it isn't likely to happen.

MAYOR: I see what you mean, all we need is a harmonizer.

CHEMIST: A tuner . . .

MAYOR: And, of course, a responsive personality.

CHEMIST: Don't worry about that. Nature loves to find the supreme harmony suddenly issuing from the human animal, which usually moves and speaks with such singular lack of it.

MAYOR: You really think it's all right for me to go – there's no risk to Isabelle?

CHEMIST: My tuner will see to that.

MAYOR: I'm going to watch what happens, all the same.

Exit the Mayor.

CHEMIST: A man who can strike the right note is safer on it than he would be on the tallest ship.

The Chemist sounds his pitch-pipe. The whole of Nature seems to take up the note and reverberate with it as the Chemist withdraws. Enter the Ghost with Isabelle.

GHOST: Have you been waiting for me?

ISABELLE: Don't apologize. If I were a ghost I should want to loiter in the twilight of these valleys where I'd only lived before as flesh and blood. Hedges, streams, nothing would get in my way any more; that's why they'd hold me. Oh, if I could be like you, and fold my shadow round all the things that I can now only touch and see; if I could acquire at will a skeleton made of a still bird on its branch, or a child, or a slanting dog-rose in bloom! The only way to get near things is to contain them . . . But what I do reproach you for is coming back this evening on your own; always alone. Haven't you been able to persuade any of your own kind to join you?

GHOST: No, none of them.

ISABELLE: We thought yesterday, after all the setbacks we'd had, that the best way to make them move, to quicken whatever nerves shadows may have, would be a sort of long cry, a monotonous reiterated howl: like that scream of a real or imagined train which sometimes wakes us humans at sunrise, or the wailing siren of steamers at night, a sound which disturbs even the soft jelly-fish floating in their estuaries. Have you made that cry? Have you spent your waking hours making it?

GHOST: Yes.

ISABELLE: Just you? Alone? Haven't thousands of kindred voices joined in?

GHOST: I had the sleep of the dead to reckon with.

ISABELLE: Do they sleep, then?

GHOST: If you can call it sleeping. They lie there, as a rule, in quivering heaps. The submerged activity is so intense that you half expect some sudden release of sound and light. During such periods, new arrivals drift into a sort of pleasant throbbing where the last eddies of their lives find peace; and the swing of the earth keeps them gently stirring for ever. But sometimes, on the other hand, the whole mass seems to stop short and freeze into a deadly sort of hibernation – and into this the new dead sink with only a last sad glimmer of the bright sunshine of living sleep.

ISABELLE: And that's how they were yesterday? Does it stay long like that?

GHOST: Centuries . . . seconds.

ISABELLE: Is there nothing one can do?

GHOST: Nothing they can do, anyway.

ISABELLE: You mustn't say that. There are some people I've seen Fate carry off who I've felt sure, from the very moment of their death, have gone for ever, wiped out at a stroke from any sort of life or death. I've dropped them into the void like stones. But there are others I've sent into death as if on some mission or exploration. Their death seemed to me more like a sudden burst of confidence. At the cemetery one had the feeling that they were off to search for an unknown continent. One didn't want to say goodbye in words, only to wave to them. The whole of the afternoon I used to feel they were busy discovering a new climate, new kinds of plant life. If it was sunny I could see them, over there, suddenly warmed by the rays of their new sun. If it was raining, then they were feeling the first drops of the rain of hell. You'll never convince me that they forget, too, and fade away once they get there.

GHOST: They haven't got there; I haven't seen them.

ISABELLE: But what about you? Are you giving up? Have you no further desire or ambition than to be a wandering ghost in a small town?

GHOST: There are sleepwalkers amongst the dead. No doubt I am one of them.

ISABELLE: You mustn't believe that. I drew you here, I caught you in a trap.

GHOST: What trap?

ISABELLE: I have a trap at home for luring the dead.

GHOST: Are you a witch, then?

ISABELLE: Mine is the most natural witchcraft. When I used to imagine what the dead might be thinking of, I didn't credit them with memories or visions. I just thought they'd be conscious of reflected or fragmented gleams of light on a chimney corner, a cat's nose or an arum leaf, tiny coloured scraps floating on their dark flood.

GHOST: So?

ISABELLE: So my room at home is, to all appearance, a room for the living – for a little provincial human like me. But if you look at it more closely you'll see it's carefully planned so that these gleams on familiar objects – the belly of a china vase, a drawer-handle – are always kept shining, in the daytime by the sun or the fire, at night by the lamp or the moon. That's my trap, so I wasn't surprised the night I saw your face at my window. You were gazing at the flame reflected on the side of

the fireguard, the moon on the tortoiseshell alarm-clock –
diamonds for ghosts – you were caught.

GHOST: In the trap.

ISABELLE: The only question now is what kept you there.

GHOST: What kept me? First of all, your voice, every evening
your voice softly tinkling in the twilight – thanks to which we
shadows now have a sound which means to us what a risen
lark does to living men. But above all it was your trust that
held me. The idea never crossed your mind for a second that
I might have deceived you and that I might be . . .

ISABELLE: Might be what?

GHOST: Alive!

*There are two shots. The Ghost falls to the ground. The Mayor runs
in, followed by the Inspector, Chemist, and Executioners.*

MAYOR: Who fired that shot? Who is that on the ground?

INSPECTOR: Look for yourself. A bogus ghost; a real corpse.

CHEMIST: Wretches: what have you done?

INSPECTOR: You should thank us. We have rid Isabelle of her
madness, the town of its haunting and the county of a
murderer.

CHEMIST: No one seriously believed in the ghost, Inspector.
Surely even you must realize that a girl has the right to rise
above her everyday self and give a bit of free play to her reason!

MAYOR: Come along, Isabelle my dear. The poor boy's been
well punished for making a fool of you.

FIRST EXECUTIONER: His heart has stopped.

INSPECTOR: Thank goodness. Nothing's more disturbing than
a dead man whose heart goes on beating.

CHEMIST: He's very good-looking. There's no finer gift to the
Almighty than a handsome corpse. Doesn't he make you
ashamed to have been right about him, Inspector? (*He kneels.*)
Forgive us, Isabelle. Forgive us, handsome corpse.

INSPECTOR: Are you mad? Forgive us for what?

CHEMIST: For the fact that the vulgar always hit the nail on the
head; that only short-sighted eyes see clearly; that there are
corpses and not ghosts.

Opposite the Executioners a Ghost, identical to the prostrate body, rises up. All those present see him one after the other. Isabelle and the Mayor pause as they are about to exit. Only the Chemist, his head bowed, sees nothing.

That the world is not worthy of you; that it's only generous with cruelty and stupidity; forgive us because the Inspector is right. (*The Ghost is fully risen.*)

FIRST EXECUTIONER: Inspector . . .

INSPECTOR: Chemist, have my eyes gone funny? There's no one there, is there?

Chemist looks up.

CHEMIST: Yes, there is.

MAYOR: Yes.

INSPECTOR: Obviously a young pine-tree swaying in the wind and given a strange shape by our overwrought nerves.

MAYOR: No, it's him.

EXECUTIONERS (*together*): He's coming this way.

INSPECTOR: Keep calm, my friends. It's a common enough phenomenon: a mirage, nothing more than a mirage. Tell me, Chemist, do you see him the right way up, or is he standing on his head?

CHEMIST: His head is held high.

INSPECTOR: It's a corona then, Chevreul's famous corona. Its composition is even less stable than water. It'll fade away at a snap of the fingers. (*He snaps his fingers; the Ghost does not fade away.*) I hope that idiot girl is satisfied now; even county officials have succumbed to mass hallucination.

GHOST: I'll see you tomorrow, Isabelle.

INSPECTOR: And now we're hearing things as well. What's he talking about with his last drop of blood?

FIRST EXECUTIONER: He's not talking about blood. He's talking about the guillotine.

GHOST: Till tomorrow, at your house, 6 o'clock. I'll be there with all the rest of them: all the rest . . .

INSPECTOR: It must be a stroke! I'm going to be paralyzed somewhere – but where?

SECOND EXECUTIONER: And I'll need amputating.

INSPECTOR: Are you coming, Mr Mayor?

MAYOR: Let's go, Isabelle. Night's coming on, and it's all over.

They all go out except the Chemist and the Ghost.

GHOST: Yes, everything begins tomorrow.

The Chemist is about to leave when the voices of the Little Girls are heard and they enter, followed by the Superintendent.

SUPERINTENDENT: Of course, Luce would have to be missing.

LITTLE GIRLS: Luce! Luce! (*Luce appears.*)

SUPERINTENDENT: Why are you so late?

LUCE: I was looking for glow-worms with my torch.

SUPERINTENDENT: Don't tell fibs. The best way to miss seeing glow-worms is to shine your torch.

LUCE: Well, I'd lost my garter.

SUPERINTENDENT: If you look at your catapult you may possibly find it.

LUCE: Well . . .

SUPERINTENDENT: Well? You'd better think of a decent excuse this time. I'm sorry, my dear Chemist, were you waiting for me?

CHEMIST: I was waiting for you.

SUPERINTENDENT: Has something ghastly happened? We heard a shot.

CHEMIST: To tell you that your hour is nigh.

SUPERINTENDENT: Which of my hours? I have so many.

CHEMIST: The hour when you can challenge your rival in the presence of the one you love.

SUPERINTENDENT: Do I love someone?

LITTLE GIRLS: Miss Isabelle! Miss Isabelle!

SUPERINTENDENT: And I have a rival?

LITTLE GIRLS: The ghost! The ghost! (*The Ghost has appeared again behind them.*)

CHEMIST: You'd better go along, my dears. (*Takes the Superintendent by the arm and leads him aside.*) Now listen carefully, Superintendent. I'm afraid you may be exaggerating the peculiarity of this whole affair. What's happening here happens every day in one or other of the thirty-eight thousand communes of France. You know what young girls are like?

SUPERINTENDENT: Of course I do . . . that is, without actually knowing. . . . (*They go out chatting. Luce is left alone on the stage.*)

LUCE (*slowly finishing her original answer*): Because I like being alone in forests at night.

SUPERINTENDENT'S VOICE: Luce!

LUCE: I've lost my beret!

As she throws her beret into the air she sees the Ghost. With a grin, she imitates his swaying movement, arms dangling, floppy legs.

SUPERINTENDENT'S VOICE: Have you got your beret yet?

Luce throws her beret up again, very high. She catches it.

LUCE: I've got it! I've got it! (*She makes an impertinent gesture at the Ghost and goes off.*)

Curtain

ACT THREE

Isabelle's room. A balcony with two windows from which one can see the square of the little town; a closed door also gives on to the square. The town band is rehearsing in a near-by hall throughout the act. The upstage door opens, and the Inspector, Mayor and Little Girls enter on tiptoe.

MAYOR: But this is breaking and entering!

INSPECTOR: Do you think at our age we can get into a girl's room, or a girl's heart for that matter, *without* breaking and entering? What time is it?

MAYOR: By the sun, half past five.

INSPECTOR: I doubt whether ghosts take their time from the sun.

MAYOR: If they take it by the Observatory, it's 5.38.

INSPECTOR: He's due at six, so we've got twenty-two minutes – plenty of time to get ourselves dug in.

MAYOR: Oh, it's trench warfare now, is it?

INSPECTOR: It may have escaped your notice, my dear Mayor, that in this moment of anguish, when our town is threatened by a peculiarly sinister invasion, we have the honour of occupying the trenches nearest to the enemy's?

MAYOR: The enemy's graves, you mean?

INSPECTOR: We must bow to the weight of evidence. After we left yesterday, Cambronne and Crapuce failed to find the body. All they found was a ring of scorched turf. Whether it's a hallucination or a real ghost, the campaign continues today.

MAYOR: But what will Isabelle say when she finds us here?

INSPECTOR: She won't find us. I put the town clock back an hour, and everyone takes their time from that. Anyway, Gilberte is going to stand guard at the window and warn us if anyone's coming.

GILBERTE: I can see the Misses Mangebois.

INSPECTOR: I should ignore the Mangebois, if I were you.

They're a full-time job in themselves. But let us know even if animals go past, Gilberte. Everything is under suspicion today.

GILBERTE: I can see the Chemist's basset-hound.

INSPECTOR (*sitting down*): That basset-hound also falls into the Mangebois category . . . It's always been a source of regret to me, Mr Mayor, that our enlightened age has failed to establish a parallel with religious exorcism, a sort of layman's benediction which would keep a place indefinitely free of superstitious accretions. You are about to witness just such a ceremony. This morning I composed my own little exorcism service, which I now propose to read to you.

GILBERTE: Am I to mention trees?

INSPECTOR: Trees don't walk, you silly goose.

GILBERTE (*gradually recoiling*): That's what I thought . . . But . . . That's what I thought . . . But . . . But, you see . . .

INSPECTOR: Viola, take over from Gilberte. She's showing signs of strain.

MAYOR: Do you wonder?

INSPECTOR: Why, Mr Mayor, is it affecting you too?

MAYOR: It certainly is, Inspector. Especially as you're making me miss the drawing of the monthly lottery: it's going on at the town hall at this moment – without me in the chair, for the first time ever.

INSPECTOR: Don't worry about the lottery. Fate will no doubt play us the same tricks as it did in the last one. You'd far better tell me the results of those inquiries I asked you to carry out among your fellow citizens. After all, we are their representatives here. Did they give you their backing?

MAYOR: Yes, they did.

INSPECTOR: You explained to them the danger they were in because of Isabelle? You asked them how they would feel when they saw all their dear departed of all ages hot on the heels of this ghost, coming back to live with them and never leaving them? He said himself last night that that's what would happen.

MAYOR: I only asked professional people, including Civil Servants of course.

INSPECTOR: Of course. We already had the opinion of the retail and building trades. What did the chief magistrate say?

MAYOR: That he suffered enough from radio programmes as it was.

INSPECTOR: The solicitor?

MAYOR: He said he knew quite a few dead people, having had to deal with them in their lifetime, and that in most cases he wouldn't recommend it.

INSPECTOR: The head fireman?

MAYOR: That since the war one was just beginning to feel secure . . .

INSPECTOR: The curator of the town archives?

MAYOR: He is afraid for the truth which he has so painfully gleaned from his archives. He says the dead will mess it all up with their faulty memories or downright lies.

INSPECTOR: In short, we are unanimously against them. The only person whose opinion I don't know is yours, Mr Mayor.

MAYOR: Inspector, my one passion is collecting; I collect rather naughty bits of Provençal pottery, and imperforated early West Indian stamps. I devote every evening to my collections, and I don't see myself classifying my chipped earthenware Venuses or preparing my gummed hinges under the united gaze of my forbears, as far back as Eve. The Merovingians, for instance . . . don't you agree, Daisy? I should look a perfect fool.

INSPECTOR: Too true. Only the living can appreciate the seriousness of living activities.

MAYOR: Of course, with the West Indies, I include the Bahamas.

VIOLA: There are some houses, Inspector.

INSPECTOR: Houses don't walk, idiot child.

VIOLA: That's what I thought; at least, that's what I used to think. But . . .

INSPECTOR: Daisy, take Viola's place, and girls, make a circle in the centre of the room. Now you know what you have to do. Repeat after me the last word of each important sentence.

LITTLE GIRLS: Sentence.

INSPECTOR: Not yet. I'm beginning now. (*He stands in the centre of the girls and reads his invocation.*) Yes, Superstition, it is I. And who am I? I am Humanity.

LITTLE GIRLS: Humanity.

INSPECTOR: What is humanity? My whole purpose in being here is to tell you, and simply by telling you, bar the way to you and all your kind. Humanity is . . . a difficult enterprise; an enterprise which is, in a word . . . superhuman.

LITTLE GIRLS: Superhuman.

INSPECTOR: Whose object is to separate man from that rabble we call the Cosmos.

LITTLE GIRLS: Cosmos.

INSPECTOR: Thanks to two irresistible forces called Administration and Compulsory Education.

LITTLE GIRLS: Education.

INSPECTOR: The Administration isolates man's body by detaching it from all places too deeply soaked in primitive virtues . . . You should really see it at work, backed by the military and local councils.

LITTLE GIRLS: Local councils.

INSPECTOR: Carving up great estates, knocking down cloisters, erecting public conveniences of slate and chinaware at the foot of every cathedral or historical monument, making sewers into the real arteries of civilization, and combating all forms of shade, especially trees. Administration! If you haven't seen her felling avenues of century-old plane trees along our national highways, you haven't lived.

LITTLE GIRLS: Haven't lived.

INSPECTOR (*still holding forth*): Compulsory Education, however, isolates the soul of man, and every time humanity sloughs off one of its spiritual skins, she presents him, gratis, with some new discovery which corresponds exactly with what he has lost. In the eighteenth century, for instance, humanity ceased to believe in the fires and sulphur of hell; ten years later it discovered steam and gas . . .

LITTLE GIRLS: Gas.

INSPECTOR: It stopped believing in spirits, and in the following decade discovered electricity.

LITTLE GIRLS: City.

INSPECTOR: Abandoned belief in the word of God and invented the tele . . .

LITTLE GIRLS: Phone.

INSPECTOR: Should it stop believing in the Divine Principle itself, Compulsory Education will be superseded quite naturally by Compulsory Light. This in turn will purge the earth of dreams and the unconscious, make the sea transparent to the very bottom of the Kuril Islands; it'll even make girls talk sense and the night, my dear Phantom, as clear as day.

LITTLE GIRLS: As day!

DAISY: Here he is, Inspector.

INSPECTOR: Here is who?

DAISY: The ghost!

INSPECTOR: What is she saying? What do you mean by ghost, you idiot girl!

DAISY: He's coming this way.

INSPECTOR: He's going to get more than he bargains for. It's some accomplice of Isabelle's who takes me for an utter fool!

LITTLE GIRLS (*in chorus, very seriously*): Utter fool.

The Inspector dashes out.

MAYOR: Come along, girls, come along.

DAISY: We were only joking, Mr Mayor. It's Miss Isabelle and the Chemist coming in by the main gate.

MAYOR: All the more reason for you to leave.

They all leave by the door which gives on to the square.
Enter Isabelle with the Chemist.

ISABELLE: Bless you, Chemist: thanks to you I've got here in time. But was it really necessary? Do you really think he'll come?

CHEMIST: He'll come, I'm sure of it.

ISABELLE: You'll stay with me, won't you?

CHEMIST: Don't you want to receive him alone?

ISABELLE: Does he want it? Since yesterday he has seen fit to make himself visible to others. He's not Isabelle's ghost any more, he belongs to the whole town. You saw all the old women at the windows. The Mangebois sisters are in permanent council on the church square. There's only one subject of conversation now: our secret. There's only one sight everyone wants to see: the ghost. The whole point of our relationship was its intimacy. Why should he bother to come back?

CHEMIST: Because he needs you.

ISABELLE: To remain on earth?

CHEMIST: No, to get away from it.

ISABELLE: You're not being very clear.

CHEMIST: Dear Isabelle, there is only one kind of damnation and one kind of ghost: those who have lost their life but can't find their way into death. I'm growing more and more convinced that your friend is one of them.

ISABELLE: Still, there's nothing common or ill-bred about him. You thought yourself he was a poet.

CHEMIST: Perhaps that's why. This state of survival we call death is not available to good talkers or profound thinkers. Talent and genius are supposed to give one an automatic right to death; but the very reverse is true. These qualities are a constant irritation to life. They eat away their owners' immortality. Poets are people dedicated to dying totally, so as to safeguard the future existence of the poet's speechless sister or humble housemaid. Remember the one who came from Paris last month, to talk to us about his work: what eloquence! His very prose unintentionally rhymed, like a horse hammering its own shoes; but it was still mortal, all of it. Except for one tiny moment when he suddenly smiled to himself and seemed to forget his speech. Probably he was thinking about his collection of walking sticks, or his cat scalding her tongue on hot milk . . . That was his only chance of one day being able to join the company of the dead.

ISABELLE: But how could a young girl like me guide him?

CHEMIST: Have you ever heard of a ghost without a young girl? Theirs is the only age which is naturally drawn to death. Only young girls think of it without either belittlement or exaggeration. They don't approach it philosophically or theoretically, but physically, through their clothes and their flesh. There are certain steps of yours, even when dancing, that are directed towards death. Even your gayest conversations include scraps of the vocabulary of hell. One day, when your ghost is by, chance will make you utter the vital word which will open the gates of the underworld to him – unless, of course, you lead him there yourself in the sort of sudden impulse or surrender that leads the living into passion or rapture. He's not far off now, I assure you . . . Goodbye.

ISABELLE: Please don't go. I can't think of any visit that wouldn't be enhanced by your presence.

CHEMIST: Just as you wish. What's the time?

ISABELLE: Time he was here.

They both go to the window. The clock sounds. There is a knock at the door. They do not move. A second knock. Only the Chemist turns round.

CHEMIST: Oh, it's the Superintendent. I'll leave you, Isabelle.

ISABELLE: The Superintendent! . . . That's right, dear Chemist; I'll see you again soon.

The door opens gently and the Superintendent comes in. He is wearing a tail-coat and yellow kid gloves, and carries his bowler hat and a gold-topped cane. Isabelle turns to him.

SUPERINTENDENT: Don't speak, Mademoiselle, please, I beg you. For the moment I neither see nor hear you. I don't think I could survive two such delights at once: both to be in Miss Isabelle's room *and* to find Miss Isabelle there herself. Let me savour them one after the other.

ISABELLE: My dear Superintendent . . .

SUPERINTENDENT: No, you're not in your room, but I am. I am alone with the furniture and all the other things which have so often beckoned to me through the open window: that secretaire which really does represent for me the very essence of secrecy (the right leg has been restored, but the body is still quite perfect), that picture of Rousseau at Ermenonville (you put your children on public assistance, you Swiss humbug, but you seem to me to be smiling), and that liqueur-stand where the quince brandy waits impatiently for the Sunday moment when it will reach your lips. Real Baccarat crystal, that decanter; real quince, too . . . for everything is real and unadulterated with her.

ISABELLE: My dear Superintendent – I don't know what to think.

SUPERINTENDENT: Everything is real with Isabelle. Evil minds think her complicated merely because she's sincere. Nothing's simple to them except hypocrisy and dreary routine. She sees ghosts because she's the only one that sees the living, In fact she's the only literally pure person in the county. She is our Parsifal.

ISABELLE: I'd just like to mention, Superintendent, that I am expecting somebody.

SUPERINTENDENT: All right, I've finished. I only wanted, for once in my life, to indulge in the luxury of telling myself, aloud, what I thought about Isabelle! People don't talk to themselves nearly enough these days. No doubt they are afraid of finding out what they really think. Well, now I know.

ISABELLE: So do I, and I think it's very sweet of you.

SUPERINTENDENT: Ah! There you are, Miss Isabelle!

ISABELLE: For heaven's sake, here I am!

SUPERINTENDENT: Well, I'm sorry about that, Miss Isabelle, I really am. I shall have to talk to you . . .

ISABELLE: What about?

SUPERINTENDENT: Me, that's all. Just me.

ISABELLE: Do you always dress up like this to talk about yourself, Superintendent?

SUPERINTENDENT: Don't laugh at my clothes, please. They're the only thing that's keeping me going at the moment. Or rather, the idea of them – the sort of people that ought to be wearing them. Yes, really, the people who should be here are the very ones these clothes belonged to: my grandfather (this is his cane), my great uncle (his watch-chain) and my father (his tail coat, which he thought far too new to go to earth in). Only this bowler is mine, and I find it disturbing to the morale. Would you mind if I put it down?

ISABELLE: Your father – your grandfather? Whatever do they want to ask me?

SUPERINTENDENT: Can't you guess? . . . Your hand, Miss Isabelle. They have the honour to ask for your hand in marriage.

ISABELLE: My hand?

SUPERINTENDENT: Don't give me an answer, please. I'm asking for your hand, not your answer. I want you not to give your answer till the day after tomorrow, thus giving me in the meantime the happiest day of my life: the twenty-four hours in which I can say to myself that at last you know everything, that you haven't yet said no, that in spite of all you are touched to know that someone on this earth lives only through you. Someone called Robert, for my father would no doubt have told you my christian name (that one at least, though I have two others which I don't care to mention). Someone brave, hard-working, honest and unpretentious, for my grandfather wouldn't have spared you any of my virtues . . . It might be better if you never answered, and let me run away with my hands over my ears.

ISABELLE: No, no, don't go, Monsieur Robert. But you've given me such a shock, and at such a moment!

SUPERINTENDENT: I chose this moment. I chose it because I'm really not unworthy of it, and it suddenly occurred to me that I'm luckier than this ghost who can bring you nothing now but confusion and pain. I realized I could challenge him in your presence, show him how powerless he is to help you, and then I could offer you the only safe road, the normal progression towards death and the dead.

ISABELLE: Oh, come now! Is there more than one way?

SUPERINTENDENT: This way leads gently to them, slowly but surely . . . it'll get us there.

ISABELLE: And what is it?

SUPERINTENDENT : Life.

ISABELLE : Life with you?

SUPERINTENDENT : With me? Don't talk about me, Mademoiselle; I hardly come into the question. No, life with a Civil
Servant. My profession is the important thing here. Don't
you see what I mean?

ISABELLE : Yes, of course! I do see. You mean that only a Civil
Servant can look death in the face, as a friend; he's not like a
banker, or a businessman, or a philosopher – he's never tried
to cover it up or hide from it?

SUPERINTENDENT : Exactly!

ISABELLE : It's simply human restlessness that's created this
contradiction between life and death. Now, a civil servant
has worked, certainly, but without over-exertion.

SUPERINTENDENT : Oh, without overdoing anything.

ISABELLE : He's lived, but he hasn't over-developed his personality.

SUPERINTENDENT : Not over-developed, no.

ISABELLE : And he has scorned wealth, because his salary always
arrives promptly, without any special effort from him, as if
there were trees giving him fruit every month in the shape of
gold coins.

SUPERINTENDENT : Just so: fruit every month, if not always in
gold. And if he hasn't tasted luxury, at least his nature has
been refined by the imaginative side of his job.

ISABELLE : Imaginative? You know, I was a bit worried about
this. I think it might make me a bit frightened of living with a
Civil Servant. Does the job of Superintendent of Weights and
Measures involve a lot of imagination?

SUPERINTENDENT : Can you doubt it?

ISABELLE : Give me an example.

SUPERINTENDENT : A thousand, if you like. Every evening
when I come home from my rounds and the sun's setting, I
have only to think of the landscape in the language of one of
my medieval counterparts – suddenly measuring the roads in
leagues, trees in feet, meadows in rods and poles, even a glow-
worm in inches – and the mere sight of smoke and mist

curling up from the towers and houses is enough to turn our town into one of those ancient villages that used to get sacked in the wars of religion, and make me feel like a Reiter or a Landsknecht.

ISABELLE: Oh, I know just what you mean!

SUPERINTENDENT: And even the sky, Mademoiselle – the celestial vault itself . . .

ISABELLE: Let me finish it for you: depending entirely on whether you describe that sky, that vault, in ancient Greek or modern terms, whether you weigh the stars in drachms or tons, and measure their paths in stadia or metres, it becomes for you, at will, the heaven of Pericles or of Pasteur!

SUPERINTENDENT: So you see, a Civil Servant's life is full of poetry as well as surprise.

ISABELLE: Surprise? I'm not sure that I quite see that – which is a pity, because it's my very favourite thing. Does your life include surprises?

SUPERINTENDENT: Surprises of a rare and discreet kind, but exciting. Just imagine, Miss Isabelle – nearly every three years we get re-posted.

ISABELLE: Three years is quite a long time, though, isn't it?

SUPERINTENDENT: Yes, but this is where the surprise comes in: from the very beginning of the three-year period, our far-sighted administration has given us the names of two towns, one of which will be chosen for our next post.

ISABELLE: You already know what town you are going to when you leave here?

SUPERINTENDENT: Well, you see, I do and I don't. I know that it will either be Gap or Bressuire. One of them, alas, will elude me, but I shall get the other one. Do you appreciate the delicacy and deliciousness of that uncertainty?

ISABELLE: But of course! For three whole years your thoughts are going to soar above our moorland and chestnut woods and swing you ceaselessly between Gap . . .

SUPERINTENDENT: Which means pine-trees, snow, a stroll after office hours among girls who have spent their day in a factory making edelweiss brooches . . .

ISABELLE: And Bressuire . . .

SUPERINTENDENT: Which means pastureland – I need hardly say that I already know the local guide-book by heart! – a marvellous fair on August 27th, and then, when September is blushing to the very reeds in the eel-ponds of the Vendée marshes, off we go to the hacking races in an open carriage starting from the corner of the rue Duguesclin and the rue Général-Picquart. Does that lack surprises? You must admit, surely, that between your method and mine, between Gap, Bressuire and immediate death, it's a pretty easy choice!

ISABELLE: I never knew all that. That's marvellous. So at Gap you'll have three years to wait for your next two towns?

SUPERINTENDENT: Yes, a choice of Vitry-le-François and Domfront.

ISABELLE: Between the flat and the hilly.

SUPERINTENDENT: Between natural champagne and bottled cider.

ISABELLE: Between the Louis XIV cathedral and the castle keep.

SUPERINTENDENT: And so it goes on in a wonderful succession of swings and crossroads, promising you (according to the type of country) either grouse-shooting or coarse fishing, bowling or wine-harvests, football matches or the Comédie Française performing at the Arena theatre; until at last, one fine day, I reach the top of the tree.

ISABELLE: Paris?

SUPERINTENDENT: You said it.

ISABELLE: Paris!

SUPERINTENDENT: And there, by some strange contradiction, is the biggest surprise of all about Civil Servants' careers: they all finish in Paris. And you needn't worry about life getting dull in Paris either, Mademoiselle, because there'll still be the uncertainty whether I'm to be posted to the first district or the second, and my dreams will still veer between Belleville, with the St Gervais meadows and St Fargeau lake, or Vaugirard with its artesian wells.

ISABELLE: What a wonderful journey your life is! One can see its wake even in your eyes.

SUPERINTENDENT: My eyes? Now that's rather gratifying. People always talk about the eyes of naval officers, Miss Isabelle. The trouble is that taxpayers don't look at the tax inspector's eyes when they pay their dues. Car-drivers, declaring their foreign acquisitions, never plunge deep into the eyes of the customs officer, nor do plaintiffs in court take the judge's head in their hands and gently, tenderly turn it towards them into the light. If they did they would see the foaming mirror of the deepest of all oceans, the wisdom of life.

ISABELLE: It's quite true. I can see it in yours.

SUPERINTENDENT: And what feeling does it give you?

ISABELLE: Confidence.

SUPERINTENDENT: Then I know what I must do! (*He rushes to the door.*)

ISABELLE: What are you doing, Superintendent?

SUPERINTENDENT: I am bolting this door. I am closing this window. I am pushing in the fire-damper. I am hermetically sealing up this diving-bell we call a human house. There, dear Isabelle: the outside world is driven outside your room. We have only to wait patiently for the fateful hour to pass. But take care not to make a wish, or express any regret, for if you do our ghost will certainly see it as a cry for help, and come rushing in.

ISABELLE: Poor ghost!

The bolted door opens. The Ghost appears, more pale and transparent than before.

GHOST: May I come in?

SUPERINTENDENT: No. That door happens to be locked and bolted. It may not look like it, but it is.

GHOST: I have brought you the key to the riddle, Isabelle. If this gentleman would kindly leave us alone together.

SUPERINTENDENT: I'm sorry, that's out of the question.

GHOST: I am speaking to Isabelle.

SUPERINTENDENT: And I am answering. I am here to protect her.

GHOST: Protect her from what?

SUPERINTENDENT: I'm not very sure myself yet, so I must be even more on my guard.

GHOST: You needn't be afraid. I'm quite harmless.

SUPERINTENDENT: Perhaps the one who sent you is not so harmless, though . . .

GHOST: Who do you mean? Death?

SUPERINTENDENT: You see! If she's called that in her own kingdom, there certainly can't be any other name for her.

GHOST: And you think that your presence will be enough to drive her away?

SUPERINTENDENT: The fact that she isn't here seems to prove it.

GHOST: How do you know? Perhaps she is here. Perhaps you're the only one who can't see her. Look at Isabelle's face. She can obviously see something strange.

SUPERINTENDENT: That's quite immaterial. There are always faces and persons prowling round women that their husbands or fiancés can't see. But as long as the husband or the fiancé is there, there's nothing to fear.

GHOST: Have you hidden your engagement from me then, Isabelle? Wouldn't a joint wedding gift from the company of the dead have tempted you? So that is Isabelle's fiancé I see standing before me.

SUPERINTENDENT: Perhaps not quite her fiancé. I've asked for her hand and she hasn't yet said no. I don't know quite what you call that sort of relationship.

GHOST: Tenuous.

SUPERINTENDENT: Anyway, it's the only one that's holding Isabelle to the earth, so I'm not going to budge while you're here.

GHOST: And you really think I won't come back tonight or tomorrow, when you've gone?

SUPERINTENDENT: I'm almost sure you won't. If the invisible powers which besiege us were capable of waiting and persevering for a quarter of an hour at a stretch, men would have been routed long ago. But nothing has so little stamina as eternity.

Your comeback is no more than a last flicker of energy or human pigheadedness. You'll never last more than a few hours. Take my advice and go. If you have to pass through closed doors, I can easily close that one for you.

GHOST: Is this what you want, Isabelle?

ISABELLE: Dear Superintendent, please . . . I appreciate your devotion, your friendship. And I will listen to you tomorrow – but let me have this minute, this last minute.

SUPERINTENDENT: You'd despise me tomorrow if I deserted my post.

ISABELLE: But can't you see that this visitor has brought me what I wanted all my childhood – the key to a mystery?

SUPERINTENDENT: I'm not in favour of solving mysteries. An unsolved one often makes you feel much nobler and fresher inside than its explanation. It's like a fish's air-bladder. It's what we don't know that gets us safely through life, not what we know. The key to what mystery, anyway?

ISABELLE: You know. Death!

SUPERINTENDENT: Whose death? The death of what? Volcanoes? Insects?

ISABELLE: Men.

SUPERINTENDENT: That's not much of a question. Do you really care about such details? Besides, does it really strike you as a mystery? In the Weights and Measures we all know what death is, it's permanent retirement. Well, it's rather absurd to torture oneself about permanent retirement. And who told you that the dead know the secret, either? If they understand death as well as the living understand life, well, I must say I congratulate them. I'm staying here.

ISABELLE: Then let our visitor say what he has to say in front of you! Perhaps he'll agree to that?

GHOST: Not on your life. I know his type only too well. In his presence the most impenetrable mystery simply evaporates and floats away.

ISABELLE: He could cover his ears.

SUPERINTENDENT: I'm sorry, that's one thing I just can't do. However hard I try, my fingers won't fit together tightly enough. If I could close my ears with a natural membrane like my eyes it would be all right, but unfortunately I can't.

GHOST: To think that fate has to make ghosts out of reinforced-concrete creatures like him!

SUPERINTENDENT: Set your mind at rest! On the contrary, if there's one thing I'm sure of it's that when my turn comes I shall be the very model of a phantom Superintendent.

GHOST: Really?

SUPERINTENDENT: And after a few days, just as I was each time I was re-posted, I shall be quite indispensable to my new colleagues.

GHOST: May we know why?

SUPERINTENDENT: Because I shall have been conscientious. Because the only thing the dead insist on before we join them is that we've led a conscientious life. That's what they question us about. What, they say, you had this magnificent war, and you didn't glut yourself on its horrors and joys? You had a Colonial Exhibition, and you never visited Angkor or sat by Guadeloupe's ornamental pond? Well, they'll have nothing to reproach me for. I've always made so many detours on my rounds, out of respect for the invisible watchers, to stroke a cat on its window-sill or peep under a child's carnival mask. And even here I'll have seen Isabelle every day of the three years I've spent in Isabelle's town. Once at midnight I rubbed out and scraped away some disgraceful scribblings on her doorpost; once at dawn I straightened the lid of her milk can, and one afternoon pushed a letter firmly into the letter-box which she had left sticking out. In my tiny way I shall have softened the malignities of fate for her. I shall have earned my death!

ISABELLE: Dear Monsieur Robert!

GHOST: What did you say, Isabelle?

ISABELLE: Nothing.

GHOST: Why did you say "Dear Monsieur Robert"?

ISABELLE: Because I am touched by the Superintendent's devotion. Am I wrong, do you think?

GHOST: No, you're right, and I'm grateful for it. I was about to commit the greatest of follies. I was about to betray for the sake of a girl. Luckily she got her betrayal in first.

ISABELLE: What have I betrayed?

GHOST: And they'll always be like that, all of them! And that's the whole story of young girls.

SUPERINTENDENT: Why bring girls into it?

GHOST: There they are, sitting in the fields with their sunshades open but lying uselessly beside them, leaning against a level-crossing and welcoming the traveller with a wave that means goodbye, or at their window in lamp-light, caught between the street's shadow and the room's. They're like flowers in summer or the thought of flowers in winter. And then they place themselves so skilfully among the great mass of men – the generous girl in a family of misers, the indomitable daughter of flabby stock – that the gods of this earth take them, not for humanity in its childhood, but for the supreme flowering, the end-product of a race whose final fruits, really, are old men. But suddenly . . .

SUPERINTENDENT: You're over-simplifying things, aren't you?

GHOST: Suddenly man comes on the scene. The girls all gaze at him. He has found ways of enhancing his earthly dignity in their eyes. He now stands on his hind legs so that he can avoid the rain and pin medals on his chest. They tremble before him with pretended admiration and fear him more than a tiger, blissfully unaware that this biped is the only carnivorous beast whose teeth decay. By then it's all up with them. The walls of reality, through which they once saw a thousand delicate traceries and heraldic devices, suddenly become opaque. It's all over.

SUPERINTENDENT: All over? If you're referring to marriage, you surely mean it's just beginning.

GHOST: Oh, the nightly pleasure is beginning, and the habit of that pleasure. Greediness is beginning. And jealousy.

SUPERINTENDENT: Dear Isabelle!

GHOST: And then revenge. And then indifference. Man's one adornment loses its prize pearl. It's all over.

ISABELLE: Why be so cruel? Save me from happiness, then, if you think it so contemptible.

GHOST: Goodbye, Isabelle. Your Superintendent is right. What you love, what men love, isn't knowledge or the quest for knowledge – it's the wavering between two truths or lies, between Gap and Bressuire. I'm leaving you on the swing for your happily gazing fiancé to push you to and fro between your two notions of death; between the hell of silent shadows and the hell of deafening noise, between pitch darkness and nothingness. I shall never speak to you again – not even the name of the charming common flower dotted over our meadows, whose scent greeted me at the gates of death, whose name fifteen years hence I shall whisper to your daughters. Take her in your arms, Superintendent! Hold her like a wolf-trap from which she will never escape.

ISABELLE: Yes, I will, just once more!

She rushes to the Ghost, who embraces her and disappears. She turns pale and faints.

SUPERINTENDENT (*calling for help*): The chemist! Where's the chemist?

The Inspector bursts in.

We're just in time. She's still breathing.

INSPECTOR: Her head is warm; her hands are cold, her legs are frozen. Our visitor from beyond the grave was clumsy to try dragging her off feet first. It was lucky for her.

ISABELLE: Where am I?

SUPERINTENDENT: In my arms . . . Oh, Inspector, she's gone again . . .

INSPECTOR: That's because your reply hardly meets the occasion, young man. Isabelle's not returning from a simple fainting fit but from disincarnation, perhaps even total oblivion. What she needs is universal truth, not personal details!

ISABELLE: Where am I?

INSPECTOR: Now watch this! . . . You are on the planet earth,

my child, a satellite of the sun. And if you feel yourself turning, as your eyes suggest, you are quite right and we are
wrong: the earth *does* turn . . .

ISABELLE: Who am I?

SUPERINTENDENT: You are Isabelle!

INSPECTOR: You are a human being of the female gender,
Mademoiselle, one of two forms assumed by the human
embryo. And a very good specimen, too . . .

ISABELLE: What a noise!

SUPERINTENDENT: That's the town band rehearsing.

INSPECTOR: Those are sound vibrations, little human female,
reacting on various parts of your dermis or endodermis, otherwise known as your senses . . . There you are, her colour's
coming back. Science is still the best smelling salt. Pass a few
atoms and ions under the nose of any young teacher who has
fainted, and she comes to in no time.

SUPERINTENDENT: Nonsense! She's gone dead again! Chemist!
Help!

*Enter the Chemist, followed by a curious crowd, including the Little
Girls and the Mangebois sisters.*

CHEMIST: Here I am, and don't worry: I've brought the anti-
dote.

MONSIEUR ADRIEN: We saw flames. Is there a fire?

CHEMIST: You've come at the right moment, Monsieur Adrien.
Please sit down at that table.

FATHER TELLIER: Shall we take her out into the fresh air? Did
she suffocate?

CHEMIST: Leave her alone and sit down. Here are some
playing-cards. As soon as I give the order, start playing
Ombre. Or Quadrille.

LITTLE GIRLS: She's still alive, isn't she, Mr Chemist? She's
still alive?

INSPECTOR: Young ladies, kindly leave the room.

CHEMIST: No, no, let them come in. I want as many as possible
here for my experiment. And when I give the signal, let them
start repeating their lessons.

INSPECTOR: You must be mad, Chemist! Anyone would think you were rehearsing a choral society.

ARMANDE: Is it true she's been burned to death?

SUPERINTENDENT: No, just fainted.

ARMANDE: Do you need any leeches?

CHEMIST: No leeches, thank you, Miss Mangebois. But do come in with your sister and chatter away when I tell you.

ARMANDE: Chatter? Us chatter, indeed?

LÉONIDE: Offer him our leeches, can't you? Don't forget the school-marm is feverish.

ARMANDE: He doesn't want them; he wants us.

CHEMIST: Fine! An excellent beginning.

INSPECTOR: Are you going to explain your extraordinary conduct, Chemist?

CHEMIST: Do I really need to explain, Inspector? Miss Isabelle is neither a drowned swimmer nor a frost-bitten mountaineer. She has fallen, either through nervous crisis or mischance, into a state of unconsciousness whose origin you can guess as well as I. The only massage or artificial respiration we can apply in this case, is to bring back her sleeping consciousness as near as possible to the noises of her everyday life. It's not a question of bringing her back to herself but of bringing her back to us. Anyway, let's try. Are you all ready? You understand what you have to do?

INSPECTOR: No.

MAYOR: Really, you haven't made it very clear.

MONSIEUR ADRIEN: Do you understand, Tellier?

FATHER TELLIER: Not a word.

LÉONIDE: What is the chemist talking about?

ARMANDE: We are going to read right through the dictionary to find a word which will wake Isabelle.

LITTLE GIRLS: That's not it! She doesn't understand!

MAYOR: Do you understand, then, Luce?

LITTLE GIRLS: We all understand.

VIOLA: It's so simple. We've got to make life round Miss Isabelle stronger than death.

LUCE: Mr Chemist wants to condense all the sounds of our town and springtime round her.

GILBERTE: Like X-rays.

DAISY: Like a symphony.

IRÈNE: And when it's right, and all the music . . .

LUCE: And all the warmth soaks into her . . .

DAISY: Some simple word or noise will reach her heart.

VIOLA: And her heart will start beating again.

CHEMIST: Well done, girls. I think you've all got it now. Mr Mayor, go out and fetch a few noises, will you?

MAYOR: The blacksmith? Some steel hammers?

CHEMIST: Or a distant cornet. And will you, Mr Inspector, deliver yourself, at regular intervals, of some of those abstract terms so recurrent in your speech.

INSPECTOR: The only abstract terms I use are those demanded by Justice and Truth.

CHEMIST: Perfect! Admirable!

SUPERINTENDENT: I love you, Isabelle.

INSPECTOR: And Democracy.

CHEMIST: That "I love you" is a bit weak, and the "Democracy" rather too loud. Right, let's begin. A moment's silence first. Now: One . . . two . . . three . . .

The card-players start to play in earnest, the women start whispering. The Inspector drones on. Instead of artificial noises, the authentic sound of life. A motor horn, a passer-by whistling: it is only a dream, a pleasant dream. The band rehearses, a canary sings. Isabelle begins to stir.

Fugue of the Provincial Choir

CHEMIST: One, two, three:

LITTLE GIRLS: The Creuse is a tributary of the Vienne.

MONSIEUR ADRIEN: Hearts, Father Tellier.

LITTLE GIRLS: The Auron is a tributary of the Cher.

FATHER TELLIER: If you catch the disease it kills you.

LITTLE GIRLS: The Sioule is a tributary of the Allier.

INSPECTOR: Hardworking peoples . . . Stagnant ponds.

LITTLE GIRLS: The Creuse is a tributary of the Vienne.

ARMANDE: There are cleaners and dyers.

SUPERINTENDENT: I love you.

LITTLE GIRLS: The Auron is a tributary . . .

MONSIEUR ADRIEN: The Queen of Spades.

LITTLE GIRLS: . . . of the Cher.

FATHER TELLIER: She's very nice . . .

LITTLE GIRLS: The Sioule is a tributary . . .

FATHER TELLIER: . . . with no clothes on.

LITTLE GIRLS: . . . of the Allier. The Creuse is a tributary . . .

INSPECTOR: Stagnant ponds . . .

LITTLE GIRLS: . . . of the Vienne. The Auron is a tributary . . .

INSPECTOR: Mentality . . .

LITTLE GIRLS: . . . of the Cher.

LÉONIDE: Margarine will never be the same as butter . . .

MONSIEUR ADRIEN: Two Byrrh with lemon!

ARMANDE: It's a woman he picked out of the gutter.

SUPERINTENDENT: I adore you.

LITTLE GIRLS: The Vienne.

Meanwhile the Chemist conducts the chorus with his baton: it swells and diminishes to his directions.

CHEMIST: We now approach the dénouement of this latest episode of Faust and Marguerite. Of course we haven't got the choir of angels, but we have instead the noise of the card-players, the Mangebois sisters and the children, a choir which now pleads for her in all its curiosity and indifference: every bit as powerful, I feel, as the heavenly one.

Chorus (while the Chemist is speaking).

LITTLE GIRLS: The Auron is a tributary of the Cher . . .	
ARMANDE: You can't make a silk purse out of a pig's ear . . .	*pp*
LITTLE GIRLS: The Sioule is a tributary of the Allier.	
INSPECTOR: Mentality . . . building plots in open country . . .	

Chemist signals a crescendo.

LITTLE GIRLS:	The Auron is a tributary of the Cher.	
MONSIEUR ADRIEN:	Hearts, Father Tellier!	
LITTLE GIRLS:	The Sioule is a tributary of the Allier.	
FATHER TELLIER:	If you catch the disease it kills you.	
INSPECTOR:	Superstition . . . Freudianism . . .	*f*
ARMANDE:	It's like my evening cape . . .	
LITTLE GIRLS:	The Creuse is a tributary of the Vienne.	
ARMANDE:	I'm going to line it with velvet!	
LÉONIDE:	Oh, for heaven's sake, no!	

ISABELLE (*trembling*): Oh, for heaven's sake, no!

ALL: What? What is it? Did she say something?

CHEMIST: I thought the word velvet would do the trick. That's right, Miss Armande, carry on as if you were talking to your sister. There's a layer of silence between us and Isabelle, too.

Chorus

LITTLE GIRLS: The Auron is a tributary of the Cher.

MONSIEUR ADRIEN: The Queen of Spades.

INSPECTOR: Hardworking peoples.

LITTLE GIRLS: The Sioule is a tributary of the Allier.

ARMANDE: Real silk velvet, I thought.

ISABELLE (*gradually awakening*): Life should be lined with silk velvet – death should be lined with . . . What am I talking about?

INSPECTOR: Poor child.

LÉONIDE: And why shouldn't I use crêpe-de-chine?

ISABELLE: Yes, why *shouldn't* you use crêpe-de-chine? The shop is still open, the band is still rehearsing . . . Ah! there you are, dear Monsieur Robert. Give me your hand!

INSPECTOR: She is lost!

CHEMIST: She is saved!

LÉONIDE: What are these gentlemen saying?

ARMANDE: That Miss Isabelle is lost and saved.

LÉONIDE: She's thoroughly deserved it!

MAYOR (*appearing with Viola*): Inspector! Inspector! The lottery!

INSPECTOR: What's the matter with the lottery?

MAYOR: It's been drawn.

INSPECTOR: Why the excitement? Outrageous results still, I suppose?

MAYOR: On the contrary, everything is back to normal. You tell them, Viola, I'm out of breath.

INSPECTOR: Normal? Who has won the motor-cycle?

VIOLA: The cripple from the orphanage.

INSPECTOR: And the big cash prize?

VIOLA: Monsieur Dumas, the millionaire.

INSPECTOR: Victory, gentlemen, victory! We have not laboured in vain. We are overjoyed to find, dear fellow citizens, that in a town where human ideas were in turmoil, our mere presence has sufficed to divide the most extravagant fantasies by that common denominator we call enlightened democracy. Permit me to take my leave of you. The Isabelle case is closed. Luce's case will not be upon us for another three or four years. I must now dash off to Saint-Yrieux, where I am told there is a nightwatchman who walks in his sleep – the worst kind of sleepwalking, as owing to the victim's profession he does it in broad daylight when everyone else is awake. Goodbye, Mr Mayor. I hand your district back to you in good order. Money is returning to the rich, happiness to the fortunate, women to the seducer. Our mission amongst you, dear fellow citizens, is completed.

MAYOR: Isabelle's soul is cured.

ARMANDE: And the poetry of civil servants very properly crowned with laurels.

CHEMIST: And so our interlude is ended.

Curtain

Ondine

based on the story by Frédéric de la Motte Fouqué

ONDINE was first performed at the Théâtre de l'Athénée on 27 April 1939 and was produced by Louis Jouvet.

ONDINE

HANS, the Knight

KING OF THE ONDINES

BERTHA

AUGUSTE

EUGÉNIE

THE KING

QUEEN YSEULT

THE CHAMBERLAIN

BERTRAM

THE POET

FIRST JUDGE

SECOND JUDGE

GRETA

KITCHEN MAID

FIRST FISHERMAN (Ulrich)

SECOND FISHERMAN

SUPERINTENDENT OF THE ROYAL THEATRES

SEAL-TRAINER

SWINEHERD

VIOLANTA

SALAMMBO

MATHO

ONDINES, KNIGHTS, COURT LADIES

ACT ONE

The scene is a fisherman's hut.
Outside a storm rages.

AUGUSTE (*the old fisherman at the window*): What on earth can she be up to, out there in the dark?

EUGÉNIE (*his old wife*): Stop fussing, Auguste. She can see in the dark, you know that.

AUGUSTE: In a storm like this?

EUGÉNIE: It takes more than rain to get her wet.

AUGUSTE: Now she's singing! I suppose it is her? Doesn't sound like her voice.

EUGÉNIE: Well, who else could it be, with the nearest house fifty miles away?

AUGUSTE: I don't know. One moment it sounds like it's coming from the middle of the lake, and the next it's up at the top of the waterfall.

EUGÉNIE: It just means that she *was* in the lake, and now she's up the waterfall.

AUGUSTE: All right, laugh! I suppose you were jumping over swollen streams at her age?

EUGÉNIE: I tried once, and they had to fish me out by my feet. Just once, that's all, and she does it all day long, jumping over ravines, and catching waterfalls in a basin. Oh, my Lord, I remember that time I tried walking on the water!

AUGUSTE: We're too soft with her, Eugénie. It isn't right, a girl of fifteen running about in the forest at this time of night. I shall have to talk seriously to her. She still insists on washing her linen on top of the rocks and saying her prayers under water – it won't do, you know. Where would we be if *you'd* been brought up like that, eh?

EUGÉNIE: She helps with the housework, doesn't she?

AUGUSTE: You may well ask.

EUGÉNIE: What do you mean? Doesn't she wash the dishes? Doesn't she clean your boots?

AUGUSTE: I don't know. Does she?

EUGÉNIE: Well, *isn't* this dish clean?

AUGUSTE: That's not the point. All I'm saying is, I've never *seen* her washing or cleaning anything – nor have you, come to that . . .

EUGÉNIE: She prefers washing outside.

AUGUSTE: Ah, yes, I know! But just you tell me one thing. Whether there's three dishes to wash or twelve, one shoe or half a dozen to clean, it always takes her just the same time – she's back inside a minute, with everything clean and shining – but the rag hasn't been used, and the polish hasn't been touched. By the by, did you ever find out the truth about those gold plates? She never gets her hands dirty, even. And you know what she's been and done today?

EUGÉNIE: Do you remember one day in all these fifteen years when she's done what we expected?

AUGUSTE: Yes, well, she's been and opened the trap of the fish-pond, and all those trout have got away that I've been collect-ing there since spring. It's too bad. I only just managed to catch one for our supper. (*The window suddenly flies open.*) Oh, now what is it!

EUGÉNIE: Don't be silly, it's the wind.

AUGUSTE: Don't you believe it. It's her! I only hope to goodness she doesn't start her nonsense of putting heads in the window, like she does on stormy nights sometimes. That old man with a beard gives me the horrors.

EUGÉNIE: I like the woman with the pearls, though. Still, if you're frightened, shut the window.

There is a flash of lightning, and the head of an old man with a crown and a long dripping beard appears in the window.

THE HEAD: Too late, Auguste!

AUGUSTE: I'll show you if it's too late, Ondine!

He shuts the window. It flies open again, and the head of a charming naiad appears in another flash.

NAIAD'S HEAD: Good evening, Eugénie!

It disappears.

EUGÉNIE: Ondine, come in this minute! Your father's very angry!

AUGUSTE: Yes, in you come, Ondine! I'm going to count up to three, and if you're not in by then, I'm going to shut the bolt, and you can sleep outside.

A crash of thunder.

EUGÉNIE: You don't mean that!

AUGUSTE: You see if I don't. Ondine – one!

Thunder again.

EUGÉNIE: Oh, these awful claps of thunder every time you speak!

AUGUSTE: It's not my fault, is it?

EUGÉNIE: Well, hurry up and finish, then, before there's another. We all know you can count up to three!

AUGUSTE: Ondine – two!

Thunder.

EUGÉNIE: Oh, you're the limit!

AUGUSTE: Ondine – three!

No thunder.

EUGÉNIE (*waiting for it*): Get it over quickly, can't you, Auguste!

AUGUSTE: It is over, as far as I'm concerned. (*He bolts the door.*) There! Now we can have supper in peace.

But the door swings wide open. Auguste and Eugénie turn round at the noise. In the doorway stands a knight in armour.

THE KNIGHT (*clicking his heels*): Ritter Hans von Wittenstein zu Wittenstein.

AUGUSTE: Auguste, sir, at your service.

HANS: I have taken the liberty of stabling my horse in your barn. The horse, as everyone knows, is a knight's best friend.

AUGUSTE: I'll go and give him a rub down, sir.

HANS: Many thanks, but I've already done so. I always do him myself, Ardennes style. I know you use the Swabian method in these parts, rubbing against the grain. Don't believe in it myself. Takes the shine out of the coat, with roans particularly. Do you think I might sit down?

AUGUSTE: Oh, please, sir, make yourself at home.

HANS: God in heaven, what a storm! It's been pouring down my neck ever since noon. Of course, it drains out again by the blood vents, but the damage is done by then. The one thing we knights simply dread in our armour, you know, is rain. Or a flea, of course.

AUGUSTE: Well, sir, perhaps you could take it off if you're going to spend the night here.

HANS: Have you seen crayfish changing their shells, Auguste? Well, it's as complicated as that! I think I'd better rest first. You did say your name was Auguste, didn't you?

AUGUSTE: Yes, sir, and this is my wife Eugénie.

EUGÉNIE: Please excuse us, sir. They aren't names for knight-errant gentlemen.

HANS: You've simply no idea, my good woman, the blessed relief of a knight errant who's spent a whole month in the forest vainly searching for Pharamond and Osmonda, when it's dinner time and he suddenly stumbles on Auguste and Eugénie.

EUGÉNIE: That's right, sir! I know it's not proper to ask a guest questions, sir, but may I just ask if you're hungry?

HANS: I should say I am. I'd be most glad to share your meal with you.

EUGÉNIE: Oh, *we* won't be having supper, sir, thank you. But I've got a trout out there. Perhaps you'd care for that?

HANS: I most certainly would. Passion for trout.

EUGÉNIE: Would you like it fried, sir, or grilled?

HANS: Ah, well, I prefer it poached, actually.

Auguste and Eugénie register dismay.

EUGÉNIE: Oh – poached? I usually fry them in butter and parsley, sir, they're very nice that way . . .

HANS: Well, you asked how I like it, and I like it poached.

AUGUSTE: She does it a treat with cheese, too, sir.

HANS: Now, just a moment. Poached means dropping it alive into boiling water, doesn't it?

AUGUSTE: Yes, sir, it does.

HANS: So that it keeps all its flavour and tenderness because the boiling water takes it by surprise?

AUGUSTE: It certainly does, sir.

HANS: That's settled then. I want it poached.

AUGUSTE: All right, Eugénie. Go and poach it for the gentleman.

EUGÉNIE (*in the doorway*): It's very nice stuffed, sir . . .

AUGUSTE: Go on.

Eugénie goes into the kitchen. The knight settles back in his chair.

HANS: You seem quite keen on knights errant in these parts?

AUGUSTE: Well, sir, we prefer them to armies. Knight errants mean the war's over.

HANS: I rather like war, personally. Not that I'm cruel or anything, I don't mean harm to anyone, but I rather like it.

AUGUSTE: One man's meat, sir.

HANS: Thing is, you see, I like talking. I've got a talkative nature, I suppose. And in war there's always someone to chat with. If you don't find your own lot congenial, you just take a prisoner. Padres are the best, of course, they never stop talking. And I mean, you pick up a wounded enemy, and he'll tell you his whole life story. Whereas being a knight errant, you can spend a month crashing through this damned forest, and never exchange a word with anyone, except possibly your own echo. Not a soul! And God knows I've got plenty to say!

AUGUSTE: They say knight errants can understand animal language. Is that true, sir?

HANS (*beginning to ramble*): Not in the way you mean, no. But of course they do speak to us too, in a way. You see, for a knight, every wild animal is a – a symbol, if you follow me; every time they bark or howl or squeak, it has a symbolic meaning, inscribed on our soul in letters of fire. You might say they write, really, rather than talk. But it's always the same word.

Each animal has only one thing to say; but it carries for miles, and it can sound pretty awe-inspiring. The stag means purity, the wild boar means disdain of worldly possessions. And for some reason, it's always the old male that does the talking. There are all sorts of enchanting little fawns and piglets in the background, but the one that makes the speech is always the ten-pointer or the senior boar.

AUGUSTE: And how about birds?

HANS: Birds have been a big disappointment to me, actually. They never bother to answer at all. They just keep up this endless chant about the evils of untruth. I don't know, I've tried to make contact with them. I've asked them how they're feeling, and if it's been a good year for laying or moulting, and if it's exhausting hatching the eggs, and so on – not a squeak. They can't be bothered.

AUGUSTE: Even larks, sir? I'm surprised at that. You'd think a lark would be more forthcoming.

HANS: I defy anyone to converse with larks while wearing a gorget.

AUGUSTE: But whoever could have made you come to a dreadful place like this?

HANS: Who do you think? A woman, of course!

AUGUSTE: Ah! Well, I won't ask you any more, sir.

HANS: Oh yes you will, this minute! Good God, Auguste, I haven't talked about her for a *month* now! You don't think I'm going to miss the opportunity, when I've actually got two human beings within earshot! Come on, now! Hurry up and ask me her name . . .

AUGUSTE: Sir . . .

HANS: Do you want to know her name or not?

AUGUSTE: What is her name, sir?

HANS: Her name, good fisherman, is Bertha. Isn't it a beautiful name!

AUGUSTE: Oh, beautiful, sir!

HANS: The other ones are called Angelica, Diana, Violanta – well, I mean, anyone can be called Angelica, or Diana, or Violanta, but she, only she deserves a name so solemn and

deep and thrilling. I expect you want to know if she's beautiful, Eugénie?

EUGÉNIE (*just coming in*): Who's beautiful, sir?

AUGUSTE: The gentleman is talking about Bertha, my dear,
Countess Bertha.

EUGÉNIE: Oh – yes. Beautiful, is she beautiful?

HANS: Is she beautiful. Listen, Eugénie. I am appointed by the
the king to select horses for his stable; and I might add that
I have a keen eye for points in women too; not a fault escapes
me. For instance, the lady Angelica has a flaw in her right
thumb-nail. Violanta has a speck of gold in her left eye. Only
Bertha is perfect.

EUGÉNIE: Oh, we *are* glad, sir.

AUGUSTE: I should think that's rather nice, though, a speck of
gold in the eye?

EUGÉNIE: Be quiet, Auguste.

HANS: Nice, you think? Oh, no, not for long. You might find it
amusing for a day, two days, perhaps. You'd enjoy looking at
it by moonlight, by torch-light – but really, by the third day
you'd be sick to death of it, you'd rather she had a fly in her
eye!

AUGUSTE: What's it like, though? A bit of mica?

EUGÉNIE: Oh, you and your speck of gold, it's getting on our
nerves. Let the gentleman go on!

HANS: Yes, I must say, Auguste, you seem to have taken a remarkable fancy to Violanta! Now Violanta, let me tell you,
when she goes hunting on the white mare, she brings the poor
beast to its knees in no time, splits 'em open, and just to make
an even prettier picture of it, dusts the wounds with charcoal.
Then again, if dear Violanta has to take a candlestick to the
Queen, she invariably contrives to slip on the marble floor and
go flat on her back. And if the old duke takes her by the
hand and starts telling her one of his funny stories, as likely
as not Violanta will start to cry.

AUGUSTE: Violanta, sir? Cry?

HANS: I imagine you'll now want to know what effect crying
has on that speck of gold.

EUGÉNIE: I'm sure he does, sir. Once he gets an idea into his head . . .!

HANS: He'll think about it till the day he sees Bertha – which won't be long now, my dear friends, because you will both come to my wedding. I invite you here and now! Bertha promised to marry me on the one condition that I returned from this forest; and if I do return, it will be entirely thanks to you. And then, Auguste, you'll see your Violanta, with her great big mouth and tiny ears and little Grecian nose and chestnut hair – and you'll see how she matches up to my dark angel! – Well, Eugénie, my dear, I think you'd better go and fetch that trout of mine. We don't want it over-poached, do we?

The door opens, and Ondine appears. She stands motionless on the threshold.

ONDINE: Oh, you're beautiful!

AUGUSTE: Why, you cheeky little wretch –

ONDINE: Isn't he beautiful?

AUGUSTE: This is our daughter, sir. I'm afraid she doesn't know much about manners.

ONDINE: It's just that I'm so happy to know that men are as lovely as that. I'm not frightened now!

AUGUSTE: Will you be quiet!

ONDINE: But I'm excited!

AUGUSTE: She's only fifteen, sir. Please try to forgive her.

ONDINE: I knew there must be some good reason for being a girl. Men are so beautiful!

AUGUSTE: Ondine, please, you're annoying the gentleman.

ONDINE: I'm not, you know. He likes me. Look at his face! What's your name?

AUGUSTE: For heaven's sake, girl, you can't address a knight like that!

ONDINE (*coming up to the Knight*): He's so lovely, though! Look at his ears, daddy – like little shells! I couldn't treat that ear like a stranger. Who do you belong to, little ear? What's his name?

HANS: His name is Hans.

ONDINE: I should have known. When you're happy and you want to say so, you say Hans. . . .

HANS: Hans von Wittenstein . . .

ONDINE: And when it's a dewy morning, and your breath goes out like a cloud, bearing all your sadness with it, you say Hans . . .

HANS: Von Wittenstein zu Wittenstein.

ONDINE: What a beautiful name! And the way it echoes itself, that's so pretty! What have you come for? To take me away?

AUGUSTE: That's quite enough from you. Go to your room this minute.

ONDINE: Oh, do – take me! Carry me away!

Eugénie returns with the trout, cooked.

EUGÉNIE: Here's your poached trout, sir. Just you settle down to that. It'll be better than listening to this mad daughter of ours.

ONDINE: Did you say poached?

HANS: Mmm – it's magnificent!

ONDINE: Mother, did you *dare* to poach a trout?

EUGÉNIE: Be quiet. It's done now, anyway.

ONDINE: Oh, my poor darling trout, you've been swimming all your life to the cold springs . . .

AUGUSTE: Now you're not going to start making a fuss about a trout . . .

ONDINE: They call themselves my parents – and they took you and threw you alive into boiling water!

HANS: I asked them to, little girl.

ONDINE: *You* did? Yes, I should have known that too. I can see, now I look at you closer. You're a beast, aren't you?

EUGÉNIE: Oh, sir, forgive us!

ONDINE: You don't know anything about anything, do you? And they call that being brave and chivalrous! You go looking for giants that don't exist, and if you find a little living creature leaping in clear water, all you want to do is poach it!

HANS: And eat it, child! It's delicious!

ONDINE: Well, it won't be delicious much longer! (*She takes the dish and throws the trout out of the window.*) Go on and eat it now! Good-bye . . .

EUGÉNIE: Ondine! Where are you going?

ONDINE: There's someone out there who hates men and wants to tell me all about them. I always refused to listen, I had my own ideas – but that's over now; now I'll listen to him.

EUGÉNIE: You're not going out again, at this hour!

ONDINE: Yes, and in a minute I'll know everything; I'll know just what they're like and what they're capable of – and so much the worse for you.

AUGUSTE: Have I got to stop you by force, then?

She slips away from him.

ONDINE: I know already that they're liars, and the beautiful ones are really ugly, and the brave ones are cowards. I know I hate them!

HANS: What if they love you, little girl?

ONDINE (*stopping, but not turning round*): What did he say?

HANS: Oh, nothing – nothing.

ONDINE (*in the doorway*): Say it again.

HANS: Suppose they love you.

ONDINE: I hate them.

She disappears into the night.

HANS: Charming manners. Congratulations.

AUGUSTE: God knows, sir, we spend our whole time telling her off.

HANS: Try thrashing her.

EUGÉNIE: Try catching her, sir!

HANS: Well, shut her up and give her no dessert.

AUGUSTE: She never eats anyway.

HANS: I envy her. Personally, I'm famishing. Go and poach me another trout, will you, if only to serve her right.

AUGUSTE: I'm afraid it was the last one, sir. We have got a smoked ham, though. Eugénie will cut you a few slices of that instead.

HANS: Oh, she allows you to kill pigs, does she? What a bit of luck!

Exit Eugénie.

AUGUSTE: I'm very sorry she annoyed you, sir.

HANS: She annoyed me because she said I was a beast, and I am. The trouble with us men, my old fisherman, is that we're all the same; vain as gamecocks. So when she said I was "beautiful", I was pleased, and when she said I was a coward I was angry, although I know perfectly well I'm neither.

AUGUSTE: It's very good of you to take it so well.

HANS: Oh, I assure you I'm not taking it well, I'm furious. I'm always furious with myself when others are in the wrong!

EUGÉNIE (*calling*): I can't find the ham anywhere, Auguste.

Auguste goes out to the kitchen.
Ondine comes in and goes softly up to the table behind the Knight, who is warming his hands at the fire and doesn't immediately turn round.

ONDINE: My name's Ondine.

HANS: It's a very pretty name.

ONDINE: Hans and Ondine. I think those are the nicest names in the world, don't you?

HANS: What about Ondine and Hans?

ONDINE: Oh, no! Hans first, he's the boy, he's got to go first. He gives the orders. Ondine's only the girl. She comes one step behind him; she doesn't even speak.

HANS: Not speak? How on earth does she manage that?

ONDINE: Hans is always a step ahead of her: in processions . . . at court . . . into the grave. Hans has to die first; it's horrible. But Ondine soon catches him up. She kills herself . . .

HANS: What are you talking about!

ONDINE: There's one awful little minute to get through, just after he dies. But it doesn't take long.

HANS: It's easy to talk about death at your age. It doesn't mean much, luckily.

ONDINE: Oh, doesn't it? Well, you just kill yourself and see; you'll see if I don't kill myself.

HANS: I've never felt less like killing myself.

ONDINE: Well, then, tell me you don't love me! You'll see. . . .

HANS: Look, you've only known me a few minutes, and here you are wanting to die for me! I thought we weren't speaking, anyway, because of that trout.

ONDINE: Oh, that. Serves it right for being so silly. It should have kept away from men if it didn't want to be caught. I'm silly too, aren't I? I'm caught now . . .

HANS: In spite of what your mysterious friend out there told you about men?

ONDINE: He was talking rubbish.

HANS: Ah, I see. You were answering your own questions.

ONDINE: Don't laugh about it. He's not far away, and he's terrible.

HANS: You're not going to tell me you're afraid of anyone or anything.

ONDINE: Yes, I am, I'm afraid of you leaving me. He said you'd leave me. Still, he said you weren't beautiful, so if he can be wrong about that he can be wrong about the other.

HANS: What about you, then? Are you beautiful or ugly?

ONDINE: Oh, that's up to you; I'll be what you make me. I'd much rather be beautiful, though, I'd much rather you loved me. I'd like to be the most beautiful . . .

HANS: You're a little liar, you know. When you were hating me just now for all you were worth, it only made you more beautiful. Did he say anything else?

ONDINE: Yes, he said if I kissed you, I'd be lost. I don't know why, because I wasn't even thinking of it – then.

HANS: And now you are?

ONDINE: Oh, yes; desperately.

HANS: There's no harm in thinking.

ONDINE: You'll be kissed tonight, don't worry. It's so lovely to wait, that's all. We'll remember this time later: the time when you hadn't kissed me.

HANS: My dear child . . .

ONDINE: The time when you hadn't told me you loved me, either. But you needn't wait any more. Come on, tell me. Here I am; my hands are shaking. Tell me.

HANS: Do you think one simply says it, just like that?

ONDINE: Oh, say it! Command me! Are all men as slow as you? I only want to do the right thing. I should be on your knees, shouldn't I?

HANS: I don't recommend it for comfort, not when I'm in full armour. Besides, it takes me a good ten minutes just to get these shoulder things unscrewed.

ONDINE: I know a way to undo armour.

The armour instantly falls apart. Ondine leaps on to Hans' knees.

HANS: Look here, you're mad! What about my arms, anyway? You don't imagine I open them to the first comer, do you?

ONDINE: Oh, I know how to open arms as well.

Involuntarily, the Knight opens his arms.

And close them.

He closes his arms. A female voice is heard outside.

VOICE: Ondine!

ONDINE (*turning furiously to the window*): Shut up! Nobody asked for your opinion!

VOICE: Ondine!

ONDINE: I don't poke my nose into your business, do I? And you never consulted me about *your* marriage!

VOICE: Ondine!

ONDINE: A fine husband, that old seal of yours! If you don't mind nostrils without a nose, that is. He got you for a string of pearls, and they didn't even match.

HANS: Who are you talking to, Ondine?

ONDINE: Oh, neighbours.

HANS: But I thought this was the only house round here?

ONDINE: There are spiteful women everywhere. They're jealous of me.

ANOTHER VOICE: Ondine!

ONDINE: Yes, you too! That dolphin only had to spout a bit of water in front of you, and you threw yourself into his flippers!

HANS: But they're charming, these voices.

ONDINE: No, they're not, it's just my name that's charming! Oh, Hans, kiss me, and make them permanently green with envy. As if you could help yourself!

A MALE VOICE: Ondine!

ONDINE: You're too late. Go away!

HANS: Is that the friend you were talking about?

ONDINE (*shouting*): I'm on his knee! He loves me!

A MALE VOICE: Ondine!

ONDINE: I can't hear you. Your voice isn't getting through. Anyway, it's too late, the thing's settled. I'm his mistress, do you hear, his mistress! Don't you understand? It's another name they call their wives.

A noise from the kitchen doorway.

HANS (*gently pushing Ondine off his knee*): Your parents are coming, Ondine.

ONDINE: Oh, you know it too! I'm sure I didn't teach you.

HANS: Teach me what, little creature?

ONDINE: How to open your arms.

Auguste and Eugénie enter.

EUGÉNIE: Please, sir, I don't know how to tell you, but we seem to have lost the ham!

ONDINE: Yes, I know, I hid it so that you'd leave us in peace.

AUGUSTE: Oh, you shameless girl . . .

ONDINE: And I haven't wasted my time, either. He's going to marry me, my dear parents! The brave Sir Hans is going to marry me!

AUGUSTE: Stop talking nonsense and help your mother.

ONDINE: That's right. Give me the cloth, Mother, I'm going to wait on Hans. From now on I am his servant, he is my lord and master.

AUGUSTE: I've got a bottle of wine up from the cellar, sir, and would be very happy to drink it with you, if you've no objection.

ONDINE: A mirror, Sir Hans, to comb your hair before the meal?

EUGÉNIE: Wherever did you get that gold mirror from, Ondine?

ONDINE: Water for your hands, my lord and master?

HANS: What a superb bowl! Even the King would be jealous of that.

AUGUSTE: First time we've seen it, sir.

ONDINE: You shall teach me all my duties, Sir Hans. I must be your model servant every hour of the day and night.

HANS: Day and night, my little Ondine! You'll have a job waking me up; I sleep like a log.

ONDINE (*sitting by Hans and clinging to him*): Oh, good! Tell me how to pull your hair and drag you out of sleep, and how to force your eyes open, with your head still struggling, and how to get your teeth apart, and kiss you and breathe life into you.

EUGÉNIE: Ondine! The plates!

ONDINE: Oh, mother, *you* lay the table. Sir Hans is teaching me how to wake him up. Let's try it, shall we, Sir Hans? Pretend you're asleep . . .

HANS: How can I, with this marvellous smell of food?

ONDINE: Wake up, little Hans! A kiss for sunrise! One for the darkness and one for the dawn . . .

AUGUSTE: Don't mind her, sir. It's only baby talk.

EUGÉNIE: She's still a child. She gets these fancies.

HANS: Now this is what I really call ham!

AUGUSTE: Smoked in juniper, sir.

ONDINE: I shouldn't have woken you up! Why wake someone you love? While he's asleep, he's all yours, but as soon as his eyes are open, he can escape! Go to sleep, my sweet Sir Hans . . .

HANS (*being offered more ham*): Well, one more slice, if you press me.

ONDINE: I'm so clumsy, that's the trouble! In the morning I'll put you to sleep instead of waking you, and at night I'll start waking you up when you should be going to sleep.

EUGÉNIE: Oh, yes, you'll make a fine wife, you will!

AUGUSTE: If you'd just be quiet for a moment, Ondine, there's something I'd like to say.

ONDINE: I *will* make a fine wife, too! You think you're wonderful just because you can smoke a ham. I don't call *that* being a wife!

HANS: Don't you now? What is, then?

ONDINE: Being everything my lord and master loves and everything he is, being his pride and his humility. Being my husband's shoes, his breath, the pommel of his sword. Being his tears, his dreams. Being the food on his plate . . .

HANS: Perfectly salted. Delicious.

ONDINE: Yes, go on, eat me, finish me!

EUGÉNIE: Ondine, your father's trying to speak.

AUGUSTE (*raising his glass*): My lord, as you are doing us the honour of spending the night under our roof . . .

ONDINE: A thousand nights. A hundred thousand nights.

AUGUSTE: Allow me to wish you the greatest triumph a knight ever had, and drink to the lady of your heart . . .

ONDINE: Oh, thank you, father!

AUGUSTE: Who awaits you in fear and trembling . . .

ONDINE: Not any more. She's finished trembling now.

AUGUSTE: And who bears the name you have called fair above all other names, although myself I rather fancy Violanta, but I know I'm inclined to favour Violanta because of that . . .

EUGÉNIE: Yes, yes, we know, that'll do.

AUGUSTE: To the most fair and noble lady, your dark angel, your betrothed, the lady Bertha!

ONDINE (*rising in panic*): What did you say?

AUGUSTE: I'm only repeating what the knight told me himself!

ONDINE: Then you're lying! He's lying! Anyway, *I'm* called Bertha now, didn't you know?

EUGÉNIE: He doesn't mean you, dear.

AUGUSTE: The knight is betrothed to Countess Bertha and he's going to marry her when he gets home. That's right, sir, isn't it? Everyone knows that.

ONDINE: Then everyone's lying.

HANS: Now look, Ondine . . .

ONDINE: Oh, he's tearing himself away from his ham! Well, is there a Bertha, yes or no?

HANS: Just give me time to explain!

ONDINE: Is there a Bertha, yes or no?

HANS: Yes, there is. Or at any rate there was.

ONDINE: So it's true what he told me about men! They ensnare you and entice you on to their knees, they kiss you till your lips hurt, they rub their dirty hands all over you, and all the time they're thinking about a black woman called Bertha!

HANS: You know I never did that, Ondine!

ONDINE (*biting her own arm*): Yes, you did! I'm a mass of bruises. Look (*To her parents.*) – look at my arm – he did that!

HANS (*to the parents*): You don't believe this nonsense?

ONDINE: I'll be your pride and your humility, he said! I'll be your naked feet, I'll be your food and drink – you heard him, mother, those were his very words! And all the things I had to do for him! Spend the whole day till midnight waking him up, die for him the minute after his death! Well, did you say that, yes or no? And all the time he had the image in his heart of this waxwork demon he calls his dark angel . . .

HANS: My dear Ondine!

ONDINE: Oh, I hate you, I spit you out of me!

HANS: Will you just listen . . .

ONDINE: I can see her from here, the black angel, with her shadowy moustache. Yes, and I can see her naked, with all that nasty black hair everywhere; and I expect she's got a little curly tail tucked up her corset, that sort of black angel always does.

HANS: Ondine, if you don't mind . . .

ONDINE: Don't touch me. I'm going to throw myself in the lake.

She opens the door. It is pelting with rain.

HANS (*rising*): I rather think, Ondine, that Bertha has ceased to exist.

ONDINE: There, you see! They betray their Berthas too. Honestly, my poor parents are blushing at your behaviour.

AUGUSTE: Don't you believe her, my lord!

ONDINE: If you don't go away this moment, I'll never come
back. (*She turns.*) *What* did you say just now?

HANS: That Bertha had ceased to exist.

ONDINE: Liar. Good-bye.

She disappears.

HANS: Ondine!

He runs out to look for her.

AUGUSTE: Well, I've made a nice mess of things.

EUGÉNIE: You certainly have.

AUGUSTE: I think I'd better tell him everything, don't you?

EUGÉNIE: I think you'd better, yes.

Hans returns, dripping.

HANS: She's not your daughter, is she?

EUGÉNIE: No, sir.

AUGUSTE: We had a daughter, sir, but she was stolen when she
was only six months old.

HANS: Who did you get Ondine from? Where do they live?

AUGUSTE: We found her, sir, by the side of the lake. No one
ever claimed her.

HANS: In fact, you will be the people to ask for her hand?

EUGÉNIE: She calls us her parents, sir.

HANS: Well, my good friends, I ask you for Ondine's hand in
marriage!

AUGUSTE: But . . . but my lord, are you in your right mind?

HANS: My right mind? You're not suggesting that your wine
has turned my head, are you?

AUGUSTE: Oh, no, sir! It's the most reliable little Moselle.

HANS: My mind has never been righter; and I've never been
surer of what I was saying. I ask you for Ondine's hand, and
it's her hand I'm thinking of, no one else's. I want that hand
to lead me to church, to battle, even to death.

AUGUSTE: One can't have two fiancées, though, sir. You can't
hold that many hands.

HANS: Which fiancée came first? Bertha, you think?

AUGUSTE: That's what you said, sir.

HANS: And do you know Bertha, that you champion her cause
so keenly? I know her now. Since I met Ondine I feel I really
know her.

AUGUSTE: You've told us how perfect she is.

HANS: Yes, apart from that dreadful laugh and a slight tendency
to froth at the mouth, she is indeed perfect.

AUGUSTE: I thought the first law of knights errant was to keep
faith . . .

HANS: With their quest, yes. And it looks as if I'll be the first
one that is, because, by God, we knights errant have been
a pretty naïve lot up to now. We discovered palaces, and crept
home to our villas. We rescued Andromeda, and retired with
a pension at sixty. We stole the giant's treasure, and were
therefore excused fish on Friday. Well, as far as I'm concerned, that's finished. I refuse to treat the quest as a sort of
bank-clerk's course in riding and fantasy. In future I'm going
to explore and plunder and marry on my own account: and I
shall marry Ondine.

AUGUSTE: But my lord, it's wrong!

HANS: Wrong? Look here, Auguste, just answer me a plain
question. Once upon a time there was a knight who set out to
look for one thing in this world that wasn't stale, flat and un-
profitable. Suddenly, on the shores of a lake, he met a girl
called Ondine. She turned pewter plates into gold. She went
out in the storm and never got wet. And not only was she the
most beautiful girl he had ever seen in his life, but he felt that
she was everything gay and tender and brave. He felt that
she could die for him, or do things for him no other woman
ever could, walk through fire, dive to the bottom of the sea
and fly like a bird. . . . And having seen and felt all this,
he bowed deeply and rode off home to marry a black-haired
girl called Bertha. Now, Auguste, what was that knight's name?

AUGUSTE: You're not putting it fairly.

HANS: I asked you a straight question and you haven't the
courage to reply. He was an idiot, though, wasn't he?

EUGÉNIE: But sir, you're engaged already.

HANS: My dear Eugénie, you don't seriously imagine that if you refuse me Ondine I shall still marry Bertha?

AUGUSTE: My lord, if Bertha loves you, I expect she'll learn to swim and dive and fly for you . . .

HANS: What a hope. Girls in love are even more silly and damp in the rain and inclined to streaming colds and twisted ankles than they are normally. Haven't you ever seen the bridegroom in church looking at his happy bride and wondering what on earth has produced this ghastly alteration? The awful truth is, she loves him!

EUGÉNIE: Auguste, tell the gentleman!

HANS: Yes, do! If you have any just cause or impediment, let me have it quickly!

AUGUSTE: My lord, you ask us for Ondine's hand. It's a great honour for us, but, you see, we can't give you what isn't ours . . .

HANS: Have you any idea who her parents are?

AUGUSTE: Well, sir, there's no question of parents, that's the whole trouble with Ondine. If we hadn't adopted her, she'd have found some way to live and grow up just the same. She never needed our hugs and kisses, and besides, once it starts raining, you can't keep her in the house. She never goes to bed, either, but lots of times we've found her fast asleep on the lake – yes, just like that, floating. I don't know – I suppose children have a sort of understanding with Nature by instinct, or maybe Ondine's own nature's bound up in it, somehow, but there's powers about that girl, no doubt of it!

HANS: Oh yes, she's the spirit of youth.

AUGUSTE: I should say she is! When I married you, Eugénie, my old dear, you were her age and you were pretty too, and adventurous, and yet the lake never changed for you – it was the same great stupid old lake I'd always known, with its idiotic flooding in winter, and those dirty storms. But, you know, sir, ever since we've had Ondine, it's changed completely . . .

HANS: It can't have. You're just a better fisherman, that's all. The advantages of age.

AUGUSTE: Oh, bless you, sir, no, it's not just that. It's something queer all right. I mean, to have a lake that never busts your nets up, and always gives you your same haul of fish, not one more nor less, and even if you find there's a hole in the bottom of your boat, like I did yesterday, not a drop comes in – well, you can't say that isn't a queer sort of lake, sir. I've never bunged a hole with water before!

HANS: Well, what do you suggest, then? Shall I ask the lake for her hand in marriage?

AUGUSTE: Please, sir, don't joke about it!

HANS: If all the rivers and lakes in the world are to be my fathers- and mothers-in-law, I shall be delighted! I've always got on very well with Nature.

AUGUSTE: Yes, but do take care, sir! It's quite true, Nature has a soft spot for humans, she's prejudiced in our favour, you might say; there's something about us that tickles her fancy. She's as proud of a nice house, or a trim boat, as a dog with a new collar. She puts up with all sorts of things from him that she never would from any other species, and all the other animals and plants are under this same blackmail. Every poisonous plant or reptile either scuttles away when man's around, or gives itself away by its colouring. But if he once gets on the wrong side of Nature, my word, he'd better look out for himself!

HANS: And you think Nature would object to my marrying Ondine, do you? But she didn't object to your adopting her. Come on, let me have her!

AUGUSTE: Let you have Ondine, sir! Where is she now, anyway? How do I know if she'll even come back? Plenty of times she's disappeared, and we've thought we'd never see her again; we've looked everywhere, there's not been a trace of her. She's never wanted any other clothes, any toys or anything; so when she goes, she leaves nothing behind. It's as if she'd never been here in the first place – as if you'd dreamed her. That's all she is, a dream. There's no Ondine, really. Do you believe in her, Eugénie?

EUGÉNIE: I believe you're starting to talk nonsense, Auguste.

It's that Moselle of his, sir. It's a bit deceptive. Like his specks of gold, sir, you know!

AUGUSTE: Ah, that speck of gold, now!

HANS: Let's forget it, shall we? And about Ondine – I'm beginning to wonder myself – perhaps you're right – I'm in a dream like you.

AUGUSTE: Of course, I remember seeing her, all right, our little Ondine; I remember her voice and the way she laughed, I can still see her throwing your trout away, a good half-pound trout; but I won't be surprised if she never comes back now, and all we see of her will be a few little storms and lightnings, and her only signs of affection will be in waves round our feet, or rain on our cheeks – or a deep-sea fish in my pike-trap, I wouldn't wonder . . .

EUGÉNIE: Please forgive us, sir. He only has to drink a glass nowadays, and he starts wandering!

AUGUSTE: Oh, there's plenty I haven't said yet. What about the shore, now, where we found her in her cradle, do you remember? It had the marks of bodies all over it, like loving couples leave in the sand, but there were hundreds and thousands of them, as if thousands of couples had been making love by the lake, and Ondine were their child . . .

EUGÉNIE: There he goes again!

AUGUSTE: Never a toe-mark though, remember that? Hundreds of bodies and not a single foot!

EUGÉNIE: I think we ought to go to bed now, sir, if you don't mind!

AUGUSTE: But all those fresh hollows in the sand, glistening with mica and mother-of-pearl!

EUGÉNIE: Oh, he's back on his mica! He's tired out, that's his trouble. Come along, now, Auguste! We'll talk about Ondine tomorrow.

AUGUSTE: Ah, if she comes back!

HANS: Well, whether she does or not, I'm going to wait.

The old couple go out and Hans settles back in the armchair. Slowly the back wall of the cabin becomes transparent and an Ondine appears.

THE ONDINE: Knight, fair knight, take me!

HANS: What?

THE ONDINE: Kiss me!

HANS: I beg your pardon?

THE ONDINE: Kiss me, fair knight!

HANS: Kiss you? For heaven's sake, why?

THE ONDINE: Shall I come to you naked, fair knight?

HANS: If you want; it's none of my business.

THE ONDINE: Do you want me on my back, or on my side?

ONDINE (*appearing*): Oh, you're so stupid! If you knew how silly you looked!

The Ondine disappears.

HANS (*taking Ondine in his arms*): My dear Ondine, what on earth is going on?

ONDINE: Oh, it's one of those jealous neighbours. They can't bear you loving me! They're saying that anyone can have you, any little slut can seduce you . . .

HANS: Let her try, my darling!

Another Ondine appears.

SECOND ONDINE: Don't touch me!

HANS: What on earth's she talking about?

SECOND ONDINE: Don't touch me, fair knight! I'm not that sort of girl.

HANS: What sort?

ONDINE: They think that if a direct attack fails, the quickest way is playing it innocent. They say men are all the same.

SECOND ONDINE: Don't undo my hair, fair knight! Don't stroke my thighs!

HANS: She's not bad, that one. Have they sent the best looking?

ONDINE: No, the cleverest. Oh Hans, darling Hans, take me in your arms. Look at that silly fool! Don't women look stupid when they throw themselves at a man! – All right, you've lost too! You can go now!

The Ondine vanishes and another rises up.

HANS: Good lord, another!

ONDINE: Oh, no, that's past a joke! Only two are supposed to come at a time!

HANS: Let her stay. She's saying something.

ONDINE: No, make her go away! It's the Song of the Three Sisters. None of our boys can resist it. Oh, please . . .

HANS: Go on, young lady.

THIRD ONDINE:

> Hans Wittenstein zu Wittenstein,
> Life is Death when you are gone.
> Alles was ist dein ist mein.
> Love me, leave me not alone.

HANS: Oh, very nice. Splendid.

ONDINE: What do you mean, splendid?

HANS: You know – simple, charming. The Sirens' Song must be rather like that.

ONDINE: It is, exactly. They copied it – oh, here's the second one. Don't listen!

Another Ondine has appeared next to the third.

HANS: Why, don't you trust me?

ONDINE: Darling Hans, don't listen, please!

HANS: Ulysses' bonds were nothing to your arms!

ONDINE (*to the fourth Ondine*): All right, then! Hurry up and get it over!

FOURTH ONDINE:

> Sometimes when on your bed you lie
> I think of you so longingly
> That in your sleep you crush my breath
> And wake me from a dream of death.

ONDINE: Have you quite finished?

HANS: Not yet, I'm glad to say. Here comes number five!

ONDINE: But can't you see, she hasn't even got legs, separate ones I mean, and she's got a tail. Ask her to do the splits and you'll see. Now I'm a real woman – I can do it – look!

HANS: Really, Ondine! – All right, young lady!

ONDINE: It's not much fun, you know, hearing other people say what you're thinking yourself and can't say.

HANS: That's the common fate of man, my dear; all except Wolfram von Eschenbach, who tends to say what he can't think . . . Ssh!

FIFTH ONDINE:

> At nightfall, when I light the fire
> To warm the shepherd and his dogs,
> I sorrow for your weak desire,
> While flames lick fiercely round the logs.

HANS: Oh, delightful! Encore! You must learn that by heart, Ondine, for our long winter evenings.

ONDINE: Go away, do you hear? That's quite enough!

AN ONDINE: You've lost, Ondine! You've lost!

HANS: What have you lost?

AN ONDINE: Her bet! He's holding you in his arms, Ondine, but he's watching me. He's kissing you, but he's listening to me. He'll deceive you.

ONDINE: Why, don't you know how men like to declare their love through a third person, some idiot like you, who sings or recites? They call them poets. That's all you are, a poet! An idiot!

AN ONDINE: If you don't mind him deceiving you with music and beauty, that's fine! You've lost!

ONDINE: No I haven't, I've won! He thinks you're silly.

AN ONDINE: I can tell them you accept, then, can I? The pact holds good?

HANS: What pact?

ONDINE: Yes, you can. You can tell envy and vanity . . .

AN ONDINE: I will!

ONDINE: Tell the frogs and snakes and rats and fish and lizards . . .

AN ONDINE: See how you like being a mammal!

HANS: What on earth are you both talking about?

ONDINE: Go on! Go and tell them!

AN ONDINE: They'll know in a minute. Do you want *him* to know too?

ONDINE: Tell him I hate him.

The Ondine disappears.

HANS: My darling, what a scene! What temper!

ONDINE: Yes. The family! (*They are seated again, and she embraces him.*) So I've really got you, this time?

HANS: Body and soul. . . .

ONDINE: No more struggling, no more silly words . . .

HANS: Crippled with happiness.

ONDINE: You took just twenty minutes to land. A pike takes thirty.

HANS: It took my whole life. I must have swallowed the hook in my cradle, and you've been drawing me in, sitting or sailing or riding, ever since, drawing me to you.

ONDINE: And you're sure it's in your heart, not just your lips or the flesh of your cheek?

HANS: It's in too deep for you ever to get it out.

ONDINE: I suppose you couldn't drop these fishy metaphors, and say you love me?

HANS (*dropping on one knee*): Certainly. I love you. There!

ONDINE: You've said that before, haven't you?

HANS: I've said similar things, but they meant the opposite.

ONDINE: You said them often?

HANS: To all the ones I didn't love.

ONDINE: Tell me who! Let me know who I've defeated, who you're leaving for me!

HANS: Oh, no one really. Just women, that's all.

ONDINE: The bad ones, the mean ones, the ones with moustaches?

HANS: The good ones, the beautiful!

ONDINE: Oh, Hans! I wanted to offer you the universe, and all I've done is take half of it away . . . the nicest half. One day you'll hate me for it.

HANS: They're nothing compared to you. You'll see them soon . . .

ONDINE: Where will I see them?

HANS: On their own ground, in the riding-schools, at the side of wells, among the velvet Greeks. We'll set off tomorrow.

ONDINE: Do you want to leave our little house and lake so soon?

HANS: I want the world to see its most perfect creature, because that's what you are.

ONDINE: I thought I might be. But will the world have eyes to see it?

HANS: You'll see the world, at any rate. You can't go on in ignorance of one another. It's a fine thing, Ondine, the world.

ONDINE: Oh, Hans, there's only one thing I want to know about the world. Do you stay together there, for ever?

HANS: What do you mean?

ONDINE: Suppose there's a king and queen, and they love each other: do they ever part?

HANS: I don't know what you're talking about, Ondine.

ONDINE: I'll try to explain. Take dogfish, for instance. Not that I like dogfish all that much. You always think they're hoarse, but they aren't really, it's only that they spend so much time with their mouths open, their vocal chords get salted up . . .

HANS: Are these dogfish getting us anywhere?

ONDINE: Yes, they're my example! You see, Hans, once a pair of dogfish have joined up, they never part company ever again, and they swim for thousands and thousands of miles, only a finger's breadth apart, with the female's head just behind the male's. Do the King and Queen live as close together as that? I mean, with the Queen just behind the King, as she should be?

HANS: That wouldn't be easy. The King and Queen each have their own rooms, and carriages and gardens . . .

ONDINE: What a horrible word that is, "each"! Why do they, anyway?

HANS: Because they have different sorts of business and leisure . . .

ONDINE: But so do dogfish, Hans – terribly different! They have to eat, you know! They have to go hunting, chase after shoals of millions of herrings, which scatter before them in a million flashes of silver. Yes, millions of reasons to turn to right or left, away from one another. But they never do, they stay side by side and parallel their whole life long, and not even a skate could come between them.

207

HANS: I'm afraid two or three whales could come between the King and Queen, several times a day. The King has to keep an eye on his ministers, and the Queen on her gardeners. Two different currents carry them apart.

ONDINE: Yes, well, if we're on currents, remember dogfish have currents to cope with too, dozens and dozens! Some are warm and some are icy. And perhaps the male dogfish prefers the cold ones and the female the warm ones – and I mean, they're strong, these currents, stronger than tides, strong enough to separate battleships; but they don't separate those dogfish, not one inch.

HANS: Which only goes to show how different men are from dogfish.

ONDINE: Yes, but you won't leave me, will you, not now, not even for a second, an inch? Because now that I love you, my loneliness begins two steps away from you.

HANS: Yes, Ondine.

ONDINE: And we can't hurt each other by rubbing together, only by being apart?

HANS: What are you trying to say, my little Ondine?

ONDINE: Listen to me, Hans, please. I know somebody who could join us for ever, somebody very powerful, who could weld us together like Siamese twins. Shall I call him now?

HANS: But what about our arms, Ondine? Don't they count for anything?

ONDINE: Men only use their arms to get free. Oh no, the more I think, the more sure I am that it's the only way to stop a wife being at the mercy of a whim or a desire. My friend's very near, and I know he'll do it, if you'll just say the word.

HANS: I'm sure those dogfish of yours aren't welded together.

ONDINE: No, I know, but they aren't out in the world. It would only be a bond of flesh to hold us in place. I've thought about it a lot. It would be quite supple, it wouldn't stop us making love.

HANS: And how about war, little Ondine?

ONDINE: Oh, I'd go to war with you. We'd be the two-headed

knight! The enemy would run for his life. I expect we'd be quite famous. I'll call him, shall I?

HANS: And if one of us died?

ONDINE: That will be all right; I've thought of that too. They won't be able to undo the bond. But I won't be any trouble, I promise, I'll shut up my eyes and ears, and you won't even notice I'm still hanging on. Shall I call him now?

HANS: No. No, I think we'll try as we are to begin with, and see what happens. You're not afraid about tonight, anyway?

ONDINE: Yes, I am. And I know just what you're thinking. She's right, of course (you're thinking), and of course I'm going to hold her tight all the day and all the night, but just occasionally, just for a second or two, I might want to leave her to have a little walk by myself, or play dice . . .

HANS: Or go and see my horse . . .

ONDINE: That's right, laugh about it! I know you'll be off to see your rotten old horse the moment I'm asleep! You're just saying to yourself, wait until she's asleep, the dear sweet little angel whom I'm not going to leave for a second, wait till she's asleep and then I'll take a minute or two off to go and see my old horse. Well, you're going to have a long time to wait, and you'll soon be asleep yourself.

HANS: I think not, my darling. I shan't sleep for sheer happiness. And besides, I really *shall* have to go and see my horse, you know; for one thing, we'll be leaving at dawn, and for another, I always tell him everything.

ONDINE: Oh, yes? We'll see about that!

HANS: Now what are you doing?

ONDINE: I'm making my own bond for tonight. You won't mind if I put this strap round us, will you.

HANS: No, my darling.

ONDINE: And this chain?

HANS: No, my sweet.

ONDINE: And this net? Of course you'll take it off as soon as I'm asleep. Look, I'm yawning already. Goodnight, my love.

HANS: Of course I will. But I promise you no man and woman were ever tied so close as we are.

Suddenly Ondine sits up again.

ONDINE: Oh yes? All right, then, *you* sleep!

She makes passes over the Knight, who falls back asleep.

AN ONDINE: Farewell, Ondine.

ONDINE: Take care of the two hundred wounded salmon for me, and the young fry – lead the two shoals under the deep-sea cascade at dawn, and under the seaweed at noon. And look out for that river Rhine; it's too heavy for them.

AN ONDINE: Farewell, Ondine.

ONDINE: You must keep watch over the pearls. You'll find them in the hall of grottoes. I made a pattern out of them – leave it there a few days. It won't mean anything to you; it's only a name, and you can't read.

KING OF THE ONDINES: Ondine, for the last time, don't betray us! Don't join the world of men!

ONDINE: I'm going to join *one* man.

KING OF THE ONDINES: He'll deceive you. He'll leave you.

ONDINE: I don't believe you.

KING OF THE ONDINES: The pact holds, then, you little fool! You accept the pact, if he deceives you! You have shamed our lake, betrayed your duty!

HANS (*turning in his sleep*): Ondine – your beauty!

ONDINE: Thank you, Hans. You see: I have two mouths to speak with now.

Curtain

ACT TWO

The hall of honour in the royal palace. The Chamberlain is giving instructions to the Superintendent of Theatres, the Seal Trainer, and the Magician, who is in fact, the King of the Ondines.

CHAMBERLAIN: Gentlemen, I appeal to your powers of invention and improvisation. In a few moments His Majesty will be giving audience in this hall to the Ritter von Wittenstein, who has finally decided, after three months' honeymoon, to present his young bride at court. It is Her Majesty's wish that the ceremony shall be followed by some entertainment . . . Well, my lord Superintendent of the Royal Theatres, what have you in mind?

SUPERINTENDENT: I thought perhaps "Salammbo".

CHAMBERLAIN: Oh, but it's so depressing, "Salammbo"; and besides, you did it last Sunday at the Margrave's party.

SUPERINTENDENT: It is rather on the sad side, but at least it is ready.

CHAMBERLAIN: More so than "Orpheus", which the Royal Zoo is providing with wolves and badgers? Or "Adam and Eve", which doesn't even require costumes?

SUPERINTENDENT: Your Excellency, if I have achieved any success in the theatre, it is because I was the first to realize that every stage has its own special advantages and problems, and that it is futile to attempt to . . .

CHAMBERLAIN: Yes, quite so, but time is running rather short!

SUPERINTENDENT: The fact is that each theatre is ideally suited to one particular play and one only, and the whole secret is to find out which. Needless to say, it's no easy matter, especially when the play has yet to be written; and you can expect an endless series of disasters, until the day when the long-awaited Hector or Mélisande appears, and gives the theatre its key, its soul, and (if I may say so) its sex . . .

CHAMBERLAIN: My dear Superintendent . . .

SUPERINTENDENT: I was in charge of one theatre, for instance, which failed dismally with the classics, and then had a sudden resounding success with a farce about Guards officers; that was a female theatre. Another one only came to life with the Sistine choir; it was queer, poor dear. And when I was obliged to close down the Park Theatre last year, in the name of public decency, its whole trouble was that it only worked with plays about incest.

CHAMBERLAIN: And in your opinion the Royal Theatre was made for "Salammbo"?

SUPERINTENDENT: Absolutely. At the very mention of "Salammbo" our chorus seems to lose its permanent frog-in-the-throat and gives out a dazzling, if somewhat discordant, sound. The cables which are always snarling up and snapping in "Faust" suddenly run like greased lightning; columns which thirty or forty stage-hands hadn't been able to lug into place without getting them caught in the flies or the curtain, swing sweetly into place at the flick of an A.S.M.'s finger. All the misery and insubordination and dust simply fly out of the theatre for good. And do you know, sometimes when we're doing a German opera and I'm up in my box, I see one of my singers bubbling with pleasure and pulling out all the stops, practically drowning the orchestra with sheer exuberance, to the applause and delight of the audience; and I realize at once that this admirable man, oblivious of his colleagues who are still conscientiously slogging on through their Nordic score, has absent-mindedly started singing "Salammbo". Yes, indeed, Your Excellency, my theatre has given "Salammbo" at least a thousand times, but I can truthfully say it is still the only piece I can ask them to improvise.

CHAMBERLAIN: No; I'm terribly sorry, but I really feel it would be most unsuitable to show a loving couple the pitiful effects of love. (*He turns to the Trainer of Seals.*) Now, sir! Who are you?

SEAL TRAINER: I train seals, Your Excellency.

CHAMBERLAIN: Really. And what do your seals do?

SEAL TRAINER: They don't sing "Salammbo", Your Excellency.

CHAMBERLAIN: What a pity. I think a pair of seals singing "Salammbo" would have made a most acceptable interlude. Besides, I gather your male seal has a beard and bears an unfortunate resemblance to His Majesty's father-in-law.

SEAL TRAINER: I can easily shave him, Your Excellency.

CHAMBERLAIN: Yes; only, as it happens, His Majesty's father-in-law shaved *his* beard off yesterday. I think we had better avoid even the shadow of a scandal. (*He turns to the Magician.*) Right! And who are you, sir?

MAGICIAN: A magician, Your Excellency.

CHAMBERLAIN: Ah. And where is your bag of tricks?

MAGICIAN: I work without materials, Your Excellency.

CHAMBERLAIN: Don't be silly. No one can produce comets with fiery tails, or make the sunken city of Ys rise from the waters with all bells tolling – without materials.

MAGICIAN: Oh, yes, they can.

A comet passes. The town of Ys rises from the waters.

CHAMBERLAIN: I tell you they can't! And they certainly can't make the Trojan horse appear with one eye smoking, or raise up pyramids complete with camels – not without materials.

Enter the Trojan horse. Pyramids rise up.

MAGICIAN: Oh, yes, they can.

CHAMBERLAIN: My dear good man . . .

Enter a Poet.

POET: Your Excellency . . .

CHAMBERLAIN: Go away . . . Or make the tree of Judaea sprout up, or Venus appear stark naked, next to the Lord High Chamberlain?

The naked Venus appears at the Chamberlain's side.

MAGICIAN: Certainly.

POET: Your Excellency! (*He bows.*) And madam . . .

Venus disappears.

CHAMBERLAIN (*staggered*): I've always wondered who these women are that you magicians produce like that. Colleagues, I suppose?

MAGICIAN: Or Venus herself. It depends on the quality of the magician.

CHAMBERLAIN. There's no doubt about yours, anyway. What act had you in mind?

MAGICIAN: With Your Excellency's permission, I shall take my cue from the circumstances.

CHAMBERLAIN: Isn't that rather trusting to chance?

MAGICIAN: I am more than ready to give you a personal demonstration, a trial run, here and now.

CHAMBERLAIN: You also thought-read, I see.

MAGICIAN: Well, that's fairly easy, as you think what the whole Court must be thinking. Yes, Your Excellency, I can show what you and every lady in town would like to see; the meeting of a man and woman who have been avoiding each other for the past three months.

CHAMBERLAIN: Do you mean *here*?

MAGICIAN: And now, Your Excellency. Just as soon as you can seat the spectators.

CHAMBERLAIN: You seem to have certain illusions – still, that's your profession. But you know perfectly well that the man in question is at this moment putting the last touches to his young bride's appearance, and gazing at her in delight, whilst the woman, on the other hand, has sworn, out of jealousy and resentment, not to appear at Court.

MAGICIAN: True. But suppose some little dog happens to pick up one of the young bride's gloves, and carries it off to this very hall – what will the husband do? And then suppose the lady's pet bird escapes from its cage and flies this way – she'll follow, won't she?

CHAMBERLAIN: Ah, but what you forget is that (a) the halberdier has strict instructions to keep all dogs out of the royal apartments, and (b) that the prince's two falcons are at liberty and unhooded next to the bird cage.

MAGICIAN: All right – then suppose the halberdier slips on a banana-skin, and the falcons are distracted from the bullfinch by a passing gazelle.

CHAMBERLAIN: Unfortunately, my dear sir, both bananas and gazelles are unknown in this country.

MAGICIAN: They *were* unknown. But it so happened that the African envoy was peeling a banana as he followed you through for his audience, and I distinctly saw gazelles among his presents for the King. I'm sorry, Your Excellency, but magic always has the last word, believe me! Now give your signal, let all the inquisitive ladies take their seats, and you shall see Bertha and the Knight come face to face.

CHAMBERLAIN (*to the Poet*): Call the ladies here, will you!

POET: Your Excellency, do you really think this is right?

CHAMBERLAIN: Why not? It's bound to happen sooner or later; and you know what the Court gossips are like.

POET: It's their business, not ours.

CHAMBERLAIN: My dear poet, when you're as old as I am you'll realize that life is a tedious entertainment, desperately in need of a little stage-managing. It shirks the big scenes and bungles the dénouements, and those who should have died of love die boringly of old age. Now that I have a magician at my disposal I am going to permit myself the luxury of watching life unfold in a way that keeps pace with human passion and curiosity.

POET: Can't you pick on a less innocent victim?

CHAMBERLAIN: This innocent victim, my dear young friend, happens to have seduced a knight from his vow; she must face her punishment sooner or later. If the Knight and Bertha meet and have it out today, instead of keeping us waiting six months as in real life, if they touch hands in the morning and kiss in the evening, instead of putting it off till the autumn or winter, it will make no difference to the course of their relationship, but will merely make it seem truer, stronger and fresher. That's the great advantage of the theatre over life, it doesn't smell rancid . . . All right, magician, on you go! – Good gracious, what was that?

A PAGE: The halberdier slipping over, sir.

CHAMBERLAIN: Ah! a promising start.

POET: Please, Your Excellency, this is wicked, trying to speed up life. You are cutting out its two saving graces of absent-mindedness and sloth. For all you know, sheer routine and carelessness might have kept the Knight and Bertha apart for the rest of their lives . . . What's that scream?

A PAGE: It's the gazelle, sir. The falcons are tearing its eyes out!

CHAMBERLAIN: Oh, splendid . . . Under cover, everybody . . . Do you think you can keep this up all day, magician?

MAGICIAN: Here's the bird . . .

Enter Bertha and the Knight from opposite sides, not seeing one another.

KNIGHT (*picking up a glove*): Ah! Got you!

BERTHA (*catching the bird*): Ah! Got you!

They each go off, still not seeing one another. The hidden spectators stick their heads out and buzz with dismay.

POET (*to Chamberlain*): Ha! Got you!

THE LADIES: Lord Chamberlain, are you trying to make fools of us?

CHAMBERLAIN: Well, magician?

MAGICIAN: A poor piece of production, you might say, my lord. I'll try again.

CHAMBERLAIN: Please do; and see that they meet this time.

MAGICIAN: To make absolutely certain, I think they had better collide.

Everyone withdraws behind pillars. Bertha and the Knight re-appear.

HANS (*picking up a second glove*): Thank God, there's the other!

BERTHA (*recapturing the bird*): Try it again, would you!

They collide violently. Bertha almost falls, but Hans catches her by the hands.

HANS: Bertha! I'm terribly sorry.

BERTHA: Entirely my fault, Sir Hans.

HANS: You're sure you're not hurt?

BERTHA: I never felt a thing.

HANS: Clumsy of me, though.

BERTHA: Yes, it was. (*They begin to move off slowly to their opposite sides. Then Bertha stops.*) Nice honeymoon, Hans?

HANS: Delightful, thank you.

BERTHA: A blonde, I hear?

HANS: Blonde, yes. She carries her sunshine with her.

BERTHA: Even at night? I prefer a little shadow.

HANS: Tastes differ.

BERTHA: Yes; I never realized how you must have hated kissing me under that oak-tree the day you left. We were right in the shadow then.

HANS: Bertha!

BERTHA: I didn't mind, though. I quite liked it, really.

HANS: Bertha, my wife is just outside.

BERTHA: Yes, it was nice in your arms. I wouldn't have minded staying there – for ever.

HANS: You could have, if you'd wanted. It was your idea to drag me off and parade me in front of your girl friends; sheer vanity!

BERTHA: Even engagement rings can be taken off to show some-one . . .

HANS: I'm so sorry. The ring didn't understand.

BERTHA: No, it rolled, as rings will. Under a bed.

HANS: Really, Bertha.

BERTHA: Perhaps not even a bed. Peasants don't bother with beds, do they, they prefer to sleep in the barn, on nice warm hay. I expect you needed a good brush down on the mornings after your nights of love.

HANS: It's quite obvious those are something you haven't had.

BERTHA: Don't worry, dear knight, I will.

HANS: I'm sure you will. If I may just give you one piece of advice, though; next time, hold on to your love a bit tighter, and don't let him go miles away just to feed your vanity. You may not believe this, but your image tends to fade at a distance.

BERTHA: I shan't let go again.

HANS: No, and whoever he is, don't pack him off in search of futile adventures and death.

BERTHA: You never know *what* you might meet in those forests.

HANS: You have a reputation for aloofness. I suggest you forget that in future, and when you see your man, throw your arms round him and kiss him in front of the whole Court.

BERTHA: I have every intention of doing so – and even in private, if necessary!

She kisses the Knight and tries to make off, but he holds on to her.

HANS: Well, Bertha! You of all people, with your dignity and pride!

BERTHA: No pride now – no shame . . .

HANS: What game are you playing? What do you want?

BERTHA: Stop squeezing my hand. There's a bird in it.

HANS: I love my wife, and nothing's going to separate me from her.

BERTHA: Please, it's my bullfinch. You'll crush it.

HANS: If I'd died in that forest, you wouldn't have given me another thought. But now that I've come back happy, you just can't bear it. Let the bird go!

BERTHA: No. I can feel his heart beating. I need this little heart to give mine courage.

HANS: What is your secret? Come on, confess!

BERTHA (*showing him the bird – dead*): There now, you've killed him.

HANS: Oh, Bertha, I'm sorry.

He drops on one knee. Bertha looks at him for a moment.

BERTHA: My secret, Hans? My mistake? I thought you'd realized by now. I believed in greatness, that was all. Not for me, but for the man I loved, the man I'd chosen as a little girl. I carved his name in the bark of an oak tree, and watched it grow as I grew, and then one evening years later I called that man to me under the same oak tree. You see, I couldn't believe a woman was a mere guide to meals and bed and sleep; I thought she should be page to a mighty hunter, and beat all sorts of wild elusive game into his ken – unicorns, dragons, even death itself. I felt I was strong enough to do that for you; because I'm dark, and I thought that if I sent my betrothed into the forest, he'd be in my sort of light, and see my shape and movement in every shadow. I only wanted to be a humble decoy and foretaste to lead him on into the heart of the true honour and glory of darkness. I wasn't frightened for him; I knew he could conquer the night, because he'd conquered me. I wanted him to be my black knight. I never thought I'd see all the pine trees in the world draw back their branches to let a blonde head through.

HANS: No, nor did I.

BERTHA: So that was my mistake. I've confessed it, and there's an end. If I want to carve any more names, I shall stick to cork-oaks. A man alone with greatness is silly enough; a woman alone with greatness is downright ludicrous. Well, that's my bad luck. Good-bye . . .

HANS: Forgive me, Bertha.

BERTHA (*taking the bullfinch from him*): Give him to me. I'll take him away.

They go off again on their opposite sides.

MAGICIAN: There now! You wouldn't have seen that till next winter without my help.

POET: It's quite enough, too! Let's stop there!

CHAMBERLAIN: Certainly not! I'm dying to see the next scene.

ALL THE LADIES: Yes, yes, the next scene!

MAGICIAN: Very well, ladies. Which one?

A LADY: The one where Hans is bending over a knight he's wounded, and realizes that it's Bertha.

MAGICIAN: I'm so sorry, madam; wrong century.

CHAMBERLAIN: The one where Bertha and the knight discuss Ondine for the first time.

MAGICIAN: Ah, you mean the following year? Certainly.

The ladies turn suddenly to stare at the Chamberlain's face.

CHAMBERLAIN: What on earth's this on my face?

MAGICIAN: Oh, dear, yes; one of the hazards of this system. You've got a six months' growth of beard.

All seek cover again. Bertha and the Knight step cheerfully on to the scene, one from the garden, the other from the courtyard.

BERTHA: Hans! I was just looking for you.

HANS: Bertha! I was just looking for you.

BERTHA: Hans, I don't want there to be any sort of cloud between us. I can't be your friend unless I'm Ondine's too. Let her come and see me tonight. I'm busy copying the Aeneid and the Tristia, and making my own illustrations. She can help me to gild Ovid's tears.

HANS: Thank you, Bertha. But I'm not too hopeful . . .

BERTHA: Ondine doesn't like writing?

HANS: No. In fact she doesn't know how to.

BERTHA: How very wise of her! She can give herself up to other people's works, then, and read stories without being jealous of the author.

HANS: No, she doesn't read them.

BERTHA: She doesn't care for stories?

HANS: I'm afraid not. You see, she can't read either.

BERTHA: Oh, how I envy her! We're going to see a real little nymph at last, among all these blue-stockings and demi-nuns! It *will* be refreshing – to see a child of nature spend her whole time in music and dancing!

HANS: No, you won't see that.

BERTHA: You don't mean you won't let her?

HANS: She doesn't know how to dance.

BERTHA: Hans, you're not serious! You haven't married a woman who can neither read, nor write, nor even dance?

HANS: Yes. And she can't recite, or play the flute, or ride, and hunting makes her cry.

BERTHA: I see. What *can* she do?

HANS: Well, she swims – a bit.

BERTHA: What an angel! Be careful, though; it's dangerous to be an ignorant girl at Court; it's teeming with willing professors, as you know. What sort of appearance does she make?

HANS: Like what she is, like love.

BERTHA: Ah, but which kind – silent or talkative? She can be as ignorant as she likes, if she only keeps her mouth shut.

HANS: Well, actually, Bertha, this is something I'm slightly worried about, between you and me. Ondine is *extremely* talkative, and she has about as much idea of grammar and syntax as a tree-frog or a March wind. We're just embarking on the hunting and tournament season, and I shudder to think of the blunders that child is going to commit, when every thrust and every figure of horsemanship has a technical name. I've been trying to teach her, but it's not much good. Every time I tell her a new word, she insists on kissing me. I tried to explain the first position for jousting yesterday, and there were thirty-three even in that.

BERTHA: Thirty-four, surely.

HANS: Good lord, you're right; thirty-four counting the *dégagé du col*. Congratulations, Bertha – I'm slipping!

BERTHA: Yes, you missed a kiss. Let me look after Ondine, Hans. She won't have that problem with me, anyway! And I'm pretty well up in hunting and jousting.

HANS: What she really ought to know, Bertha, is all the special customs and privileges of the Wittensteins, and of course they're secret.

BERTHA: Well, I was nearly one of the family. Ask me and see.

HANS: I'll give you a prize if you get this right: what colour shield should a Wittenstein carry when entering the lists?

BERTHA: Royal blue, quartered, with a squirrel, souffrant.

HANS: My dear Bertha! And how should he pass the barrier?

BERTHA: Lance at the ready, mount ambulant.

HANS: Bertha, you're going to make some knight very happy.

Exeunt together. The spectators emerge.

CHAMBERLAIN: Bravo! And how right Wittenstein is! The Countess Bertha is a mine of knowledge and skill, she'd make a perfect wife. The money she spends on books! – On quickly to the next scene, magician, we can't wait!

A LADY: The one where Bertha catches Ondine dancing naked in the moonlight with her gnomes.

MAGICIAN: You're getting muddled again, madam.

CHAMBERLAIN: The row between Bertha and Ondine?

POET: How about a year's grace?

A PAGE: Your Excellency, it's nearly time for the reception.

CHAMBERLAIN: Good gracious me, so it is! I think I've just got time to go and fetch the young lady in question and try to give her some advice about how to keep her little mouth shut and not to be too tactless – today at any rate . . . Now you won't go and do any scenes while I'm out of the room, will you, magician?

MAGICIAN: Only one very tiny one, my lord.

CHAMBERLAIN: Nothing to do with the plot, I trust?

MAGICIAN: Nothing to do with anything. But it'll give a lot of pleasure to an old fishing friend of mine.

Exit Chamberlain. Enter from one side the lady Violanta, from the other Auguste. The old fisherman goes up to the lady.

AUGUSTE: Are you the Countess Violanta, my lady?

VIOLANTA: Yes, my good man. (*She leans towards him, and he sees the gold speck in her eye.*) What did you want?

AUGUSTE: Nothing more, my lady. I was right, it's marvellous. Thank you, my lady.

They disappear. The Chamberlain comes down the staircase with Ondine, giving her his hand and making her rehearse curtsies.

CHAMBERLAIN: Absolutely out of the question!

ONDINE: But I would like it so much . . .

CHAMBERLAIN. I'm sorry, but to change a formal reception, third class, into an aquatic display is a practical impossibility. And in any case the Chancellor of the Exchequer would put his foot down. Every time we fill the pool it costs us a fortune.

ONDINE: I could get it done for nothing.

CHAMBERLAIN: I can't help that. Even if His Majesty was receiving the King of the Ocean in audience, he would have to do so on dry land for purely economic reasons.

ONDINE: But I should feel so much more at home in the water!

CHAMBERLAIN: I daresay, but we wouldn't – I certainly wouldn't . . .

ONDINE: You would, though. It would suit you specially. You've got clammy hands, and no-one would notice that in the water.

CHAMBERLAIN: I have *not* got clammy hands.

ONDINE. Oh yes you have. Just feel them.

CHAMBERLAIN: Your Ladyship, do you think you could pay attention, just for two or three seconds, to the friendly advice I am trying to give you about how to get through this afternoon without being tactless and upsetting everybody?

ONDINE: Of course! For an hour – two hours, if you like!

CHAMBERLAIN: Without interrupting?

ONDINE: I promise. Nothing easier.

CHAMBERLAIN: Your Ladyship, the Court is a sacred place . . .

ONDINE: Oh, sorry, just a second! (*She goes over to the Poet, who has been standing aside and now comes forward to meet her.*) You're the poet, aren't you?

POET: So they say.

ONDINE: You're not very beautiful.

POET: They say that too – not usually quite so loud, but poets' ears are attuned to whispers, so I hear it all the better.

ONDINE: I thought writing made you beautiful.

POET: Oh, it does. I used to be much uglier!

She laughs with him. He withdraws.

ONDINE (*returning to the Chamberlain*): I'm so sorry. Do go on.

CHAMBERLAIN: Your Ladyship, the Court is a sacred place where one has to control the two traitors one can never be rid of: one's words and one's face. If you're afraid, they must express courage; if you're lying, they must express truthfulness. If you happen to be telling the truth, incidentally, it's not a bad idea for them to express a hint of falsehood; it gives the truth that equivocal look which is so helpful when faced with hypocrisy . . . Now, instead of the smell of burning which I usually quote, let us take the example which you

chose yourself, in your innocence: my hand. Yes, my right
hand *is* clammy – only my right, by the way, my left is as dry
as a bone, it actually burns in summer. However, I have
known this fact, and suffered from it, ever since my childhood. My nanny, in fact, when I used to touch her breast,
could never tell my fingers from my lips, and it was no conso-
lation to me when I heard the legend that I inherited this
peculiarity from my forebear Onulph, who carelessly plunged
his right hand into some holy oil. Still, however clammy my
hand may be, my arm is long. My hand touches the throne,
and controls rewards and punishments. If you offend me, you
are risking not only your own future at Court, but your
husband's too, especially if you laugh at my physical defects –
defect, I should say. I need hardly add that I have no moral
defects . . . Now, my pretty Ondine, if you have followed
what I have been saying, tell me, as an experienced lady of the
Court, how you would describe my hand?

ONDINE: Clammy, like your feet.

CHAMBERLAIN: She hasn't understood a word! Your Ladyship . . .

ONDINE: Would you mind, just a second?

CHAMBERLAIN: Yes I would mind, very much!

Ondine goes over again to the Poet, who again comes forward.

ONDINE: What was your first line of poetry?

POET: The best.

ONDINE: The best you ever wrote?

POET: I, or anyone else. As far above the rest as you are above
other women.

ONDINE: You're very modest in your vanity. Tell it to me,
quickly . . .

POET: I can't. I wrote it in a dream, and when I woke up, I'd
forgotten it.

ONDINE: You should have written it down at once.

POET: That was the whole trouble, I did – in the dream.

She laughs pleasantly to him, and he withdraws once more.

CHAMBERLAIN: Your Ladyship, let us admit that my hand is
clammy – though when you've shaken all the hands at Court,
you may not think it quite so bad – let us admit that, and let
us admit that I admit it. But would you go and tell His
Majesty that his hands were clammy?

ONDINE: Of course not.

CHAMBERLAIN: Bravo! Because he's the king!

ONDINE: No, because they're dry.

CHAMBERLAIN: You really are impossible. I'm saying supposing they *were* clammy.

ONDINE: Well, you can't, because they aren't.

CHAMBERLAIN: Then what if the king asks you about the wart
on his nose? I suppose you agree that he *has* got a wart? –
And please don't make me shout like this! – Suppose he
asks you what it looks like?

ONDINE: I should be very surprised, if the first thing a king does
upon meeting you is to ask you what his wart looks like.

CHAMBERLAIN: But Your Ladyship, we are talking theoretically! I am merely trying to make you think, if *you* had a wart
on your nose, the sort of things you would like to have said
about it!

ONDINE: Oh, I'll never have a wart, don't worry.

CHAMBERLAIN: She's mad, mad . . .

ONDINE: They come from touching tortoises, did you know
that?

CHAMBERLAIN: I neither know nor care!

ONDINE: They're not as bad as carbuncles, though. You get
those from rubbing against a catfish.

CHAMBERLAIN: I'm sure you do . . .

ONDINE: And not nearly as bad as a mean spirit, which comes
from smothering eels! Eels are noble fish; their blood should
flow!

CHAMBERLAIN: The girl's impossible.

POET: Madam, all the Chamberlain is trying to say is that you
mustn't hurt ugly people by talking about their ugliness.

ONDINE: But they don't *have* to be ugly! I'm not ugly, am I?

CHAMBERLAIN: The whole point is, Your Ladyship, that

politeness is the best sort of investment; look at the dividends!
When you get older, thanks to it people will keep saying how
young you are. When you get ugly, they'll tell you you're
beautiful – and all this for such a tiny premium.

ONDINE: But I shall never grow old . . .

CHAMBERLAIN: What a child you are!

ONDINE: Do you want to bet? – Oh, sorry, just a moment.

She runs over to the Poet.

CHAMBERLAIN: Your Ladyship!

ONDINE: Isn't it the most beautiful thing in the world?

POET: Of course it is: leaping down from the rocks, splashing
the larkspur and belladonna!

ONDINE: A waterfall, the most beautiful thing in the world?
You must be mad!

POET: Ah, I understand. You mean the sea?

ONDINE: What, that old brine bath with St Vitus? How rude of
you!

CHAMBERLAIN: Your Ladyship!

ONDINE: Oh, there he goes again. What a pity: we were getting
on so well!

She returns to the Chamberlain.

CHAMBERLAIN: What are you two talking about! Your Ladyship, we had better continue this lesson another day. I've
just got time to tell you about the question His Majesty will
undoubtedly ask you today, as he asks all debutantes, about
the hero Hercules, whose name he bears. He received the
name in his cradle, having sat down on a blindworm which
happened to have blundered in there by mistake, and killed
the unfortunate beast. You are the sixth debutante of the
year, and he will ask you about the sixth labour of Hercules.
So if you will please listen, and repeat it after me, and *not* go
rushing off to exchange chit-chat with the poet . . .

ONDINE: Oh, goodness, I was forgetting – thanks for reminding
me! It's terribly urgent!

CHAMBERLAIN: I *forbid* you to move!

She runs over to the Poet.

ONDINE: I think you're nice.

POET: That's terribly kind, but the Chamberlain's waiting for you. What did you want to say that was so urgent?

ONDINE: Oh, that was all.

CHAMBERLAIN: They're completely crazy. Your Ladyship!

ONDINE: Springs, that's what I meant just now: underwater springs, spring-time springing from the bottom of a lake. The great game is to find them at their source. Suddenly there's this great leap of water lashing about in the middle of the other water. You try and get your hands round it, but you can't. You're soaked with this water which has never touched anything but water in its life. There's one quite near here, in the big pool. Go and stand over it and look at your reflection, and you'll see yourself as you really are, the most beautiful man in the world.

POET: So the Chamberlain's lessons are bearing fruit after all.

CHAMBERLAIN: Walter, this is all your fault! – Your Ladyship, when Hercules had killed the fish . . .

ONDINE: What? Hercules killed a fish?

CHAMBERLAIN: Yes, the biggest one of all, the Lernaean Hydra.

ONDINE: Then I'm not going to listen any more! I don't want to hear about murderers!

CHAMBERLAIN: This is diabolical! (*A great noise is heard outside. The Magician appears.*) And what scene are you giving us now?

MAGICIAN: The next one? It's not my doing.

A LADY: Hans kissing Bertha for the first time?

MAGICIAN: No, much worse than that: his first quarrel with Ondine. And here it comes, on cue.

Enter Hans.

A PAGE: Your husband, madam.

ONDINE: Oh, Hans darling, do come here: the Lord Chamberlain's teaching me how to tell lies.

HANS: Not now; I want a word with him.

ONDINE: Touch his hand and feel how dry it is! There now, Chamberlain, wasn't that a good lie!

HANS: Be quiet, Ondine.

ONDINE: You're ugly, and I hate you – and I'm not lying this time!

HANS: Shut up! – Your Excellency, will you kindly explain my position at table? You have put me below Salm, haven't you?

CHAMBERLAIN: I have, my lord.

HANS: I am entitled to third place after the King, and the silver fork.

CHAMBERLAIN: You *were*. In fact you would have been entitled to first place and the gold fork, if a certain union had taken place. Unfortunately, however, your marriage relegates you to fourteenth place and the silver spoon.

ONDINE: Hans darling, what does it matter, anyway? I've seen the food: there are four whole oxen for a start! I'm sure there'll be plenty for everyone.

Laughter.

HANS: And what are you laughing about, Bertram?

BERTRAM: I laugh when I feel happy, my lord.

ONDINE: You're not going to stop people laughing, are you, Hans?

HANS: He happens to be laughing at you.

ONDINE: Not nastily, though. He thinks I'm amusing, that's all. I don't try to be, but I am. He laughs in sympathy with me.

BERTRAM: Exactly, madam.

HANS: Nobody is going to laugh at my wife, sympathetically or otherwise.

ONDINE: Then I'm sure he won't laugh again, because he wouldn't want to offend me – would you, my lord?

BERTRAM: I shall do nothing, madam, but what you desire.

ONDINE: Don't be angry with my husband. It's really very flattering of him to be so particular about me – don't you think so, my lord?

BERTRAM: I envy his being the only one who can.

HANS: No one asked your opinion, Bertram.

ONDINE: Yes, darling, I did! You ought to have lessons from the Chamberlain, you know, Hans. Don't be so jittery, just do as I do. Even thunder and floods won't wipe this smile off my face. (*The Magician has come close to her. Recognizing her uncle, she speaks to him aside.*) What are *you* doing here, and why are you disguised? What sort of mischief are you preparing?

MAGICIAN: You'll find out. Forgive me for intruding, but it's for your own good.

ONDINE: I'll forgive you on one condition.

MAGICIAN: Which is?

ONDINE: Oh, uncle, if only I can keep calm! Please, just for this afternoon, stop me seeing what other people are thinking. It's so awful!

MAGICIAN: What am I thinking?

ONDINE (*terrified as she reads his thoughts*): Go away!

MAGICIAN: You'll be calling for me in a minute, Ondine.

The King is announced. He enters with the Queen and their attendants, among whom is Bertha.

KING: Hail, Sir Knight! And hail, little Ondine!

But Ondine has spotted Bertha, and seems unable to take her eyes off her.

CHAMBERLAIN: Madam, your curtsey!

She curtsies automatically, still staring at Bertha.

KING: I am receiving you here, my dear child, as I receive all whom I wish to know and love, in this hall dedicated to Hercules. I adore Hercules, and his is the dearest of all my names. I am not among those who believe the name to derive from Hercele, the gentleman who collected tree-frogs. There are no tree-frogs in the story of Hercules. In fact the frog is about the only animal one simply cannot envisage in connection with Hercules. The lion, the tiger, the hydra, by all means. The frog, no. Don't you agree, Master Alcuin?

MASTER ALCUIN: In this case, sire, you would require a rough breathing, and the epsilon rather than the eta.

KING: Quite, quite. I've got off the point, haven't I, Ondine? His labours, now. I expect you know how many labours Hercules managed to complete?

CHAMBERLAIN (*prompting her*): Nine . . .

ONDINE (*still gazing at Bertha*): Nine, Your Highness.

KING: Well done. The Chamberlain is prompting you rather loudly, but your voice seems to have distinct charm, even in such a short sentence. I'm afraid he may find it harder to whisper to you the complete description of the sixth labour; but if you look at that fresco on the wall, little Ondine, it may help – just above your head, that's right. Now, who is that woman trying to seduce Hercules, with such a charming face and such a treacherous heart?

ONDINE (*still looking at Bertha*): Bertha . . .

KING: What did she say?

Ondine goes up to Bertha.

ONDINE: You're not going to have him!

BERTHA: Have who?

ONDINE: He'll never belong to you – never!

KING: What is wrong with the child?

HANS: Ondine, the King is speaking to you.

ONDINE: If you speak one word to him, or touch him, I'll kill you.

HANS: Ondine, will you be quiet!

BERTHA: She must be mad!

ONDINE: Oh, Your Majesty, save us, please!

KING: Save you from what, my dear girl? What possible danger can you be in at a reception given in your honour?

HANS: Forgive her, sire. And forgive me . . .

ONDINE: You be quiet too! You're on their side already, you're just playing those women's games whether you mean to or not . . .

KING: Ondine, what is all this about?

ONDINE: Oh, your Majesty, it's so terrible! You have a husband

and you've sacrificed everything in the world for him; he's strong, he's brave, he's beautiful. . . .

HANS: Ondine, for heaven's sake . . .

ONDINE: Oh, shut up. I know what I'm saying. You're stupid, but you are beautiful, and all those women know it. And they're saying to themselves: Isn't it lucky he's so stupid, seeing how beautiful he is! He's so beautiful, they'd all like to be in his arms, kissing him; and it'll be easy to seduce him, because he's so stupid. He's so beautiful, they all want him to make up for their poor withered old husbands and trembling lovers. But they won't need to bother their little hearts about him, because he's so stupid!

BERTRAM: You marvellous girl!

ONDINE: I'm right, aren't I, my lord?

HANS: Ondine! What are you thinking of?

ONDINE: What is your name, you who think I'm marvellous?

BERTRAM: Bertram, madam.

HANS: Will you be quiet, sir!

BETRAM: When a woman asks my name, my lord, I am in the habit of answering.

KING: Please, gentlemen, please.

CHAMBERLAIN: The Viscounts and Viscountesses are approaching to kiss His Majesty's hand!

BERTHA: Father, don't you think it's going a bit far for a peasant to insult your adopted daughter in your own palace?

HANS: Your Highness, allow me to take my leave of you for ever. I have an adorable wife, but she is not made for society.

ONDINE: You see, they're in league together! They're liars, both of them!

KING: Bertha is not a liar, Ondine.

ONDINE: Yes, she is. I bet she's never told you about your . . .

CHAMBERLAIN: Your Ladyship!

KING: My being related to Hercules through my remarkable ancestress Omphale? I'm not ashamed of that, my little Ondine.

ONDINE: I don't mean that, I mean your wart, which is the prettiest wart a monarch ever bore, and must have come from some rare foreign tortoise. (*She sees that she has been tactless, and tries to cover it up.*) Where did you touch it? I expect it was by the Pillars of Hercules, wasn't it?

CHAMBERLAIN: The Margraves are now coming forward for the ceremony of the garter . . .

KING: Please, my little Ondine, do calm down. It's all right, I like you very much. It's quite an event for this old hall to ring with the voice of love, and I really find it rather a pleasant change. But let me give you a few bits of advice, my dear, for your own happiness . . .

ONDINE: Ah, you, I shall believe you without question.

KING: Bertha is a sweet, good girl and she only wants to be your friend.

ONDINE: Oh, no! You really are wrong about that!

HANS: Do for God's sake be quiet.

ONDINE (*to Hans*): I suppose you call a girl who kills bullfinches sweet and good?

KING: What's all this about bullfinches? Whatever would Bertha go and kill bullfinches for?

ONDINE: To upset Hans!

KING: I can assure you that Bertha . . .

BERTHA: Father, this is what happened. My bullfinch had got out of his cage, and I'd just caught him when Hans came in and greeted me and took my hand. He pressed too hard, that was all.

ONDINE: He didn't press too hard. The weakest woman's fist becomes a cage of marble to protect a living bird. If I had a bird in my hand, Your Highness, even your old Hercules could squeeze as hard as he liked. But Bertha knows what men are like – monsters of egoism who can be shattered by the death of a single little bird. That bullfinch was perfectly safe in her hand, but she let it die.

HANS: Because I pressed too hard.

ONDINE: Because she killed it!

CHAMBERLAIN: Your Highness, the barons and baronesses . . .

KING: Ondine, whether it was her fault or his, you must promise me on your oath to leave Bertha in peace from now on.

ONDINE: If you order it, I swear.

KING: Well, I do order it.

ONDINE: Then I swear – on condition she shuts up!

KING: But you do all the talking!

ONDINE: Oh, she's talking to herself, and I can hear everything
. . . Be quiet, Bertha!

KING: Say you're sorry to Bertha, Ondine.

ONDINE: My hair? I like that! I'd rather have my mop of tow,
as she calls it, than those awful black snakes of hers. Look at
her, Your Highness, they're snakes, not hair!

HANS: Apologize this minute!

ONDINE: But you can't hear her! None of you can hear her!
Now she's saying that I'll regret making this scene, and if I go
on playing the fool for a few more days I'll lose my husband,
and then she'll only have to wait for me to die of sorrow!
That's what your sweet gentle Bertha's saying – shouting! Oh,
Hans, darling, take me in your arms, now, in front of her, just
to humiliate her!

HANS: Don't touch me.

ONDINE: Let her see you kiss me! I've brought the bullfinch
back to life, by the way. It's back in its cage.

BERTHA: She's raving!

ONDINE: You killed him, and I brought him back to life! So
which of us is mad, which is the murderer?

QUEEN: Poor child!

ONDINE: Can't you hear him? He's singing.

KING: Is the interlude ready, Your Excellency? I hope so, and
I hope it's good.

ONDINE: Are you angry with me, Hans darling?

HANS: I'm not angry with you, but you've thoroughly disgraced
me, that's all. We shall be the laughing-stock of the whole
Court.

ONDINE: Then don't let's stay. The King's the only nice man
here, and the Queen's the only beautiful woman. Let's go,
please.

CHAMBERLAIN (*to Hans, at a signal from the Magician*): Give
the Countess Bertha your arm, my lord.   ·

ONDINE: Give her his arm? Certainly not!

CHAMBERLAIN: It's the protocol, Your Ladyship.

HANS: Your hand, Bertha.

ONDINE: Leave her hand alone! All right, then, Hans, you'd better know everything. I'll tell you all about Bertha . . . Stop, everyone, and listen. I'll tell you about Countess Bertha and the sort of protocol she deserves!

HANS: Ondine, this is the limit.

QUEEN: Leave me with her. I want to speak to this child alone.

ONDINE: Oh, yes, I've got a secret to tell Her Majesty!

KING: An excellent idea, Yseult.

ONDINE: Yseult! Oh, King, is she really Queen Yseult?

KING: Didn't you know?

ONDINE: And Tristan? Where's Tristan?

KING: I'm afraid I don't see the connection, Ondine . . . See if you can calm her, Yseult.

Everyone goes out except the Queen and Ondine.

QUEEN: Your name's Ondine, isn't it?

ONDINE: That's right. And I am an ondine.

QUEEN: How old are you? Fifteen?

ONDINE: Fifteen, yes. But I've been alive for centuries and I'm never going to die.

QUEEN: How did you land up here, then? Whatever attracted you to our world?

ONDINE: It looked marvellous from the shores of the lake.

QUEEN: And does it still, now that you're living dry?

ONDINE: Oh, there are lots of ways to keep the water in front of your eyes.

QUEEN: Ah, yes! So when you want to see the world again in all its splendour, you think of Hans dying; or if you want our ladies to look beautiful again, you think of them taking Hans away from you?

ONDINE: They want to take him, don't they?

QUEEN: It looks very much like it. You over-value him, you know.

ONDINE: Yes, my secret! That's my whole secret, Queen; if they

234

take him away from me, he'll die, I know he will! It's awful!

QUEEN: Don't worry, my dear. They aren't as cruel as that.

ONDINE: He will, though, he will! He'll die because I agreed that he should die if he deceived me.

QUEEN: What on earth are you saying? Is that the normal punishment with ondines?

ONDINE: Oh, no! Ondine husbands are never unfaithful, except by some sort of muddle or mistaken identity; you know, a double, or the water being cloudy. But we arrange it so that anyone who does it by mistake never finds out.

QUEEN: Then how can they know that Hans may deceive you? Do they even know what the word means?

ONDINE: Oh yes, they knew it at once – the moment they saw him. There'd never been any question of unfaithfulness up to then, never till Hans arrived. And then they saw this beautiful man on horseback, with loyalty in his face and truth in his mouth, and suddenly the word "deceive" went humming through the waves.

QUEEN: Poor ondines!

ONDINE: And then everything about Hans which made me trust him – his straight look, and his open speech – seemed to them the very token of mischief and hypocrisy. I suppose men's virtue is a dreadful lie in itself. And he told me he'd always love me . . .

QUEEN: And the word "deceive" was heard among the waves.

ONDINE: Even the fish learnt to spell it. Every time I went out of the cabin to tell them about Hans's love and snap my fingers at them, they shouted that word at me in splashes and bubbles. "He's furious about losing his trout," I told them, "he's getting hungry." "Yes," said the pike, "he'll deceive you." "I've just hidden the ham," I said. "Yes," said the dace, "he'll deceive you." Do you like dace or not?

QUEEN: I don't think I've ever met one.

ONDINE: Nasty, vulgar, flashy little beasts. I could tell you plenty about dace. And then they tempted him with the ondines. Well, I thought, from what I'd heard about men, that he'd really behave badly when they appeared and throw

himself at them, because my uncle had chosen ones without
fins and gills. But he didn't kiss them or touch them or anything: I was so proud of him. And I challenged them, and
told them he'd never deceive me; but they just laughed. Then
I did something awful. I made the pact.

QUEEN: What pact do you mean?

ONDINE: My uncle, the King of the Ondines, said: "Will you
let us kill him, then, if he does deceive you?" Well, if I said
no, it was humiliating him in front of them, it was as good as
saying I didn't trust him, or I was ashamed of him. So I said
yes.

QUEEN: They'll forget, though. They'll change their minds.

ONDINE: Oh no, they won't. You don't realize what a tiny part
of the universe it is where people forget, or forgive, or change
their minds – what you call humanity. With us, it's the same
as with wild beasts, or ash-trees, or caterpillars: there's no
forgetting, no pardon.

QUEEN: But what power have they got over him now?

ONDINE: All that is wave or water watches him. If he goes near
a well, the water climbs up to meet him. If it's raining, it falls
on him twice as thick. He gets furious! And you watch when
he walks past the fountains out there: they're so angry, they
shoot up to twice the height.

QUEEN: Do you want some advice, my little Ondine?

ONDINE: Oh, yes, I am an ondine.

QUEEN: You can afford to listen, you're only fifteen.

ONDINE: Fifteen next month. But I've been alive for centuries,
and I'm never going to die.

QUEEN: What made you choose Hans?

ONDINE: I didn't know you had to choose, with men. You don't
have to with us, you see; we're chosen by our passions, and
the first ondine boy that comes along is for ever and only.
Hans was the first man I'd seen, so how could I choose?

QUEEN: Ondine, go away, leave, now!

ONDINE: What, with Hans?

QUEEN: If you don't want to suffer dreadfully, if you want to
save Hans, dive into the first stream and go!

ONDINE: With Hans? But he's so ugly in the water!

QUEEN: My dear, you've had three months of happiness with him; you should be satisfied with that. Go while there's still time.

ONDINE: And leave Hans? But why?

QUEEN: Because he wasn't made for you, and he has a small soul.

ONDINE: I haven't got any soul, that's much worse.

QUEEN: The question doesn't arise for you, or for any creatures except humans. The world's soul breathes in and out through every bird and fish and animal; but man wanted his soul to himself. So, like a fool, he chopped up the human spirit into bits so that every man could have one – a wretched little allotment with a few miserable flowers and vegetables. What you needed was a whole human soul, whole like the seasons, or the wind, or love – but that's appallingly rare. There was just one, by pure accident, in this universe and century; but I'm sorry, it's already taken.

ONDINE: I'm not sorry at all.

QUEEN: You wouldn't know what it was like, an ondine with a great soul.

ONDINE: Oh, I would: we had one too! He always swam on his back so that he could see heaven. He used to take the skulls of dead ondines between his flippers and meditate on them. He had to go off and fast for a fortnight before making love. He wore us all out; even the oldest ones avoid him now. No, the only man worthy of being loved is the one who is like all men, whose words and features are all men's and who you can only distinguish from the others because he's even stupider and clumsier than they are.

QUEEN: Hans?

ONDINE: Yes, Hans.

QUEEN: But don't you see, all the great things about you Hans could only love in miniature. You are light, but he loved a blonde. You are grace, but he just thought you were pretty. You are adventure, but all he saw was *an* adventure. And as soon as he finds out his mistake, you'll lose him.

ONDINE: He'll never realize. Bertram would realize, if it was

Bertram. But I knew this might happen, so I chose the stupidest knight of all.

QUEEN: Even the stupidest see clearly enough to be blind.

ONDINE: Then I shall tell him I'm an ondine!

QUEEN: No, that would be even worse. I expect he thinks of you already as a sort of ondine – but not a real one, that's the point. Hans's idea of a real ondine wouldn't be you, it would be a sort of fancy-dress version of Bertha with a fish's tail.

ONDINE: Well, then, if men can't stand the truth, I'll tell lies.

QUEEN: My dear child, whether you tell the truth or lies, you won't fool anybody and you'll only give men the one thing they loathe.

ONDINE: Faithfulness?

QUEEN: No. Simplicity. That terrifies them. They feel it's the most dreadful secret of all. Once Hans sees that you're not an accumulation of ideas, desires and memories, he'll be scared, and you'll be lost. Believe me: go away now and save him!

ONDINE: Oh, Queen, it wouldn't save him even if I went. If I go back to the ondines, they'll all flock round me, they'll be attracted by the human smell. Then my uncle will want me to marry one of them, and I'll refuse and he'll be so angry he'll kill Hans. No, I've got to save Hans on dry land; I've got to find some way of hiding it from my uncle, if he stops loving me one day and deceives me. But he still does love me, doesn't he?

QUEEN: Certainly he does, with all his heart!

ONDINE: Then I needn't look any further, Queen. I've got the answer. It came to me just now when we were having that quarrel. Every time I tried to get Hans away from Bertha, I only succeeded in driving him towards her. As soon as I said anything nasty about her, he took her side. Well, I'm going to do just the opposite from now on. I'm going to tell him twenty times a day how beautiful she is, how right she is. Then he'll lose interest in her, and think she must be wrong. Every day I'll see that he meets her when she looks absolutely marvellous, in her Court dress with the sun shining and everything.

Then he'll only look at me. I've got another idea too: I think
Bertha ought to come and live with us in Hans's castle, so
they'll always be together and she might be miles away for all
the notice he'll take of her. I'll spend my whole time leaving
them together, walking and hunting, and it'll be as if they
were in a thick crowd. They'll sit there elbow to elbow reading
their manuscripts; he'll watch her eye to eye, illuminating her
capitals; they'll keep rubbing and brushing against each other,
and they'll feel so far apart there won't be any desire at all. So
Hans will be all mine at last! That's my solution: you see how
well I understand men! (*The Queen rises and comes to kiss her.*)
Oh, Queen Yseult, what are you doing?

QUEEN: I am saying thank you.

ONDINE: Thank you? What for?

QUEEN: For a lesson in love. Heaven will be the judge. Let's try
Ondine's prescription.

ONDINE: Yes, I am an ondine.

QUEEN: And a fifteen-year-old's philtre.

ONDINE: Fifteen next month. But I've been alive for centuries,
and I'm never going to die.

QUEEN: They're coming back . . .

ONDINE: Oh, good! Now I can say I'm sorry to Bertha. (*Enter
the King, with Hans, Bertha and the others.*) Bertha, I'm sorry.

KING: Well done, my child.

ONDINE: I was right, really. But you can't say sorry unless
you're wrong, so – I was wrong, Bertha. Forgive me.

HANS: Well done, Ondine, my darling.

At this moment the Magician appears and Ondine sees him.

ONDINE: Yes, it was. I do think she might say something.

HANS: What?

ONDINE: Well, here I am grovelling to her, and I'm far better
than she is! I've humbled myself, although I feel so full of
pride I could burst – and she won't even answer!

BERTRAM: I agree, Bertha might answer.

ONDINE: She might, mightn't she, Bertram?

HANS: If you'd kindly mind your own business . . .

ONDINE: It is his business. I'm his business.

HANS: We'll see about that presently, Bertram!

KING: Bertha, the child's admitted her mistakes. Try to forgive and forget, for all our sakes.

BERTHA: All right, I forgive her.

ONDINE: Thank you, Bertha.

BERTHA: On condition she carries my train in processions.

ONDINE: Yes, Bertha.

BERTHA: All twelve feet of it.

ONDINE: The more feet there are between us, Bertha, the happier I shall be.

BERTHA: That she doesn't call me Bertha in future, but Your Highness.

KING: That isn't right, Bertha.

BERTHA: And that she declares publicly that I didn't kill my bullfinch.

ONDINE: Yes, I will, though of course it will be a lie.

BERTHA: Father, do you hear her impertinence!

KING: Please don't start all this again . . .

ONDINE: Her Highness Bertha never killed the bullfinch. Hans never took her hand, and when he did he never squeezed it.

BERTHA: She's insulting me!

ONDINE: Her Highness Bertha never spends her time poking her finches' eyes out to make them sing, oh no! And in the morning when Her Highness Bertha jumps out of bed, she never steps on a carpet made of a hundred thousand dead finches, oh goodness no!

BERTHA: Father, are you going to let her insult me like this?

KING: Why did you provoke her?

HANS: Kindly remember, Ondine, that you are speaking to His Majesty's adopted daughter!

ONDINE: His Majesty's daughter! Do you want to know who His Majesty's daughter really is? Shall I tell you? You're all so scared of her!

HANS: Oh, Ondine, now I see what it is to come of common stock!

ONDINE: Common, my poor blind gentleman! You want to

know who's common, do you? I suppose you think your Bertha came from a race of heroes! Well, I happen to know her parents, and they're fisherfolk by the lake, and their names aren't Parsifal and Kudrun, they're Auguste and Eugénie.

BERTHA: Hans, make her stop, or I'll never see you again!

ONDINE: Uncle, you're there – come and help me!

HANS (*trying to drag her away*): You're coming with me . . .

ONDINE: Uncle, show them the truth, please! Show them what really happened! Oh, listen to me, just this once! Help me!

Suddenly the lights go out, and the Chamberlain announces:

CHAMBERLAIN: Your Highness, the interlude.

The back of the stage is illuminated, representing the lakeside with Auguste's cottage. The King of the Ondines is standing there, looking at a cradle of reeds containing a baby girl brought to him by the ondines. Then enter, from opposite sides of the stage, an actor and actress in the costumes of Salammbo and Matho.

MAGICIAN: Who the devil are these two? They don't belong here.

CHAMBERLAIN: They're going to sing "Salammbo". We couldn't stop them.

MAGICIAN: Well, you'd better stop them now.

CHAMBERLAIN: Stop them singing "Salammbo"? The eighth labour of Hercules, my dear fellow!

THE INTERLUDE

AN ONDINE (*looking at the little girl*):
    How shall this babe be known for sure?

KING OF THE ONDINES: Leave her the cross her mother wore.

MATHO (*singing*): A mercenary I, no more!

A LITTLE ONDINE: Ah! She bit my finger, King!

KING OF THE ONDINES: Leave her too that bauble thing
                 Which Auguste with fingers worn
                 Carved her from a narwhale's horn.

SALAMMBO (*singing*): Hannibal's niece, sir, I was born!

AN ONDINE: Ah, my lord, she's scratching me!
KING OF THE ONDINES: Every token treasured be,
      Marks that, when I will it so,
      The secret of her birth may show.
SALAMMBO: Yet, poor wretch, I worship thee!
MATHO: Thee I worship, blessed foe!
AN ONDINE: Tell us, shall the babe be found
    By a prince amid the reeds,
    And its cradle royal-crowned?
KING OF THE ONDINES:
    Yea, to us dwellers in the weeds,
    Wilt thou, my little vanity,
    Dwindle by human dignity,
    Not fisher-girl but Queen to be,
    Haply some joy thou yet may'st find . . .
ALL THE ONDINES: The proud of heart were ever blind!
KING OF THE ONDINES:
    But should a day dawn dank or dry
    When to our race thou giv'st the lie . . .
SALAMMBO: Carthage is thine, and so am I!
KING OF THE ONDINES: How high soever be thy name,
      How noble in the world thy fame,
      Cross and bauble shall unearth
      The secret of thy humble birth.
MATHO: Thy face revealed, O heaven on earth!
AN ONDINE: But a cross may soon be broken . . .
ANOTHER ONDINE: Bauble by a thief be taken . . .
SALAMMBO: I feel a sneaping breeze awaken!
MATHO: Let this veil thy limbs embrace!
KING OF THE ONDINES: This to forestall, my children dear,
      See how on her shoulder here,
      Marks that naught shall e'er efface,
      Cross and bauble now I trace.
SALAMMBO: The veil!
MATHO: The veil?
SALAMMBO: At last, at last,
    The veil of Tanit!

MATHO: Not so fast!

KING OF THE ONDINES:

> Also on thy skin so white
> An A and now an E I write,
> Lest thy pride should e'er disdain
> The breeding of thy parents twain.
> Therefore in this mighty hall
> Stand forth in the sight of all,
> Stand forth, Bertha, if you dare,
> And show the world your shoulders bare!

The light bursts on again.
Consternation in the hall.
Bertha rises.

ONDINE: Dare, Bertha!

BERTHA: Dare yourself.

ONDINE: All right!

She tears Bertha's veil away.
The marks appear on Bertha's shoulder.

SALAMMBO AND MATHO (*together*):

> Nothing but love on earth below!
> Nothing but love!

ONDINE: Are they there, Uncle?

MAGICIAN: Just arriving now.

Auguste and Eugénie burst into the room and rush towards Bertha.

AUGUSTE: My daughter! Oh, my dear daughter!

BERTHA: Get away! Don't touch me! You stink of fish!

ALL THE ONDINES (*reproachfully*): Oh! Oh!

EUGÉNIE: Oh, my child! I prayed to God for you!

BERTHA: And I pray Him to make me an orphan, quickly!

KING: You disgraceful girl! So all you cared for was my throne!
You're nothing but a treacherous upstart! Ask your parents'
forgiveness at once – and Ondine's.

BERTHA: No, never!

KING: Very well then. If you refuse to obey me, you are banished from this town, and you can finish your life in a convent.

BERTHA: It is finished now.

Exeunt all except Ondine, Bertha and Hans. Auguste and Eugénie remain standing at the far end of the hall, and when Ondine speaks of their royalty, golden crowns seem to light on their heads.

ONDINE: I'm sorry, Bertha!

BERTHA: Leave me alone.

ONDINE: You don't have to answer now. I don't need it any more . . .

BERTHA: Pity is harder to bear than treachery.

HANS: We won't desert you, Bertha.

ONDINE: I go on my knees to you, Bertha! You, the daughter of a fisherman, you're my Queen from now on! The ondines call Auguste His Highness.

HANS: What will you do now, Bertha?

BERTHA: I've always behaved according to my condition.

ONDINE: Oh, I envy you so much! Just to be an ordinary fisherman's daughter!

HANS: Let her be, Ondine.

ONDINE: No, but Hans, I want to make her understand what she's become. And you should understand it too. Don't you see, Auguste is the great King of a mighty kingdom; and when he frowns, thousands of trout tremble.

HANS: Where will you go, Bertha?

BERTHA: Where can I go? Everyone is casting me off already.

ONDINE: Then come with us. You won't mind my sister coming, will you, Hans? Because Bertha is my sister now, my elder sister. So lift up your head, Bertha – there! You get your dignity from Eugénie, because Eugénie is Queen among us. As noble as Eugénie, that's what the chub say.

HANS: Ondine's right, Bertha. We don't want to live at Court any more. Come with us tonight.

ONDINE: Bertha, forgive me, and forgive my tempers. I always forget that with men, when a thing's happened, it's happened. It's so difficult living here, with you, with all sorts of things you only said once but you can't take back, all sorts of gestures which are fixed for ever. It would be so much better if other people's hateful words turned into kisses as they hit you! That's how it is with me about you.

CHAMBERLAIN (*putting his head round the door*): His Majesty wishes to know if all is forgiven.

ONDINE: Absolutely.

HANS: Come on, then, Bertha. My castle is huge. You can live there just as you please, quite alone if you want, in the wing looking over the lake.

ONDINE: Oh! Is there a lake by your castle, Hans? Then Bertha had better have the other wing.

HANS: The one by the Rhine? Whichever she likes.

ONDINE: The Rhine? Do you mean the Rhine goes past your castle too?

HANS: Only to the east. There are waterfalls to the south. Come along, Bertha.

ONDINE: Oh, Hans, don't you have a castle in the middle of a heath somewhere, with *no* lakes or rivers?

HANS: Go on, then, Bertha; I'll be with you in a minute. (*Bertha goes; he turns back to Ondine.*) Why this sudden fear of water? What's going on between you and the water?

ONDINE: Me and the water? Nothing.

HANS: I'm not blind, you know. You never let me near a stream any more, never mind the sea; if I so much as sit down by a well, you drag me away.

ONDINE: You must beware of water, Hans.

HANS: Oh, I must, must I? Well, my castle's practically surrounded by water; I shall take my morning shower under the waterfall, at mid-day I shall go out on my lake and fish, and in the evening I shall dive into the Rhine. And I know every current and whirlpool of it, so if the water thinks it can frighten me, it's much mistaken. The water hears nothing and understands nothing.

He goes out, and suddenly all the jets of water round the hall leap high into the air.

ONDINE: But it does! It heard him!

She goes out after him.

CHAMBERLAIN (*to the Magician*): Oh, well done, marvellous! I can't wait to see the dénouement. When can we go on?

MAGICIAN: Straight away, if you wish.

CHAMBERLAIN: But – but what's happening to my face? Look here! I'm all wrinkled! I've gone bald!

MAGICIAN: It was your idea, Your Excellency. You see, ten years have passed in an hour.

CHAMBERLAIN: And I have false teeth, and mumble?

MAGICIAN: Do you still want to go on, Your Excellency?

CHAMBERLAIN: No, no! Curtains! Curtains!

Curtain

ACT THREE

The courtyard of Hans's castle, on the morning of his marriage to Bertha. They are talking to some servants.

SERVANT: The choir, my lord, attends you in the chancel.

HANS: What are you talking about?

ANOTHER SERVANT: He means the singers for your marriage service, my lord.

HANS: Well, is that the best you can do, then? Can't you speak plain German?

SERVANT: Good luck to you, Lady Bertha! Long live the bride!

HANS: Oh, get out.

BERTHA: Hans! What is there to be angry about, on a day like this?

HANS: Not you too!

BERTHA: I'm going to be your wife, and you look at me like that!

HANS: You! Now you've started talking like them!

BERTHA: Why, what was wrong with them? They were only congratulating us!

HANS: Say that again! Now, quickly! Just as you said it, without changing a word!

BERTHA: Why, what was wrong with them? They were only congratulating us!

HANS: Good! Thank you!

BERTHA: Hans, you're frightening me! You've frightened me for days now . . .

HANS: All right; as you know so much about the Wittensteins, you'd better learn something else about them. Whenever something terrible's going to happen, the servants, for no reason at all, start speaking in a sort of solemn language, noble and rhythmic. Grooms and washerwomen suddenly turn into poets. All sorts of little people start seeing things they never saw before: the curve of a river, the pattern of a honeycomb. They start thinking about Nature, about their souls – and that same evening comes the disaster.

247

BERTHA: But they weren't talking verse. It didn't even rhyme.

HANS: When a Wittenstein suddenly hears them speaking in rhymes and poetry, it means death is coming.

BERTHA: Oh, Hans, all it means is that every sound is made noble for a Wittenstein at the great moments of his life! Surely it applies just as much to weddings as to funerals!

HANS: Even swineherds, they say. Well, let's find out. (*To a Servant.*) Where's the swineherd, do you know?

SERVANT: On the gorse-covered hillside . . .

HANS: Shut up. Go and fetch the swineherd here . . .

SERVANT: Under an acacia tree . . .

HANS: And be quick about it!

Exit Servant.

BERTHA: Oh, Hans, I'm grateful to the servants for leaving me their simple words this morning to tell you how I love you. Hans, you're holding me in your arms – why look like that? Whatever can be wrong today?

HANS: Only that I didn't punish her for her crime, and force her to confess in front of the whole town what she was.

BERTHA: Ondine disappeared six months ago – and you still can't forget? Surely you can forget anything today.

HANS: No, less than ever. I offer myself to you today suspicious, mean and humiliated – and it's all her fault. The way she lied to me!

BERTHA: She didn't lie to you. Anyone except you would have guessed she wasn't one of us. She never complained, never disobeyed you, she was never angry, or ill, or arrogant – nothing that a real woman is!

HANS: Yes, she was, though – she deceived me.

BERTHA: You were the only one that couldn't see it. You never realized that she wouldn't use the word woman. Did you ever hear her say: You can't say that to a woman, you can't do that to a woman? No, everything about her said: You can't say that to an ondine, you can't do that to an ondine.

HANS: Forget her – forget Ondine – as if she'd let me! That cry, that woke me on the morning of her flight: I've been unfaithful with Bertram! Every morning now it comes echoing up from the rivers and springs and wells! The castle and the town ring with it, all day long, through their fountains and aquaducts! The wooden ondine on the great clock cries it at mid-day! Why does she have to go on shouting out to the whole world that she was unfaithful with Bertram!

ECHO: With Bertram!

BERTHA: Be fair, though, Hans. We'd already deceived her, remember. Perhaps she'd caught us at it, and this was her revenge.

HANS: But where is she? What's she doing? I've had all my huntsmen and fishermen searching for her the last six months, and not a trace. And yet she can't be far away. Look what they found this morning, hung on the chapel door – a bouquet of starfish and sea-urchins! Obviously her idea of a joke.

BERTHA: I doubt it. Adventuresses haven't that much stamina. Once they've been shown up, they simply vanish, dive back into obscurity. That's a good metaphor for ondines, I think. She's dived back.

HANS: Unfaithful with Bertram! Who said that?

ECHO: With Bertram!

BERTHA: We're paying for your mistake, Hans. Whatever could have fascinated you about that girl – what on earth gave you the idea that you were born for adventures? You, a hunter of fairies! I know you too well, my dear. Why not be honest and admit that what really excited you in a haunted forest was to see some derelict woodman's hut and crawl into it and find a mildewed chair or two and a few remains of a fire so that you could light your filthy old pipe and roast a couple of thrushes for your supper. As for so-called enchanted palaces, I can just see you: I bet the last thing you wanted was to go opening cobwebby cupboards and taking out robes and old helmets to put on your head. You thought you were looking for magic, but the only trail you ever followed was the human trail.

HANS: Not with much success.

BERTHA: You lost it, but you soon found it again. You found it that winter night behind the old castle when you told me you

249

still loved me – remember? – and I ran away, and you followed my footprints in the snow. They were clear and deep – as clear as my distress and exhaustion, as deep as my love. They weren't like Ondine's footprints, which were like faint ripples on dry land, even your dogs couldn't see them. No, they were the prints of a real woman bearing human life, bearing your future son – your wife, Hans! But I left no footprints coming back, because you carried me in your arms.

HANS: Yes, as Bertram must have carried her. (*Enter a servant.*) What do you want?

SERVANT: The swineherd's here, my lord. You wished to see him.

HANS: Well, swineherd – and how are your pigs?

SWINEHERD: My pipe is willow, boxwood is my knife!

HANS: I didn't ask you that, I asked about your pigs, your sows!

SWINEHERD: Under the acacia tree . . .

HANS: Shut up!

SERVANT: Be careful, sir, he's deaf!

SWINEHERD: Whose filigree leaves . . .

HANS (*to servant*): Put your hand over his mouth, quickly!

SERVANT (*having done so*): Into my hand he speaks – of hexagons . . .

HANS (*to another servant*): Stop his mouth too!

SECOND SERVANT (*putting his hand over the first one's mouth*): I don't know what's the matter with them, sir, they're all talking verse!

HANS: Go and fetch the kitchen-maid, do you hear? We'll see what the kitchen-maid has to say!

Enter two fishermen.

FIRST FISHERMAN (ULRICH): My lord! My lord!

HANS: Say it twice more and it's poetry!

SECOND FISHERMAN: We've got her! She's caught!

HANS: Ondine caught!

ULRICH: Yes, sir, she was down there in the Rhine, singing!

SECOND FISHERMAN: Like blackcocks, sir, you can steal up on them while they're singing!

HANS: Is it really her? Are you sure?

ULRICH: Sure as light, sir. She's got her hair down over her face, but there's that marvellous voice of hers, and her skin like velvet, so you can hardly keep your hands off her; she's the monster all right, sir!

SECOND FISHERMAN: The judges are coming up with her now.

BERTHA: What judges?

ULRICH: The Imperial and Episcopal Judges, sir, that have to judge supernatural cases. They were doing their circuit round here.

SECOND FISHERMAN: They came over from Bingen to hang a werewolf.

BERTHA: But why hold their assizes in the castle? Isn't the Courthouse free?

ULRICH: Well, you see, Countess, they say ondines have to be tried on a hill.

SECOND FISHERMAN: And quite a way from the river, too, and you've still got to watch out they don't go slithering back on their belly like eels do to a lake. Besides, His Lordship's going to be plaintiff, aren't you, sir?

HANS: I am, yes. I've been waiting for this for six months. Leave us, Bertha.

BERTHA: Hans, you mustn't see Ondine again!

HANS: I'm not going to. You heard what they said. I'm going to see *an* ondine, a creature which is no longer human, can't speak human language, and won't even recognize me.

BERTHA: Hans, let me tell you something. When I was a little girl, I fell in love with a lynx. Only an imaginary lynx, he didn't really exist. But we used to sleep together, we even had children. Well, you know, even now, when I go into a menagerie and see the lynx's cage, I find myself trembling all over. He'll have forgotten me, I know that; he won't remember how I made him a purple cap, and how he saved me from the giant dwarfs, and how our twin daughters Ginevra and Berthelinga married the Emperor of Asia. There he is, furry and bearded and rank. And all the same, my heart beats fearfully. I wouldn't feel right going to see him on my wedding day.

SERVANT: My lord, the judges.

HANS: Only a moment, Bertha, and then we'll be at peace.

Enter the Judges, with a crowd at their heels.

FIRST JUDGE: Perfect! Exactly the correct altitude – above the realm of water, and below the realm of air.

SECOND JUDGE: It was on such a hummock as this, good people, that the great ship settled when the Flood sank down, and Noah had to pass right judgement on the sea-monsters, which had crept in by the portholes two by two, and defiled his Ark. Our compliments to you, my lord.

HANS: You've come at the right moment.

FIRST JUDGE: Our living among the supernatural, my lord, gives us premonitions unknown to our legal or preaching colleagues.

SECOND JUDGE: And of course ours is a more arduous mission.

FIRST JUDGE: Oh, indeed, yes, it is a far simpler matter to decide questions of demarcation between neighbouring vine-yards than between mankind and spirits. However, our case today promises to be unusually straightforward; I don't think I ever remember one before in which the ondine made no attempt to deny being an ondine.

SECOND JUDGE: Those creatures will resort to almost any subterfuge, my lord, to evade our questioning. Why, some-times they even contrive to catch us out on points of learning.

FIRST JUDGE: Yes, indeed. You will remember that they did so only the day before yesterday, my dear colleague, in that case at Kreuznach, when we were trying the magistrate's servant, a girl who called herself Dorothea. Now you were entirely satisfied that she was a salamander. We put her to the stake, to find out, and she burned; which showed that she must have been an ondine after all.

SECOND JUDGE: Well, and even yesterday, my dear President, if you remember, at Tübingen, there was that wall-eyed girl with red hair, Gertrude I think her name was, a barmaid. Her tankards used to fill up of their own accord, and what was even more remarkable, without a trace of froth. Now you were absolutely convinced that she was an ondine. So we threw her into the water, bound in wire, and she drowned, proving that on the contrary, she was a salamander.

HANS: Did you bring Ondine with you?

FIRST JUDGE: My lord, before we bring her in, it would be particularly helpful for us to know, as you are the plaintiff, what punishment you are asking for the accused?

HANS: What I'm asking? I'm asking what all these serving-girls and grooms are asking: the right of men to a little privacy on earth! God hasn't granted us much, after all; a couple of yards of air between heaven and hell! And it's not such a very attractive proposition, life, with hands to be washed all the time, and noses to be blown, and your hair falling out! All I ask is to be able to live without feeling these non-human lives swarming around you the way they do – herrings with women's bodies, bladders with babies' heads, spectacled lizards with thighs like nymphs. All I ask, on my wedding day, is to be alone at last in a world free of their whims and their pryings and couplings – alone with my bride.

FIRST JUDGE: You're asking rather a lot.

SECOND JUDGE: Indeed, my lord, you are. We may find it rather embarrassing that they should take such obvious pleasure in watching us kissing our wives, or maids, or having a footbath, or spanking our children. But the undeniable fact is that every human action, from the basest to the most noble, is surrounded by a prancing audience of goblin mimics, who have hurriedly slipped into carcasses or velvet skins, with their snouts to the ground or their bottoms in the air, to imitate our eating or praying for miracles.

HANS: Has there been a single age, a single century they haven't infested?

FIRST JUDGE: An age, a century? To the best of my knowledge, my lord, there has been at most one day. Yes, there was one single day when I felt the world suddenly freed of these presences, these hellish doppelgaenger. It was last August, in the foothills beyond Augsburg; they were bringing in the harvest. And for the first time in my life I saw the ears of corn

253

with no shadows of darnel behind them, no blight on the cornflowers. I was lying under a service-tree, and a magpie was in the branches overhead, with no black crow at his side. Our dear Swabia stretched away to the Alps, all green and blue, and for the first time I could see no Swabia of the air hovering over her, teeming with sharp-beaked angels, and no Swabia of hell below, with its legions of red demons. A soldier on horseback was jogging along the highway, and for once he had no companion with a scythe. The harvesters were dancing in pairs round the maypoles, with no slimy pike-headed third winding into their revels. The mill-wheel ground gently round, with no great wheel circling beyond it, flailing damned souls with its spokes. Everywhere you looked there was shouting, and work, and dancing, and yet for the first time I could feel real, human solitude. Yes, and the posthorn rang through the hills, with no trumpet of doom echoing it. It was the one moment in my life, my lord, when I felt that the spirits had departed and left the earth to men; they'd been called away by some unexpected summons, to other haunts, other planets. If that had lasted, I need hardly say, my dear colleague, you and I would have been out of a job. But not a bit of it! In a moment, in the twinkling of an eye, the soldier was rejoined by Death, the dancing couples became three-somes, spears and broomsticks hung down from the clouds. The other planet had proved a disappointment; they were back, all back, in a second. They had left everything else, comets and galaxies and all the fireworks of the skies, to come and watch me mopping my brow or blowing my nose with a chequered handkerchief . . . Ah, here is the accused! One of you guards, see that she stays upright. If she gets down on her belly, it'll be like that eel-woman last Sunday, down to the Rhine before we can stop her.

Ondine is brought in.

SECOND JUDGE: Her hands aren't webbed, I see. She's wearing a ring.

HANS: Take it off her.

ONDINE: No! No!

HANS: It's a wedding ring. I shall be needing it in an hour or so.

FIRST JUDGE: My lord . . .

HANS: And that necklace, too, with the medallion. It's got my portrait on it!

ONDINE: No, leave me the necklace!

FIRST JUDGE: My lord, I must respectfully ask you to let me take charge of the proceedings from now on. I am afraid that your indignation, however justified, can only tend to obscure the issues. May we first proceed to identify the accused?

HANS: It's her!

FIRST JUDGE: Yes, yes. But which is the fisherman who caught her? Will the fisherman who caught her please step forward!

ULRICH (*stepping forward*): It's the first time I ever caught one, my lord judge. I'm very pleased about it!

FIRST JUDGE: I am sure we all congratulate you. Now will you tell us what she was doing?

ULRICH: You know, I just felt I was going to catch one today. Well, I mean, I've felt that for the last thirty years, but this morning, somehow, I was *sure* . . .

FIRST JUDGE: My dear man, I asked you what she was doing!

ULRICH: And I took her alive, too! That one they caught at Regensburg, they went and bashed her to death with an oar. But all I did was knock her head against the side of the boat, just to stun her, like.

HANS: Yes, you brute, she's still bleeding from it.

FIRST JUDGE: Would you mind answering my question! Was she swimming when you caught her?

ULRICH: Oh, yes, sir, she was swimming, you could see her throat, sir, and her little behind. She can stay under the water ten minutes, sir – I counted.

FIRST JUDGE: And was she singing?

ULRICH: No, sir, not singing, more like barking, really; no, not exactly barking neither; sort of yapping. I can remember what she was yapping too: "I've been unfaithful with Bertram."

FIRST JUDGE: Don't talk such nonsense. Or perhaps you can interpret yappings?

ULRICH: Not usually, sir, no; I mean, a yap's a yap. But that one, yes, I could.

FIRST JUDGE: She smelt of brimstone, did she, when you pulled her out?

ULRICH: No, sir, not brimstone. Seaweed she smelt of, and hawthorn blossom.

SECOND JUDGE: Well, those are hardly the same thing! She smelt of seaweed *or* hawthorn blossom – which?

ULRICH: Seaweed *and* hawthorn blossom.

FIRST JUDGE: Let it pass, my dear colleague, let it pass.

ULRICH: She smelt a sort of smell that said: "I've been unfaithful with Bertram."

FIRST JUDGE: Oh, so smells are speaking to you now?

ULRICH: Yes, I know, sir, you're quite right, a smell's a smell. But that one spoke, sir.

FIRST JUDGE: I suppose she struggled a lot?

ULRICH: No, sir, she didn't, that was the funny thing; she let herself be taken. Only thing she did, she shivered; her haunches sort of shivered, like they were saying: "I've been unfaithful with Bertram."

HANS: Have you finished howling, you bloody idiot!

FIRST JUDGE: Forgive him, my lord. It's hardly surprising that he wanders a bit. The simple soul's an easy prey to such stratagems. However, we needed the testimony of a professional fisherman to identify her as an aquatic monster, and he seems to have no doubts about that.

ULRICH: I swear to God she is one. Spit and image of that one in Nuremberg they brought up in a fishpond. They put a seal in with her, too; they used to play ball together. Even had kids, I believe. She might be that one, after all; I wonder? Anyway, sir, the reward's double for live ones, isn't it?

FIRST JUDGE: Yes. You'll be paid tonight. Thank you.

ULRICH: Sir, my net – can I have my net back?

FIRST JUDGE: You'll get it back at the proper time – two days after the adjournment.

ULRICH: Oh, no, sir! I've got to have it now! It's the implement of my trade, sir. I'll be fishing tonight!

SECOND JUDGE: Yes, yes. Now will you please go. The net is confiscated. Besides, it's broken.

FIRST JUDGE: Proceed with the examination, my dear colleague.

HANS: Hey! What do you think you're doing?

SECOND JUDGE: I happen also to be a doctor, my lord. I am about to examine the girl's body.

HANS: Nobody's going to examine Ondine.

FIRST JUDGE: My colleague has the highest possible qualifications, my lord. It was actually he who established the Electress Josepha's virginity, for the annulment of her marriage, and she paid particular tribute to his tact.

HANS: I can certify that this person is Ondine, surely that's enough?

SECOND JUDGE: My lord, I fully realize how painful it must be for you to see your erstwhile spouse examined, but I assure you I can do it without even touching her. All I have to do is to study, with the aid of my magnifying glass, certain portions of her body where divergences from the human invariably manifest themselves.

HANS: You can do that from where you are, and with the naked eye.

SECOND JUDGE: You don't seem to realize, my lord, I am looking for an almost invisible network of tiny trilobate veins running under the ondine's armpit, the mark of the tempter serpent! I hardly think I can be expected to see that with the naked eye! Couldn't she at least take a few steps in front of us, and get that net off, and put her legs apart?

HANS: Ondine, don't move!

FIRST JUDGE: Far be it from us, my lord, to make an unnecessary issue of this. I think the evidence as it stands is perhaps sufficient . . . Do any of you good people doubt that this woman was an ondine?

GRETA (A SERVING GIRL): She was so good to us, though!

SECOND JUDGE: Yes, a good ondine, that's all.

SWINEHERD: She loved us, and we loved her!

SECOND JUDGE: Even lizards have been known to show affection.

FIRST JUDGE: Yes, well, I suggest we proceed with the hearing. Now, my lord, you stand here as plaintiff, both as husband and landowner, to accuse this girl of having, by the very fact of being an ondine, disrupted your public and private life?

HANS: What – I say that? Never!

FIRST JUDGE: You mean you don't accuse her of having introduced something strange, supernatural and demoniac into your household?

HANS: Demoniac – Ondine? What absolute rubbish!

FIRST JUDGE: *We* are conducting this trial, my lord. What do you find so odd about the question?

KING OF THE ONDINES (*in the guise of a man in the crowd*): Demoniac – Ondine!

FIRST JUDGE: Who are you, my good man?

ONDINE: Tell him to be quiet! He's lying!

SECOND JUDGE: This is an open trial, and anyone can give evidence.

KING OF THE ONDINES: Demoniac! On the contrary, that ondine has disowned her race, disowned and betrayed them. If she had wanted, she could have kept all their power and knowledge; she could have worked what you call miracles twenty times a day, made her husband's horse grow a trunk, or his dogs grow wings. At a word from her, the Rhine and the very vault of heaven would have answered and brought forth wonders. But what did she do? She gave it all up in favour of twisted ankles, hay fever, and greasy cooking! Is this the truth, knight, or is it not?

FIRST JUDGE: Ah, so you accuse her, if I understand you rightly, of having hypocritically put on the most flattering and favourable disguise, in order to find out our human secrets?

HANS: I most certainly do not!

KING OF THE ONDINES: Your secrets? Look, sir, if anyone didn't care for human secrets, it was Ondine. I know men have got all sorts of treasures – gold, jewels and that – but what she liked best was the plainest, commonest things – like spoons, or a wooden stool. And they've got silk and velvet; but what she really loved was flannel. Oh, she tricked them all right, that sister of the elements; she loved fire for the bellows and firedogs, water for the sinks and jugs, and air for the sheets they used to hang out on the willows. If you want to write something down, master clerk, write this: she was the most human being that ever lived, because she was human by choice.

FIRST JUDGE: Some witnesses have claimed that she used to lock herself into her room for hours at a time.

KING OF THE ONDINES: Certainly. And what was your mistress doing, Greta, when she locked herself in like that?

GRETA: Making cakes, sir.

SECOND JUDGE: Cakes?

GRETA: Yes, sir, she spent two months getting her shortcake right.

SECOND JUDGE: One of the most delectable of human secrets. We also heard, however, that she reared animals in some obscure courtyard.

SWINEHERD: Yes, sir, rabbits. I used to take them clover.

GRETA: And hens, sir. Why, she even peeled their tongues for them, sir, when they got the pip.

SECOND JUDGE: You don't happen to remember, my dear, if her dogs and cats were in the habit of talking?

GRETA: Oh, no, sir. I used to talk to them, mind. I like talking to dogs. But they never answered, though.

FIRST JUDGE: Thank you for your evidence. We shall bear it most carefully in mind when we come to our judgement. After all, if incubi and succubi and other tiresome visitors are able to appreciate the excellence of the human state, the marvels of our ingenuity, our pastry, our hardware, and our sticky papers for cuts and rashes, we can hardly hold it against them, can we?

SECOND JUDGE: Personally, I adore shortcake. Do you remember if she used butter in her final recipe?

GRETA: Oh, yes, sir, lots!

FIRST JUDGE: Silence, please. I thin we are coming to the

heart of the matter; and I think at last I understand your position, my lord . . . Woman, the Knight accuses you of having insinuated yourself into his household, in place of the woman who loved him and was to have married him, but whom you succeeded in supplanting for a time – you, a creature entirely given over to the petty acts and contemptible satisfactions of life, entirely selfish and unfeeling . . .

HANS: Ondine not love me? Who says she didn't?

FIRST JUDGE: My lord, it is becoming very hard to follow you.

HANS: She loved me as no man has ever been loved before.

SECOND JUDGE: Are you sure of that, my lord? Look at her now; she's trembling with fear at your words.

HANS: Fear? You'd better use your magnifying glass, judge. That isn't fear she's trembling with. It's love! Yes, all right, as it's now my turn to do the accusing, I'll accuse. Have you got your pen ready, clerk? Oh, and judge, I should put your cap on if I were you; a little warmth keeps the head clear. So: I accuse this woman of trembling with love for me, of having no other thought, or nourishment, or god but me! I am this woman's god, do you hear?

FIRST JUDGE: My lord . . .

HANS: You don't believe me? All right . . . Ondine, what is your only thought?

ONDINE: Hans.

HANS: What is your bread and your wine? When you sat at my table and lifted your glass, what were you drinking?

ONDINE: Hans.

HANS: Who is your god?

ONDINE: Hans.

HANS: You hear that, judges? Her love is blasphemy!

FIRST JUDGE: Let us be fair, my lord, and not confuse the issue. All she means is that she adores you.

HANS: Not at all; I know what I'm saying. I've got proof, too. You kneel in front of my image, don't you, Ondine? And you used to kiss my garments? And you made your prayers in my name?

ONDINE: Yes.

HANS: I was the saints. I was the holy festivals. And on Palm
Sunday, who did you see riding into Jerusalem on a donkey,
with feet dangling to the ground?

ONDINE: Hans.

HANS: Women were shouting my name, and waving over my
head – what? It wasn't palms – what was it?

ONDINE: Hans.

FIRST JUDGE: My lord, where is all this leading us! We are here
to pass judgement on an ondine, not on love.

HANS: But it's love that's on trial. Let's have the boy in the box
this minute, with his beribboned bottom and his quiver. He's
the real defendant. I accuse the truest love of falsehood, the
most passionate love of worthlessness – because this woman,
who only lived for love of me, was unfaithful with Bertram!

ECHO: With Bertram!

FIRST JUDGE: My lord, this is becoming quite absurd! How
could a woman who loved you like that have been unfaithful
to you?

HANS: Well, answer them, you! Were you unfaithful with
Bertram?

ONDINE: Yes.

HANS: Swear it, go on, swear it in front of the judges!

ONDINE: I swear that I was unfaithful with Bertram.

FIRST JUDGE: It's quite simple then: she doesn't love you! Her
statements prove nothing, after all; you leave her so little
margin in her replies. My dear colleague, you succeeded in
catching out Geneviève de Brabant herself, when she declared
that she loved her pet doe better than her husband, and the
doe's muzzle better than her husband's face; so ask Ondine
the three canonical questions. Firstly . . .

SECOND JUDGE (*indicating Hans*): Ondine, when this man runs,
what do you do?

ONDINE: I gasp for breath.

FIRST JUDGE: And secondly . . .

SECOND JUDGE: When he has hurt his finger?

ONDINE: I bleed.

FIRST JUDGE: And thirdly . . .

SECOND JUDGE: When he snores in his sleep – forgive me, my lord – what do you hear?

ONDINE: Sweet, sweet music.

SECOND JUDGE: Not a single mistake. She must be telling the truth. This man means everything to you, and yet you were unfaithful to him?

ONDINE: Yes, with Bertram.

KING OF THE ONDINES: Don't shout so loud, I heard . . .

SECOND JUDGE: You love only him, he is the only one in your life, and yet you were unfaithful?

ONDINE: With Bertram.

HANS: There! Now you know everything!

SECOND JUDGE: I imagine you know the punishment for an adulterous woman? And you know that confession makes the guilt heavier, not lighter?

ONDINE: Yes, but I was unfaithful with Bertram.

KING OF THE ONDINES: It's me you're talking to, isn't it, Ondine? Me you're rebuking? All right, then. Now I start questioning, and it'll be tougher than the judges, I warn you. First, Ondine, where is Bertram?

ONDINE: In Burgundy. I'm to join him there.

KING OF THE ONDINES: Where was it you deceived your husband with him?

ONDINE: In a forest.

KING OF THE ONDINES: Morning or evening?

ONDINE: Noon.

KING OF THE ONDINES: Was the weather hot or cold?

ONDINE: Freezing. I remember Bertram said the ice would preserve our love. You don't forget remarks like that.

KING OF THE ONDINES: I see . . . Bring Bertram into Court. We'll see if he confirms your statements.

FIRST JUDGE: Bertram unfortunately disappeared six months ago, and all the powers of justice have so far failed to unearth him.

KING OF THE ONDINES: They can't be very powerful, then . . . Here he is!

Bertram suddenly appears.

ONDINE: Bertram, my beloved!

FIRST JUDGE: You are Count Bertram?

BERTRAM: I am.

FIRST JUDGE: This woman has declared that she was unfaithful to her lord with you.

BERTRAM: If she says so, it's true.

FIRST JUDGE: Where did it happen?

BERTRAM: In her room, here in the castle.

FIRST JUDGE: Morning or evening?

BERTRAM: Midnight.

FIRST JUDGE: Was it hot or cold?

BERTRAM: Boiling. There was this great log fire blazing away in the hearth. I remember Ondine saying it was a foretaste of hellfire. You don't forget remarks like that.

KING OF THE ONDINES: Thank you; perfect. Now we know where we are.

ONDINE: What's so perfect about it? Why do you disbelieve us? If our answers don't tally, it's because we made love so wildly and passionately that it's burnt itself out of our memories, that's all. It's only guilty people who rehearse what they're going to say beforehand!

KING OF THE ONDINES: Count Bertram, would you please take this woman in your arms and kiss her . . .

BERTRAM: I only take orders from her.

FIRST JUDGE: Doesn't your heart command you?

KING OF THE ONDINES: All right, then, Ondine: ask him to kiss you. Because we shan't be able to believe you if you don't let him.

ONDINE: Certainly. Kiss me, Bertram.

BERTRAM: You really want me to?

ONDINE: I command you to. Kiss me! . . . No, no, just a moment! . . . If I seem to shrink from you, Bertram, if I struggle at all, pay no attention, it won't mean a thing.

KING OF THE ONDINES: We are waiting.

ONDINE: Couldn't I just have a cloak or a wrap on?

KING OF THE ONDINES: No. Stay as you are.

ONDINE: All right; good. I love Bertram stroking my bare

shoulders when he kisses me. Do you remember that wonderful night, Bertram? . . . No, please, not quite yet! . . . If I
scream when you take me in your arms, Bertram, it's only that
my nerves are on edge, it's been such an awful day. Don't be
angry, will you? I shouldn't think I will scream, anyway.

KING OF THE ONDINES: Make up your mind.

ONDINE: Or suppose I faint – well, if I faint, you can do anything you like with me, Bertram, anything you like!

KING OF THE ONDINES: Then get on with it.

BERTRAM: Ondine!

He kisses her. She struggles frantically.

ONDINE: Hans! Hans!

KING OF THE ONDINES: There, judges, there's your proof.
His lordship's case and mine is concluded.

ONDINE: What proof? (*The judges rise.*) Proof of what? What
are you all thinking? You think if I shout for Hans when
Bertram kisses me, I can't have been unfaithful to Hans? That
isn't true! If I keep shouting Hans all the time, it's only
because I don't love him any more, because his name is
oozing away from me, and every time I say it, there's less of
him left. Besides, how could I help loving Bertram? Look at
him! He's the same height as Hans! He even looks a bit like
Hans!

SECOND JUDGE: The Court will now pass sentence.

FIRST JUDGE: My lord, our part in this case I think is ended
now, and with your permission I will give my judgement.
This ondine girl has wrongfully laid aside her true nature and
led us into temptation; it is clear, however, that she brought
with her nothing but goodness and love.

SECOND JUDGE: Rather too much, perhaps. That degree of love
doesn't exactly make life easy.

FIRST JUDGE: As for her trying to make us believe in her liaison
with Bertram, the reason for that escapes us, and as it falls
within the sphere of your private married life, we intend to
pursue it no further. The girl will be spared torture and public
execution. We decree that her neck be severed this night from

her body, no witnesses being present, and we appoint as her warders till then the executioner and this gentleman (*indicating the King of the Ondines*) in gratitude for the assistance he has given the court.

SECOND JUDGE: And now, my lord, as the bridal procession is waiting outside the chapel, pray allow us to follow you and add our sincere good wishes for your future happiness!

Suddenly, the kitchen-maid comes forward. To some she appears the soul of beauty; to others, the merest slut.

HANS: Who is that girl?

FIRST JUDGE: Which one, my lord?

HANS: That one, coming straight towards me as if she was blind – or seeing visions . . .

FIRST JUDGE: I never saw her before.

SERVANT: She's the kitchen-maid, my lord. You said to bring her here.

HANS: She's beautiful!

FIRST JUDGE: Beautiful, that little hag?

GRETA: She's beautiful!

SERVANT: Beautiful? She's at least sixty!

FIRST JUDGE: Lead on, my lord, we'll follow.

HANS: No, no, I must hear the kitchen-maid first. She's going to tell us how all this will end . . . Go on, kitchen-maid, we're listening.

SECOND JUDGE: He's mad . . .

FIRST JUDGE: Poor man. It's hardly surprising . . .

KITCHEN-MAID: I wash the plates with loving care;
My body's foul, my soul is fair.

HANS: That rhymed, didn't it?

FIRST JUDGE: Good heavens, no.

KITCHEN-MAID: The humblest tasks are my delight,
I darn the socks at dead of night.

HANS: Now you're not going to tell me *that* didn't rhyme!

FIRST JUDGE: Rhyme? You must have singing in the ears, my lord. However do you make that out to be verse?

SWINEHERD: She *is* speaking verse!

SERVANT: Tell that to your pigs! It's prose as far as we're concerned.

KITCHEN-MAID: I live on stale and greasy bread,
But noblest suffering bows my head;
My tears are fine of temper as
The tears of kings and emperors,
And for the fickle stable lad,
He makes me every whit as sad
As the poor queen, when her dear lord
Absents him from her bed and board.
O Christ, that high in heaven art,
How wilt Thou tell our souls apart,
Bleeding and bruised as we shall be
With the same indignity?
Thou shalt confound us in Thy feast,
A crown upon my head be placed,
And "Welcome", Thou shall say at last,
"My queens, your suffering is past."

HANS: Well, now, was that a poem or wasn't it? Was that a poem, sir?

FIRST JUDGE: A poem, my lord! All I heard was a wretched little woman moaning about someone accusing her of stealing the silver.

SECOND JUDGE: Yes, and how her chilblains had been bleeding since last November.

HANS: That's a scythe she's holding, isn't it?

FIRST JUDGE: A distaff, my lord.

GRETA: A scythe, a golden scythe!

SERVANT: It's a distaff.

SWINEHERD: No, it's a scythe, and a sharp one too! Lord, I know a scythe when I see it.

HANS: Thank you, kitchen-maid. I shall be there . . . Come, gentlemen.

SERVANT: The service is starting, my lord.

Everyone moves away, except Ondine, her uncle, and the executioner. With a wave of his hand, the King of the Ondines transforms the executioner into a blood-red snowman.

KING OF THE ONDINES: The end draws near, Ondine.

ONDINE: Don't kill him.

KING OF THE ONDINES: The pact, Ondine. We must. He deceived you.

ONDINE: Yes, he deceived me, and I tried to make you think I deceived him first. But you mustn't judge human feelings by our ondine standards. Unfaithful husbands often love their wives; the unfaithful ones are sometimes the most faithful of all. Some even deceive those they love so as not to be too proud, to humble themselves and feel small beside the women they worship. Hans wanted to make me into a marble statue, a rose of constancy, always right, always perfect . . . he was too good . . . he deceived me.

KING OF THE ONDINES: Poor Ondine, you're almost a woman!

ONDINE: I don't see what else he could have done, really.

KING OF THE ONDINES: No, you never had much imagination.

ONDINE: You know on nights when there's been a fair in the village, you see the husbands slinking home with gifts in their hands. They've just been unfaithful to their wives; and the wives now shine with unimaginable splendour.

KING OF THE ONDINES: He made you unhappy.

ONDINE: Of course he did. But that's what human beings are like. Just because I'm unhappy, it doesn't mean I'm not happy as well. You don't seem to understand; if you search round the whole wonderful world till you find the one thing most likely to involve you in doubt, and treachery, and lies, and then hurl yourself at it like a mad thing – that's what men call happiness. People think you're very odd if you do anything else. The more you suffer, the happier you are. And I'm happy; I'm the happiest woman in the world.

KING OF THE ONDINES: He's going to die, Ondine.

ONDINE: Save him.

KING OF THE ONDINES: What does it matter to you? In a few minutes you won't even have a human memory any more. Your sisters will call three times, and you'll forget everything. I'm going to let him die at the very same second as you forget.

That should be humane enough, shouldn't it? And besides,
I don't even have to kill him; he's dying as it is.

ONDINE: But he's so young, and strong!

KING OF THE ONDINES: He's dying, and you killed him. As
you're so fond of dogfish metaphors, Ondine, perhaps you
remember that couple that split away from each other?
They'd swum right across the ocean, through storms and
tempests, and come to a quiet warm bay, and suddenly a tiny
wave came along and the link between them snapped. All the
iron of the sea was in that tuft of foam! Then for about a week
their eyes grew paler, their faces thinner. Nothing was the
matter, they said. But in fact they were dying. And that's how
it is with men. Woodmen don't break themselves on oaks, or
judges on crimes, or knights errant on monsters. What finally
cracks them is a slip of willow, or innocence, or the love of a
child. He'll be dead within the hour.

ONDINE: But I've let Bertha take my place. Everything's fine for
him now.

KING OF THE ONDINES: Oh, no. His head's spinning; already
he has the music of death in his brain. When the kitchen-maid
was carrying on about the price of cheese and eggs, it sounded
to him like poetry. He's not even with Bertha, he's not in the
chapel, no-one knows where he is. As a matter of fact he's
with his horse. And his horse is saying to him: "Farewell,
beloved lord, Heaven be thy reward" – because even his
horse speaks verse to him now.

ONDINE: I don't believe you. Listen to the singing! That's his
wedding service.

KING OF THE ONDINES: He's not bothered with his wedding!
The whole affair has slipped off him like an oversized ring
from his finger. He's wandering through the castle now, talk-
to himself, rambling in his wits. That's the only way men can
cope with the situation, when they've bumped up against
some truth, something simple or precious. They call it going
mad. Suddenly they start behaving logically, stop submitting
to circumstances, refuse to marry women they don't love; they
have the reasoning of plants, or water, or God. They are mad.

ONDINE: But he hates me!

KING OF THE ONDINES: No, he's mad. He loves you!

At this moment Hans appears, and comes up behind Ondine, just as she had come up behind him, back in the fisherman's cottage.

HANS: My name's Hans.

ONDINE: It's a pretty name.

HANS: Ondine and Hans. I think those are the best names in the world, don't you?

ONDINE: Or Hans and Ondine.

HANS: Oh, no! Ondine first. That's the title, Ondine. They'll call this story Ondine, and I'll keep cropping up in it like a great clown, just a stupid . . . man. Not that I had much part in it, really. I loved Ondine because she wanted me to, I deceived her because I had to. You see, I was born to live for my horses and hounds; and instead, I was trapped like a rat between nature and destiny.

ONDINE: Forgive me, Hans.

HANS: Why do they always get it wrong, though, whether their names are Artemis, or Cleopatra, or Ondine? Why don't they look for little professors with big noses, thick-lipped gentlemen with private incomes, or bespectacled Jews? Those are the men cut out for love, with time to feel and enjoy and suffer it all. But no, they have to pounce on a poor soldier called Antony, a poor knight called Hans, a wretched average man; and he's doomed from that moment on. I hadn't a moment of my life to spare, what with fighting, and grooming, and hunting, and trapping! And I certainly hadn't reckoned with fire in my veins, poison in my eyes, spices and gall in my mouth. I've been shaken and pounded and flayed alive from heaven to hell. And the sad thing is that I'm not even bright enough to see the picturesque side of it all. It's so unfair.

ONDINE: Good-bye, Hans.

HANS: There you are, you see! One day, they just up and leave you. The very day when everything falls into place, and you realize you'd only loved them all the time, and you'll die if they leave you even for a moment – they go. The day when you find them again, and everything's set for eternity – it's quite simple, their ship weighs anchor, their wings open, their fins begin to beat, and they say good-bye.

ONDINE: Hans, I'm going to lose my memory.

HANS: And you see, it really is good-bye, this time! Most lovers who say good-bye on the threshold of death are destined to meet again on the other side, and be eternally joined and blended as shades in the same kingdom. They are only parting to be eternally together. But Ondine and I are setting out for eternity in opposite directions; limbo to larboard, oblivion to starboard. We must do it justice, Ondine, ours is the first true farewell ever to be said in this world.

ONDINE: Try to live, Hans. You will forget, too.

HANS: Try to live! That's easy to say, isn't it. If only I cared about living! Since you went away, I've had to force my body to do things it should do automatically. I no longer see unless I order my eyes to see. I don't see the grass is green unless I tell them to see it green. And it's not much fun, black grass, I can tell you. I have five senses, thirty muscles, even my bones to command; it's an exhausting stewardship. If I relax my vigilance for one moment, I may forget to hear or to breathe. He died, they'll say, because he could no longer bother to breathe. He died of love . . . What have you come to tell me, Ondine? Why did you let them catch you?

ONDINE: To tell you I shall be your widow Ondine.

HANS: My widow? Yes, I'd been thinking about that. I shall be the first Wittenstein who hasn't left a widow behind to mourn for him and say "I must be beautiful, though he no longer sees me, I must speak for him, though he no longer hears." All there will be is an unchanging Ondine who will have forgotten me. And that's not very fair either.

ONDINE: Of course not. But don't worry, Hans; I've taken my precautions. Do you remember how you used to say sometimes I was silly always to go the same ways through the house, with the same steps and the same gestures? That was because I felt that some day I might have to lose my memory and go back under the water. So I was training my body, and forcing it into a fixed routine. And when I'm deep in the Rhine again, even without a memory, it will go on repeating the motions of my life with you. The impulse that carries me from the cave to the tree-roots will be the same that used to take me from my table to the window, and when I roll a shell along the sand it will be the same as when I rolled out my pastries. I shall climb up to the attic, and look out. So you see, there'll always be one little bourgeoise among all those crazy ondines . . . Hans! What is it?

HANS: I'd forgotten, that's all.

ONDINE: Forgotten what?

HANS: To see the sky was blue. Go on!

ONDINE: They'll call me the human one, because instead of diving head-first to the bottom I'll be going down stairs in the water. I'll be reading books and opening windows in the water. Everything's ready down there. You know those things you lost when I went – my clock, and chairs, and chandelier? I threw them in the river! They're all in place now, waiting for me. But I can't get used to it, somehow. They don't seem quite solid any more; they wobble. Still, I'm afraid tonight they'll be as firm and sure to me as all the currents and eddies are. I shan't know exactly what they mean, but I shall live with them around me. And I expect I'll use them, too. I'll sit in my armchair and light up the Rhine with candelabra. I'll look at myself in the mirrors. The clock will strike; I'm time-less, but I'll know the time. I shall have our room at the bottom of the river.

HANS: Thank you, Ondine.

ONDINE: We shall be parted by oblivion, by death, by race and by the ages, but we shall understand one another, we shall still be faithful.

FIRST VOICE: Ondine!

HANS: They're calling you back!

ONDINE: They have to call three times; I shan't forget until the third . . . Hans, little Hans, make the most of our last mo-ments, ask me, ask me something! Revive my memories;

they'll soon be ashes. Oh, Hans, what's the matter? You're so pale . . .

HANS: I'm being called too, Ondine; called by something pale and cold. Take back your ring, and be my true widow under the water.

ONDINE: Oh, ask me, quickly!

HANS: What did you say, Ondine, the first evening I saw you, when you came in out of the storm?

ONDINE: I said: "Oh, you're beautiful."

HANS: And when you caught me having poached trout?

ONDINE: I said you were a beast.

HANS: And when I said there was no harm in thinking?

ONDINE: I said we'd remember this time later; the time when you hadn't kissed me.

HANS: We've no time now for the pleasures of waiting. Kiss me, Ondine.

SECOND VOICE: Ondine!

ONDINE: Ask me, go on, ask me more! Everything's starting to fade!

HANS: We can only talk or kiss, Ondine, we can't do both.

ONDINE: Then I'll be quiet!

HANS: Ondine, the kitchen-maid is there! Her body's foul, her soul is fair . . .

The kitchen-maid appears. Hans falls dead.

ONDINE: Help! Help!

Enter Bertha, with a servant and Greta. The flagstone on which Hans lies rises up, and he folds his hands in death. Enter the King of the Ondines.

BERTHA: Who called?

ONDINE: Hans isn't well! Hans is dying!

THIRD VOICE: Ondine!

BERTHA: You've killed him! Was it you?

ONDINE: Killed – who? What do you mean? Who are you?

BERTHA: Don't you know me, Ondine?

ONDINE: You, my lady? Oh, you're beautiful! But where am I?

I can't swim here! Everything's hard – or empty. Is this the earth?

KING OF THE ONDINES: This is the earth.

AN ONDINE (*taking her by the hand*): Let us leave it, Ondine. Quickly!

ONDINE: Yes, let's leave it . . . Oh, wait! Who is this beautiful young man on the bed? Who is he?

KING OF THE ONDINES: His name is Hans.

ONDINE: What a pretty name! Why doesn't he move?

KING OF THE ONDINES: He's dead.

ANOTHER ONDINE (*appearing*): It's time. We must go!

ONDINE: I like him so much. Couldn't you bring him alive again?

KING OF THE ONDINES: I'm afraid not.

ONDINE (*allowing herself to be led away*): What a shame! I should have loved him!

Curtain